Terrorism, the Worker and the City

Terrorism, the Worker and the City

Simulations and Security in a Time of Terror

LUKE HOWIE
Monash University, Australia

GOWER

© Luke Howie 2009

All rights reserved. No part of this publication may be reproduced, stored in a retrieval system or transmitted in any form or by any means, electronic, mechanical, photocopying, recording or otherwise without the prior permission of the publisher.

Luke Howie has asserted his moral right under the Copyright, Designs and Patents Act, 1988, to be identified as the author of this work.

Gower Applied Business Research
Our programme provides leaders, practitioners, scholars and researchers with thought provoking, cutting edge books that combine conceptual insights, interdisciplinary rigour and practical relevance in key areas of business and management.

Published by
Gower Publishing Limited
Wey Court East
Union Road
Farnham
Surrey, GU9 7PT
England

Ashgate Publishing Company
Suite 420
101 Cherry Street
Burlington,
VT 05401-4405
USA

www.gowerpublishing.com

British Library Cataloguing in Publication Data
Howie, Luke.
  Terrorism, the worker and the city : simulations and
  security in a time of terror.
  1. Business--Effect of terrorism on. 2. Industries--Defense
  measures. 3. Business enterprises--Security measures.
  4. Business--Effect of terrorism on--Australia--Melbourne
  (Vic.) 5. Industries--Defense measures--Australia--
  Melbourne (Vic.) 6. Business enterprises--Security measures-
  Australia--Melbourne (Vic.)
  I. Title
  658.4'73-dc22

ISBN: 978-0566-08889-6

Library of Congress Cataloging-in-Publication Data
Howie, Luke.
  Terrorism, the worker, and the city : simulations and security in a time of terror / by Luke Howie.
     p. cm.
  Includes bibliographical references and index.
  ISBN 978-0-566-08889-6 (hardback) 1. Terrorism--Economic aspects. 2. Business--Security measures. 3. Terrorism--Prevention. I. Title.
  HV6431.H695 2009
  363.325'17--dc22

2009018882

Printed and bound in Great Britain by
MPG Books Group, UK

Contents

Acknowledgements		*vii*
Chapter 1	Working in the Theatre of Terrorism	1
Chapter 2	Working People as Witnesses and Victims of Terrorism	17
Chapter 3	The Consequences and Meanings of Terrorism for Businesses	41
Chapter 4	Terror and the Mediated City	77
Chapter 5	Working in a Time of Terror	109
Chapter 6	Simulated Security: A Business Response to Terrorism	137
Chapter 7	Terror-work	163
Bibliography		*179*
Index		*191*

Acknowledgements

A book is an outcome, a consequence and a product of a complex network of colleagues, friends, family, publishers, research assistants, organizations and corporations, universities, households, the media, and the points where these people, places and institutions intersect. It would be impossible to acknowledge everyone and everything that helped make this book possible but I want to try and name a few of these people, places and institutions.

First, I am deeply indebted to my colleagues, co-workers and friends in the School of Political and Social Inquiry at Monash University. In particular, my friends and colleagues in the Behavioural Studies department – the academics, the PhD students and the staff – are a constant source of support and inspiration. It is a support that stretches well beyond our work, research and teaching. Special thanks go to Peter Kelly, Francesca Collins and Roseanne Misajon. I must single Peter Kelly out here for special praise – his constant support, supervision, expertise and advice over many years is the reason the words on these pages exist. Thanks also to Gary Bouma, Keith Abbott, David Wright-Neville, Pete Lentini, Chris Hadfield, Denise Cuthbert, Brett Hutchins, Greg Barton, Gavin Kendall, Craig Snyder, Michele Huppert, Chad Whelan, Stuart Koschade and Athol Yates who have, at one point or another, offered thoughtful comments, criticisms and advice at various stages of the project that resulted in this book.

Special thanks also go to friends and colleagues in the Global Terrorism Research Centre (GTReC) at Monash University and the Australian Homeland Security Research Centre (AHSRC) in Canberra.

Thanks also go to the publishers at Gower. Most of their work goes on behind the scenes and, as such, I do not have a full list of people I would need to thank, but I do know that Rachel Lynch and Martin West at Gower devoted considerable time and effort in reading the manuscript and helping me improve the final product. They truly make the daunting process of bringing a manuscript to print an enjoyable and valuable experience.

I would also like to thank the informants in my research who offered their time so we could all benefit from the stories they had to tell.

Lastly and most importantly I thank Perri Campbell – my friend, partner, life companion, editor, fan and critic – to whom this book is dedicated and without whom nothing is possible.

CHAPTER 1

Working in the Theatre of Terrorism

As things fell apart nobody paid much attention
Talking Heads

Introduction: Ground Zero

On 11 September 2001 witnesses throughout the world watched as commercial passenger airliners were crashed into each of the Twin Towers of the World Trade Center in New York City, the Pentagon in Washington DC and the ground in Pennsylvania. These attacks sparked a startling chain of events. After '9/11' witnesses worldwide watched as the US government deployed their military muscle – supported symbolically and militarily by the so-called 'Coalition of the Willing' – in Afghanistan and then later in Iraq. Hundreds of thousands of people have been killed as a consequence of the responses of the 'willing' governments to the attacks of 9/11. Witnesses watched as those who resisted the invading coalition were labelled 'terrorists' and detained by the invading armies. Many so-called 'enemy combatants' were flown out of Afghanistan and Iraq to Guantánamo Bay, Cuba and illegally imprisoned without charge. Witnesses watched as revelations of torture emerged from this prison and another in Iraq – the now notorious Abu Ghraib (Dickinson, 2006).

Witnesses continued to watch as some commentators expressed outrage while others engaged in troubling debates about the potential benefits and morality of torture (Pearson, 2005: 20). Witnesses watched as major airlines throughout the world grounded flights; the media reported terrorism and terror scares incessantly; the stock market crashed and quickly recovered; and as discriminatory 'revenge' attacks targeted mosques and people who appeared to be Muslim. Television audiences witnessed soldiers drape the American flag over a statue of Saddam Hussein and witnessed captured journalists and invading troops being beheaded, and there were revelations that American soldiers had murdered and raped helpless civilians (von Zielbauer, 2006). People throughout the world witnessed the President of the United States, George W. Bush, prematurely declare 'mission accomplished' in 2003 (Elliott, 2003) at a carefully staged media event. Yet at the time of writing, unrelenting wars continue in Afghanistan and Iraq.

More than anything, witnesses watched the 9/11 attacks replayed over and over again, beamed onto televisions throughout the world. Witnesses watched and watched and it soon became a mundane and routine part of life.

The day after 9/11, I spoke to many friends and colleagues about what had happened. One friend in particular – at that time an undergraduate journalism student, now a journalist with a major Melbourne daily newspaper – told me that 9/11 would be the 'biggest' thing that *we* will ever witness. He said that *we* should just be thankful that *we* watched these attacks on television and not on our streets. Of course for New Yorkers and many other people in the US, it was not just terrorism on television, but terrorism in their cities. What reaction would my friend's statement have received if he had been talking to a New Yorker? Would it still make sense to speak of a *we* who witnessed 9/11? I was a final year business and management student. Added to the initial shock and horror I could not help but consider the consequences for the many organizations and corporations housed in tall and prominent buildings in cities throughout the world. I thought that every aspect of business was sure to be changed forever and in many respects these initial thoughts have changed little.

Ground Zero, Underground Zero and Spain's 9/11

The fears, anxieties, and shock of 9/11 were reproduced in many other theatres throughout the world. On 12 October 2002 nightclubs in the tourist resort region of Bali were targeted killing 202 people including 88 Australians. On 11 March 2004 – what Whitaker (2007: 30) describes as 'Spain's 9/11' – the public transport network in Madrid was targeted during peak hour killing 191 people. In London on 7 July 2005, 52 people were killed when the public transport network was again targeted at peak hour – John Tulloch (2006: 5) described these attacks as 'underground zero'. These events represent the smallest sample of major terrorist attacks that have occurred since 9/11. With the elevated interest in terrorism that followed the 9/11 attacks one could be forgiven for assuming that terrorism was a contemporary phenomenon. But the fact is that terrorism has been frequently employed throughout history. While many argue that the term was first coined during the French revolution, retrospective analysis has suggested that terrorism has been employed as a tactic for political and social change for thousands of years.

Whilst it is often acknowledged that terrorists seek to target civilians, innocents and non-combatants it is rarely acknowledged that contemporary terrorists have targeted working people in major cities. Working people were victims on the passenger airliners that struck the Twin Towers and the Pentagon and crashed into a field in Pennsylvania – many were engaging in their routine and mundane commute to business meetings and workplaces in cities where their organization's offices are housed in accessible and central urban locations. Within the World Trade Center thousands of working people employed at 'domestic and international companies from all sectors of the economy' died during the attacks including 2000 from the financial industries alone (Alexander and Alexander, 2002: 124). Some businesses lost most of their employees. Within the reinforced walls of the Pentagon, security and military employees and bureaucrats were busily trying to understand the devastation in New York and soon were aware that they too were targets. In Bali the targets were affluent Western tourists, many of whom happened to be from Australia, and in Madrid and London, the logic of targeting working people was unmistakeable – the public transport networks during peak hour would seem to be an ideal terrorist target not only for the death and destruction that was caused but also for the ongoing fear and anxiety that it was sure to generate. As Zygmunt Bauman (2006: 2) argues: 'Fear is at its most fearsome when it is diffuse, scattered, unclear, unattached, unanchored, free floating, with no clear address or cause'. If terrorists were to target one particular location over and over again, then all one would need to do to avoid terrorism is avoid that location. But when terrorists strike seemingly at random but still in a targeted way – as in targeting the amorphous public transport network – *terror* is the likely outcome. This situation is all the worse because terrorists are not random enough. Perhaps living in a time of truly random terror would force us all to do our best to ignore the threat – certainly if terrorism was truly random, capable of killing anyone at any time, then worrying about it would not help. Residents of the late capitalist, bureaucratic and industrialized West will often work in centralized locations such as cities and will often need to travel to work. Many travel long distances. Many do not view travelling to work as a choice – work is essential for survival. When terrorism defies our ability to make choices and take reasonable steps to mitigate our already risky, precarious and vulnerable existence, *terrorism is diabolical*.

If terrorism is theatre, and most literature exploring the meaning of terrorism suggests that it is, then working people are the ideal theatrical targets. On 9/11 images of business people in identifiably business attire could be seen staggering from the wreckage of the Towers or out of one of the 23 surrounding buildings that were damaged or destroyed in the attacks. In London on 7/7, the images of women and men in the encoded attire of business and work are lasting artefacts of the day Londoners on peak hour public transport became instrumental victims in the theatre of terrorism. These women and men were engaging in the most routine and banal of daily activities – going to work. Many were killed, maimed, and otherwise severely injured. The terrorist penchant for business targets is unmistakeable. The theatre of terrorism in the globalized, media-saturated, and complex world of the twenty-first century provides terrorism with its power to terrify. As Jenkins (1987) has argued, terrorists want a lot of people watching, not a lot of people dead. Indeed it has long been the cornerstone of many definitions of terrorism that terrorists seek to distinguish between the victims and the victimised – those who are killed and those who bear witness.

This is how I have encountered contemporary terrorism – I was a distant witness and a worker in Melbourne, Australia. But my emplacement in Melbourne was not a causal factor for being a witness and a victim of terrorism. I could have been anywhere in the world in front of a television.

Following Bryan Turner (2006) and Zygmunt Bauman (2006) I argue that people share commonalities that define our everyday lives. Humans constantly grapple – in routine, mundane, and everyday ways – with their precarious and vulnerable existence and their fears of the unknowable and unfathomable risks and dangers of contemporary city living:

Human beings experience pain and humiliation because they are vulnerable. While humans may not share a common culture, they are bound together by the risks and perturbations that arise from their vulnerability. Because we have a common ontological condition as vulnerable, intelligent beings, human happiness is diverse, but misery is common and uniform.

(Turner, 2006: 9)

I suggest that these shared perceptions of precariousness, vulnerability and fear of unknowable and unpredictable dangers ensure that global events like 9/11, 3/11 and 7/7 will continue to have local consequences. Business leaders, managers and working people in all of the world's cities – not just in New York, Washington DC, Madrid and

4   Terrorism, the Worker and the City

London – need to account for these commonalities and the consequences of international terrorism on the everyday lives of workers, customers, clients and the public. The potential consequences of doing too *little* or too *much* to prevent and mitigate the impact of terrorism represents the complexity and power of terrorism as a tactic and as theatre to portray millions of people throughout the world's cities as *witnesses* and *victims*. It is the theatre of terrorism – generated by a series of *images* and what I choose to call *simulations* – that distinguishes terrorism from other threats, dangers and risks that are the consequences of living and working in the city.

Images of Terrorism

In this study of the consequences and meanings of terrorism for working people and businesses in cities, social theory, media analysis and qualitative interviews are employed to gain a deeper understanding of what it means to be a witness and a victim of terrorism. The size and distribution of the audience of terrorism is testimony to its power as a tactic and to the terrorists' goal to have a lot of people watching, not just a lot of people dead (Jenkins, 1987). Stated differently, I want to explore how the undifferentiated *witnesses and victims of terrorism* become differentiated across time and space. Terrorists have used violence and its image producing power in various sites in contemporary times. Often, cameras of the world's major news networks are already rolling when terrorists strike, beaming the attacks live onto televisions throughout the world. On 9/11 the images that were generated made these attacks particularly memorable. In many respects 9/11 was, as Jean Baudrillard (2002: 3–4) has argued, the 'mother' of all events.

Contemporary terrorism has created not only death and destruction but images – images that are described in some social theory as 'hyperreal' and 'simulations' (Baudrillard, 1983; 1994; 2002). These incessantly replayed images bear witness to terrorism long after the attacks and provide for a larger audience – images of contemporary terrorism have been viewed by many more people on television than viewed the events on the streets of New York, Washington DC, Madrid and London. Even many people who lived and worked in these cities at the times they became terrorist targets learnt of the attacks on television. The media, as creator and disseminator of these images, have reported terrorism in detail. Baudrillard (2002) argued that before the 9/11 events occurred but none have had the same impact of terrorism as an image-event. It is 'the unforgettable flash of images' (Baudrillard, 2001) that gives terrorism its power. This 'unforgettable flash' has provided terrorism a power not drawn from violence alone, but from a combination of violence and images. The impact of this combination has made 9/11, the Madrid attacks and London's underground zero, stand-outs in the history of terrorism and referents through which all terrorism and image events are understood:

> *When it comes to world events, we have seen quite a few – from the death of Diana, Princess of Wales, to the World Cup. And violent, real events, from wars right through to genocides. Yet, when it comes to symbolic events on a world scale … we had had none. Well, the strike is over now. Events are not on strike anymore.*
>
> (Baudrillard, 2002: 3)

In the discussion and analysis that follows theoretical positions such as Baudrillard's will be used extensively to explore how violent acts after 9/11 are infused with new and altered meanings in the post-9/11 world. The mother of all events proves pivotal in understanding how terrorism – past, present and that which has not happened, but, we are told, is waiting to happen as a consequence of 9/11 – has consequences for people throughout the world.

It can be argued that people's responses to terrorism are often disproportionate to any physical danger it poses (Schmid, 1993; Friedland and Merari, 1985; Jenkins, 1987). Michaelsen (2005), for example, argues that this has been particularly evident in Australia where many believe terrorism will inevitably occur. The debates surrounding terrorism have gained considerable public and media attention in the process. When this occurs terrorism has an impact far beyond the damage and death it initially causes. A 2005 opinion survey reported that terrorism had become one of the most feared international threats for Australians (Cook, 2005) and 9/11 has been instrumental in shaping these concerns. Other attacks have reinforced feelings of vulnerability and insecurity. In October 2002 bombs were detonated in and around nightclubs in Bali killing 212 people including 88 Australians (Chulov, 2006: 91). In Madrid on March 11, 2004 terrorists targeted train commuters on the Spanish rail network at peak hour killing 192. The London 7/7 attacks that targeted the British rail network at peak hour on July 7, 2005 killed 52. Bali was again targeted in 2005 killing more than 20 people in a popular restaurant district (*Herald Sun*, 2005a: 8–9). I argue that these events may seem less important than 9/11 and not just because they destroyed fewer buildings and killed fewer people. I suggest that these attacks, in some respects, lacked the real-time, powerful and terrifying images that 9/11 generated: images that allowed many to witness 9/11 in differing configurations of time and space even as it was occurring. Nonetheless, acts of terrorism that are part of a post-9/11 theatre of terrorism have still produced terrifying images and consequences. Perhaps they are most terrifying for the memories of 9/11 that they invoke, although this could not be considered universal. It will be argued in this book that the 'post-9/11' world holds the 9/11 attacks in special regard. As devastating as the attacks in Madrid, Bali and London have been, they are most terrifying because they reinforce the potential for terrorists to inflict massive damage and carnage as they did on 9/11.

Distance from terrorism and the healing power of time collapse in the face of images of terrorism that make terrorism feel close and that are capable of generating *terrorism as spectacle*. For this reason, I argue that traditional definitions of terrorism will not be useful for understanding the consequences of terrorism for working people and businesses. The spectacular effect of terrorism should be the most significant concern for business leaders and managers in a time of terror. For the purposes of this book *terrorism as spectacle* can be understood as the use of terrorism in ways that translate readily into terrifying mediated images: into terrifying symbolic events. In doing so, such events can be viewed and consumed by global audiences. These audiences occupy diverse configurations of time and space. Often this audience is not in close geographic proximity to the flashpoint of terrorist violence. Terrorism as spectacle seeks the largest possible audience. The spectacle terrorist plans to combine violence with image production to create something more powerful than the violence alone. As Nacos (2006: 208) argues, terrorists have long used the publicity producing power of violence to their advantage:

Contemporary terrorists commit violence in order to spread their propaganda, but modern communication technology has equipped today's terrorists far better than their predecessors. Well aware of the news media's appetite for featuring violence-as-crime and violence-as-terrorism, terrorists have staged increasingly shocking and deadly acts with the knowledge that the resulting news coverage will further their goals. They believe that the most spectacular and the bloodiest events will result in the most extensive media coverage.

In this view the target of terrorism is the media and the media is the primary source for public information about terrorism as spectacle (Nacos, 2006: 208–209). Contemporary terrorists have undoubtedly surpassed their expectations for success. Not only were their audacious plans of hijackings, bombings and death on passenger airliners in the US and on the public transport networks in Madrid and London successful, but on 9/11 the Twin Towers buckled under the heat and weight to spectacular effect. The sledgehammer produced the most profound chain reaction as the blunt force of the aircraft set off a type of system failure. The Twin Towers, designed for wind resistance at high altitude, not endurance through extreme heat, crumbled and made spectacular terrorism more spectacular.

Media representations of terrorism have come in many forms and sites including round-the-clock television news coverage as the events unfolded; ongoing television news reporting in the following months and years; a multitude of sites on the internet; coverage on radio including radio talkback; and reporting and opinion writing in newspapers. We have also witnessed Hollywood disaster movies depicting 9/11. *United 93* (2006) is the fictional tale of one of the hijacked aircraft: 'The story of the doomed 91-minute flight is told in *real* time' (Koltnow, 2006: 12, my emphasis). The producers also hired government and airline workers to play themselves in the movie to enhance the *feeling* of reality. The film's creator, Paul Greengrass, used a 'real flight attendant and two real pilots in the cast' (Koltnow, 2006: 12). These were all strategies to improve the reality of the movie. Since contemporary terrorism has been fiction-like for some (Baudrillard, 2002) the transferability of this imagery to disaster movies is perhaps not surprising. As Baudrillard (2001) argued after 9/11: 'One could almost say that reality is jealous of fiction, that the real is jealous of the image … it is as if they duel, to find which is the most unimaginable'.

Many of my friends, family and colleagues have become overnight news junkies, consumers and experts of international events, politics and terrorism. On 12 September 2001, foggy-eyed students attended schools and universities, and sleep deprived workers attended factories, suburban malls, and buildings in major cities after a long night in the audience of the theatre of spectacular terrorism. They discussed 9/11 and meditated on its meaning over lattés and flat whites, near photocopiers and water-coolers and during thank-god-it's-Friday drinks. An event, that until then was a happening reserved for James Bond movies and Hollywood disaster epics, became a routine and everyday topic of conversation in a post-9/11 world.

We witnessed 9/11 as it occurred and we witnessed destruction, military invasion, and torture as the consequences of 9/11. We witnessed the feature films and the television portrayals of terrorism and 9/11. We witnessed Jack Bauer fight terrorists in real time on *24*, Jennifer Garner demonstrated spy chic in *Alias*, and *United 93* (2006) and *World Trade Center* (2006) took American anti-terror cheerleading to a new level. This cheerleading was countered by conspiracy theorists who believe that 9/11 was staged by the US government and others who questioned the US government's actions before and after 9/11. Movies such as *Loose Change* (2005) and *Fahrenheit 9/11* (2004) became signposts in a 9/11 counterculture that disputed a number of the 'facts' reported about 9/11. Documentaries, news programmes, religious ministers, teams of academics and experts, and government spokespeople and diplomats all weighed into the debate about terrorism and its meanings and consequences. Opinion columnists and 'shock jocks' fashioned debates on the merits of bombing civilian populations, detaining innocent people and the difference between wholesale torture or mere rendition and coercive interrogation. As the material, often murderous, consequences of terrorism endure, so too have images of terrorism. They have become a routine and banal part of life. Despite all this, perhaps the strangest, most surreal aspect of contemporary terrorism is how ordinary it all seems. It has been shocking and amazing, even horrific, but something about it is so normal, so regular and mundane. We watched and took notice, and then we went back to work. It was perhaps a demonstration of evil and it was unusual to see the US – and Spain and the UK – targeted in such a way. But it was also banal, just like the response of witnesses.

Spectacular Terrorism, Images and Simulations

Laqueur (2003: 238) argues that one need not succinctly define terrorism to know what it is. Richardson (2006: 1) similarly argues that terrorism may not necessarily be definable but everybody knows it when we see it. Seeing terrorism through tele-visual images, however, not only shocks and terrifies but appears to some, at first glance, to be like a Hollywood disaster movie (Žižek, 2002a). How then would we know terrorism when we see it? Through this logic it could be argued that the movies *Independence Day* (1996), *Die Hard* (1988) and *Deep Impact* (1998) were acts of terrorism. If it were simply a matter of seeing, these movies would have to be considered terrorism. I suggest terrorism is something more that seeing. As some theorists have argued, in the theatre of contemporary terrorism the movie is real (Baudrillard, 2002: 29; Žižek, 2002a). Or, as Baudrillard (2002) argued, it is better than mere reality – it is hyperreal. Hyperreality becomes a driving force of terrorism as spectacle: 'it is only the radicality of the spectacle, the brutality of the spectacle that is the original and irreducible. The spectacle of terrorism imposes the terrorism of the spectacle' (Baudrillard, 2001). Hyperreality manifests within media imagery and discourse an analysis of which is the subject of Chapter 4.

Hyperreality communicates terrorism in a different form than just violence alone. It is a combination of images and violence. Terrorists rely on this to communicate their ideological and political message. Since the image is what remains once an event has passed into history, it takes on an eternal presence that preserves the life of the event long past its expiration. The event no longer exists as mere reality, it exists as something more: 'more real than the real, that is how the real is abolished' (Baudrillard, 1994: 81). This is hyperreality: something existing as a once-was-real, synthesized visual portrayal (Baudrillard, 1987a). However, the seduction of the aesthetically pleasing and concise image is, as Baudrillard (1994: 79, 81) argued, destructive – or 'implosive' – of the event itself. As witnesses become more and more reliant on images for information about the world, the event fades further into the background: 'As simulacra, images precede the real to the extent that they invert the causal and logical order of the real and its reproduction' (Baudrillard, 1987a: 13). It is when the image most imitates the real that it is most diabolical. The power of images of terrorism proves that terrorism is more than just violence. In responding to terrorism business leaders and managers must understand this power.

Baudrillard's (1983; 1994) conceptualization of hyperreality – the image real, more real than the real – is closely related to his concept of 'simulations'. Simulations is a term that is deployed extensively in this book, and a detailed explanation of its meaning is required.

Simulations

A simulation is an image that evolves the past being merely an image. As the act of terrorism that generated the simulated image vanishes into the past, the simulation stands alone as a new referent – it no longer needs the original act to cause terror in witnesses and create more victims. The origin of the image is real, but its continued existence is a simulation. It is in this context that Baudrillard (1983: 3) argued 'the era of simulation is inaugurated by a liquidation of all referentials'. The simulated image becomes the new cause of terror, fear, stress and anxiety. The image can be replayed again and again – terrorism only needs to happen once. Gilles Deleuze (2004: 295) argues that to describe a simulation as 'a copy of a copy' is to miss the core difference between simulations and the original event. For Deleuze (2004: 295) 'The copy is an image endowed with resemblance, the simulacrum [simulation] is an image without resemblance'. Put simply, the simulation is an original act of terrorism – it does not need to copy. The difference between a simulation and the *real thing* is inconsequential. Both will produce the same *effect*. I intend to suggest that the simulation is powerful – simulated symptoms present as real symptoms and the impact of acts of violence labelled 'terrorism' and the impact of its simulated image are difficult – if not impossible – to distinguish. It should be of no surprise therefore to see Australian private security and counter-terrorism organizations embrace simulation technologies to provide anti-terror commodities to business and government. By simulating cities on computer servers – a technique increasingly adopted on the internet in virtual worlds such as Second Life – the impact of terrorism can be predicted through precise calculations that determine blast direction, power and reflection, directions of crowd movement during mass panic, and the best practices for evacuation and response. I suggest that such computer-assisted simulations are perhaps not necessary. Maybe an examination of the 'real' world would be just as effective as a simulated test ground.

Following in a tradition of describing management problems through metaphor – a practice employed by critical management theorist Martin Parker (1995; 2002) – I often share the following metaphor – and return to it throughout the book – with colleagues when attempting to explain what I mean when I argue that terrorism is a simulation. Shawn Levy's film *Night at the Museum* (2006), based on the novel by Milan Trenc, tells the story of a security guard at a natural history museum where the exhibits come to life during the night. Among these exhibits are Attila the Hun, Sacagawea, Octavius and Teddy Roosevelt as well as garrisons of Roman soldiers, Mayan warriors and gunfighters from the Wild West. The hero, Larry Daley (played by Ben Stiller), is living a mundane and unsuccessful life before taking a job watching the museum during the graveyard shift. One of the museum's statues, former US President Theodore Roosevelt (played by Robin Williams), offers inspirational words to Larry, fitting of an American President, and convinces him that he can turn his mundane life around and be a great man. Larry's rigorous studies into world history (following the advice of Teddy Roosevelt) are supplemented by conversing with the come-to-life characters that by day are stagnant depictions of historical figures. As Larry again becomes disillusioned with his life he turns to Teddy Roosevelt ('TD' to Larry) for help. Following more wise words from the President, Larry, exasperated by his hopeless situation, replies angrily: 'I'm not you, okay? I didn't build the Panama Canal. I wasn't President of the United States!' Teddy leans forward as if to not let anyone else hear so as to not reveal a well-kept secret: 'Actually, I never did any of those things. Teddy Roosevelt did. I was made in a mannequin factory in Poughkeepsie ... I am made of wax, Larry'. The previously authoritative and powerful demeanor of Roosevelt is replaced briefly, for Larry's benefit, to explain to him that he is not really real, only real as a simulation.

Cannot the same be said for contemporary terrorism? Violence and images of spectacular terrorism were watched by near and distant witnesses on television. The image, by virtue of its existence as an image, confirms that it is made of wax – a mere depiction of something that exists, severed from its grounding. It is a simulation with all the semblances of terrorism, yet somehow it is different to terrorism. And, just like Larry's epiphany (Of course this is not Teddy Roosevelt! And now that I think of it, I never thought it was), so too does the witness and victim of terrorism know that they see these events as images on their televisions and not violence in their living rooms. Yet, it would seem that clear distinctions between *real* images and *real* events remain problematic. Kellner (2004: 2) argues that 'the spirit of terrorism' creates a 'global specter' where 'Western capitalism and culture' can be targeted 'anytime and anywhere'. The power afforded to terrorism by the image seems to affirm the effect of this 'spirit'. The movie ends with the *confession of the simulation* being lost. Museum tour operator, Rebecca (played by Carla Gugino), is introduced to the wax sculpture of *Sacagawea herself* by Larry: 'You rock!' is how she greets the subject of her intellectual obsession. And why not? Cut away from its grounding which is unreachable, ambiguous and trapped in a different configuration of time and space, the image – the simulation – becomes far better than reality for witnesses of images and violence.

Whilst simulations and events have a complex and problematic relationship, the simulation is able to stand alone, cut away from its grounding as a 'distinct totality that breaks with the continuity in life in general' (O'Connor, 2006: 58). As Jean-Luc Nancy argued (2000: 9, 12–13) the image is not a representation of reality, rather it presents a new reality where intangible events are made obvious. The simulation holds itself out as an absolute – an absolute, however, that has a limited yet groundless meaning. Even if images of terrorism are cut away from their ground ([Under]Ground Zero as it were) and its source, witnesses feel sympathy for the 'victims' and feel fear for their safety – it is an indication that the simulation has real symptoms. The groundlessness of the image inverts the relationship of the image to the event. If it seems that reality is a precondition for the image it is because the image has incorporated all the best characteristics of reality and improved upon them. Simulations of terrorism and simulations of violence in disaster movies are both real simulations. On 9/11, 3/11 and 7/7 terrorism was not only an image – it was real. This realness of terrorism, according to Baudrillard (2002: 29), is 'superadded' to the simulated image and can be viewed as a 'bonus of terror'. In this way, the images and simulations of terrorism precede the violence of terrorism for most witnesses and victims. The adding of image to reality creates the hyperreal, hyperknowable simulated event that can be recorded, scrutinized, and analyzed. Most of all, it can be replayed over and over again. Images of contemporary terrorism and the Hollywood disaster movies that they so resemble merge to create something more powerful and terrifying than either terrorism, images and simulations of terrorism, or the Hollywood movie alone.

The City: The Desert of the Real

Many millions of witnesses and victims of terrorism have experienced violence through images transmitted to many distant locations even as it was occurring. For most witnesses to terrorism it was a moving picture on a screen. Baudrillard (1987a) argued that in this way the image is seductive and destructive of the event it seeks to represent. For people living in New York, Washington DC, Madrid and London, terrorism will always haunt its organizations, its tall buildings, its major gatherings and sporting events, its public spaces, its retail strip malls, its public transport networks, and a host of other potential terrorist targets. Thanks to images and simulations of terrorism, people in cities throughout the world, think about their own cities in the same way. For this reason, social theorist Slavoj Žižek describes the world post-9/11 with the ironic phrase: 'Welcome to the desert of the real!' (Žižek, 2002b: 15).

In the desert of the real there is little certainty of security, an acute awareness of human vulnerability and precariousness, and the institutions that fashion and sustain existence are fractured and disorganized. The desert of the real is the post catastrophe city. This city can be seen in Hollywood disaster movies such as *The Matrix* (1999) from which Žižek takes this quote. It can also be seen in the footage of passenger airplanes being crashed into the Twin Towers and in images of the decimated rail and public transport networks in Madrid and London. Consider for a moment a fundamental proposition of psychological studies literature of the function of the senses. In particular, consider the so-called visual association area of the brain. In this view, the eyes are neutral organs. They transmit stimuli that they do not understand to a part of the brain where visual interpretation occurs. Indeed, it is the brain that we can say truly does the *seeing* (Plotnik, 2005: 232). How then are we to distinguish between the real and the simulated if it is little more than a matter of association, a matter of considering the new information in light of information that we already possess? How does the witness distinguish between what is an image of fictitious violence and what is an image of real violence?

> *For the great majority of the public, the World Trade Center (WTC) explosions were events on the TV screen and when we watched the oft-repeated shot of frightened people running towards the camera ahead of the giant cloud of dust from the collapsing tower, the framing of the shot itself was reminiscent of spectacular shots in catastrophe movies, a special effect which outdid all others, since reality is the best appearance of itself.*
>
> (Žižek, 2002a: 11)

The implication here is that fiction and reality are not easily distinguishable when they are both images. Baudrillard (2002) argued that on 9/11 the real absorbed the energy of the fiction. This is perhaps why some changed the channels on their televisions so they could be sure that 9/11 was really happening. The images are comparable to those in catastrophe movies with one notable exception: images of terrorism are real.

But Baudrillard (2002: 28–29) argued that 'the fascination with the attack is primarily a fascination with the image (both their exultatory and its catastrophic consequences are themselves largely imaginary)'.

In arguing that terrorism appears as an image and a simulation to most witnesses does not mean that I am suggesting that contemporary acts of terrorism were fictitious conspiracies, or that the attacks literally never took place, or perhaps that the Twin Towers are still standing. Rather, I am arguing that what has come to be relied upon as information and meaning does not convey the events only as a violent act, but also as an image and a simulation. Without going to New York, Madrid or London and seeing holes in the ground, the witness to the image can never verify that the Towers are gone or that a devastating act of terrorism has taken place. Witnesses, however, accept that the Towers are gone and that the public transport networks were treated as military targets – it is an unwavering faith in images that confirms that these events occurred. Žižek (2002a: 11) posits this problem as a continuation of a trend where the 'product is deprived of its substance' but retains a 'hard resistant kernel of the real'. It is one in a series of commodities that embody an absence: things that are 'deprived of their malignant properties' (Žižek, 2002a: 11). Milk and cream without fat, beer and spirits without alcohol (think of the 'Claytons' drink: the drink you have when you are not having a drink), cakes and biscuits without sugar, coffee without caffeine, cyber-sex as sex without sex, internet communities as societies without human contact, war without casualties and multiculturalism as Others without Otherness. As I seek to demonstrate in Chapters 5 and 6, witnesses and victims of terrorism in Melbourne have never viewed terrorism as *real* event. It was violence as an image. It was violence without any violence. Only a small percentage of terrorism's witnesses have watched and witnessed the violence as a 'really real' (Žižek, 2002a: 3–12) event.

Terrorism and the City

Now that I have explained in some detail the meaning that I intend when I describe terrorism as a *simulation*, I move to a description of the city and its significance for understanding the meanings and consequences of terrorism for businesses and working people.

Rapoport (2006) argues that the shrinking of time and space through advancements in communication and transport technologies have empowered terrorists in communicating their 'propaganda by deed' (Laqueur, 1977: 134–135). Terrorists have exploited contemporary technology well. Passenger airliners were used as weapons and crashed into buildings and the image was exploited to communicate terrifying and powerful images to many parts of the world. These images were beamed into televisions, computers and reproduced in newspapers in many distant cities. Where many cities, particularly in the United States and Australia, were perhaps insulated at one time by distance from the impacts and consequences of foreign violence, this distance is problematic when the impact of images of terrorism is considered. To be a witness one only needs to see. I argue that the particular vantage point differentiates witnesses and victims across time and space.

The city possesses all the characteristics for the theatre of terrorism. Cities are home to major sporting, cultural and social events, businesses, workers and managers, as well as criminals and terrorists. People who live and work in the city congregate on public transport and in public spaces that are difficult to secure without significantly undermining the openness and freedom enjoyed by visitors and dwellers alike (Graham, 2004; Bergin and Yates, 2006; Coaffee, 2003). These are critical sites that are attractive targets for terrorists seeking to generate powerful and terrifying images. According to Graham (2004: 4): 'The last two decades have seen a geopolitical and strategic reshaping of our world based heavily on a proliferation of organized, extremely violent acts against cities, those who live in them, and the support systems that make them work'.

The city of Melbourne, Australia is the location for the stories of nine key respondents that I interviewed at length. Each of the informants work in Melbourne's central business district and their responses were given at critical moments between February and November 2005. These witnesses were subject to what Virilio (2002: 23) refers to as 'the curiosities of the black museum of journalism'. The media, with its sponsorship deals and corporate backing, and its thirst for market share and sensationalism over quality of content, are complicit in the reactions of witnesses and victims and the impact of images and simulations of terrorism. For these reasons this book also includes an analysis of Australia's major newspapers at two crucial moments when terror scares hit the newsstands in October and November 2005. Media coverage at these times of terror provides an opportunity to explore terrorism in images and its impact on people who live and work in the city.

Terror-work

In this book, I do not intend to provide exhaustive lists of what businesses should and should not do to magically stop terrorism from having consequences. I do not intend to prattle on endlessly about the need to train employees in security and terrorism awareness, hire new staff, and consider security in the strategic context of business decision-making although these things should still form an important part of an organization's conduct in a time of terror. I also do not intend to merely add variables to almost meaningless attempts to quantify risks. These things are all important in one context or another, but I hope to strip these superficial business realities back and deal with some of the root vulnerabilities of businesses, corporations, and organizations and the working people and the cities that generate and sustain them. I intend, instead, to articulate some of the crucial dilemmas that working people, business leaders and managers encounter when responding to terrorism and engaging in counter-terrorism, and contribute to a better understanding of precarious and vulnerable witnesses and victims of terrorism living and working in the world's cities.

There is an unmistakeable logic that binds and unites the business world. It is a logic that has been accused of alienating the working classes, of polluting the environment and exploiting laws and social norms. It is also a logic that delivers efficient and effective production results, generates employment and revenue and produces wealth and quality of life for millions of people. Parker (1995), in his critical examination of organizational narratives in contemporary business, has argued that business managers and leaders in their attempts to control, organize and secure their organizational sites and structures, resources and employees work to know everything that can be known about the risks, problems and dilemmas that threaten organizational efficiency, effectiveness and productivity. However terrorism resists attempts to understand it – certainly it does not fit neatly in risk management models. Even scholars, diplomats, practitioners and politicians have toiled for many years to define terrorism with little success (Laqueur, 2003).

Nonetheless, businesses, managers and employees are at home in the risky and threatening city. The city is a place to which millions of people flock to benefit from the social, cultural and employment opportunities that organizations in cities provide. As such, the city and the people who live and work there, have been, and likely will again be, an attractive target for terrorists. For Grosz (1995: 105) the relationship between people and their cities is clear – 'Humans make cities. Cities are reflections, projections, or expressions of human endeavour'. For Grosz (1995) the human body and the city are linked in powerful ways:

> *The city is a reflection, projection, or product of bodies. Bodies are conceived in naturalistic terms, pre-dating the city, the cause and motivation or its design and construction. More recently, we have heard an inversion of this presumed relation: cities have become (or may have always been) alienating environments that do not allow the body a 'natural', 'healthy', or 'conducive' context.*
>
> (Grosz, 1995: 105)

Managers and business leaders in organizations are compelled by moral, financial and legal imperatives to take all reasonable steps towards protecting the people that work and move within organizational spaces. This is not a simple task. I argue that this task is as much a process of image creation – a process of generating a simulation of security and safety – as it is of securing organizational spaces. Full, complete, no gaps security will likely always prove elusive. The best that managers and business leaders can hope for are *simulations of security*. Responding to images and simulations of terrorism with images and simulations of security and safety would seem to be a reasonable way for managers and business leaders to tackle the terrorism problem.

Workers in businesses housed in major cities face a variety of security dilemmas in the everyday performance of doing business but the need for corporate counter-terrorism is a distinctively post-9/11 problem. With the 'specter of terrorism' (Alexander and Alexander, 2002: 149) looming over the corporate world, the city and the workplace have been transformed into public laboratories for counter-terrorism – places where untried counter-terrorism practices can be tried and tested in practical conditions. As such, organizational spaces have been fortified, workers have been emotionally, psychologically and physically prepared for the worst, and legal frameworks compel managers and business leaders to consider the 'risks' of terrorism. However, terrorism will defy risk-management attempts to capture its danger and threat. I argue that security operations may do little to stop a determined terrorist, but visibly improved security can generate feelings of safety and security. In many respects, this is the true counter-terrorism operation. Business leaders and managers cannot hope to win a war against the amorphous political tactic labelled as 'terrorism', but they stand a fighting chance against the human emotion *terror*.

As 9/11 unfolded in Manhattan, witnesses both near and far tuned into the television coverage, some as close as a mile away (see Miller, 2002; Barnett, 2002: 249). These images were recorded, reproduced and replayed. Contemporary terrorism is radicalized by images that problematize traditional understandings of time and space. For some, witnessing terrorism is little more than a 'Google' away. As I have already indicated my intent in this book is to explore and analyze the witnesses to the spectacle of terrorism and the consequences and meanings of terrorism for working people and businesses. Through media analyses, combined with interview data collected across several months in Melbourne, Australia I examine the impact of terrorism on people working in this international city. The research and writing was conducted under interpretivist research methodologies and ontologies, and critical social theories. In total, 55 participants were interviewed from which nine key respondents were identified.

Heidegger's (1962) concept of *da-sein* – the literal being-there in time and space – is a conceptualization of the essential characteristics and contingencies of human existence. The image problematizes these contingencies by presenting an image-reality differently bound to time and space. A rigorous discussion of Heidegger's philosophy is beyond the scope of this book but his writings offer a space in which a critical analysis of the consequences and meanings of terrorism can occur.

In this book I intend to demonstrate that understanding perceptions of terrorism is complex. It involves witnesses and victims, simulations and images of violence, distance and cities that re-animate contemporary terrorism as an image-event. Much of the literature that examines terrorism, its nature and its impact on people, does not fully account for the important role that the image plays in generating terrorism as spectacle. I aim to contribute to a growing understanding of this role and how it affects working people and businesses in contemporary cities. To achieve this I explore terrorism studies literature and highlight its silence in accounting for the role of the image in generating witnesses and victims (Chapter 2). In doing so I detail how contemporary terrorism has consequences and meanings for working people and businesses in cities. I explore the organization and the corporation as a space and target of terrorism and I propose that these spaces can be viewed as laboratories and clinics where counter-terrorism experimentation can occur in the hope of producing a true counter-terrorism that may not only prevent violent attack but can alleviate the crippling feelings of dread and terror experienced by audiences of witnesses and victims (Chapter 3). I present research that employs media analysis and interviews as tools in an exploration of the situated stories of witnesses of terrorism living and working in a major city (Chapters 4–6). I conclude by demonstrating how these literatures, analyses and stories create a space for the emergence of what I call *Terrorwork* (Chapter 7). Terrorwork is the everyday and routine incorporation of terrorism and the threat it poses into workplace well-being, safety and security.

Conclusion: Working in the Theatre of Terrorism

In this book I want to tell the stories of people who work in the contemporary city and the businesses, organizations, enterprises, firms and corporations that employ them. In telling their stories I explore the meaning of human security, precariousness and vulnerability in organizational, managerial, city-dwelling and workplace settings. Working people, particularly those in major cities, have been the preferred targets for contemporary terrorism. Life in the city has perhaps always been risky, but the post-9/11, post-Madrid, post-7/7 city is filled with witnesses and victims of terrorism going about their work and lives in routine, mundane and everyday ways – I argue that this is the essence of *terrorwork*.

Business leaders, managers, and security professionals responsible for the safety and security – simulated and otherwise – of organizations, business, places and people were painfully aware that 9/11, and the wave of contemporary terrorism that seemingly flowed from these attacks, changed the landscape of working in major cities. The responses of workers, business leaders, managers and security professionals to terrorism and the threats and dangers it poses must accommodate a myriad of characteristically human responses. A heightened awareness of precariousness and vulnerability combined with a sometimes paralysing, unfathomable and unanchored fear has and must be incorporated into the routine, mundane, everyday and banal organizational and working life of witnesses and victims of terrorism.

The images and violence generated by 9/11 were spectacular and breath-taking and witnesses throughout the world were compelled to watch. Although Debord (1983: 14) argued that the spectacle is a version of the world that has 'invented a visual form of itself', in the contemporary city there can be little clarity when distinguishing images from the world, reality from fiction and terrorism from mere violence. Terrorism attracts the camera's lens and a willing viewing audience. The power of images and the generation of terrorism as spectacle make it likely that terrorism will remain an object of journalism's black museum, the witnesses' desire, and of commodification. In this sense the consequences of terrorism are not only felt in New York, Washington DC, Madrid and London, but also in distant cities touched by the image.

CHAPTER 2
Working People as Witnesses and Victims of Terrorism

Introduction

This study of how working people perceive contemporary terrorism places the simulation, the image and the spectacle at the centre of an understanding of terrorism. It employs the notion of *terror-work* as a way of understanding how terrorism remains different from other dangers, risks and anxieties that are induced by the precariousness and vulnerability of living and working in the contemporary city. My argument is based on four fundamental assumptions: that terrorists seek to affect the behaviour and attitudes of people who do not die in the attack but bear witness, becoming victims in the process; that this is achieved by combining simulations and images of violence and destruction in creating a spectacle; that people both small and large distances from terrorism's 'flashpoint' were, and are, significantly affected by terrorism; and that the city is a site and a theatre for the re-animation of terrorist events. The relationship between these four themes – witnesses and victims, simulations and images of violence, distance, and cities as theatres – has powerful implications for understanding the consequences of terrorism for working people and businesses. If witnessing the violent images of terrorism affects the people who live and work both near to, and far from, terrorism's flashpoint then understanding this process becomes central to coming to terms with the meanings of terrorism. At times when witnesses are bombarded with images of terrorism, such as on the occasion of anniversaries of terrorist attacks or following a so-called 'failed' attack, fears and anxieties that were caused by these attacks are reinforced (see Gupta, 2002). This argument is driven by a powerful logic that suggests that seeing is believing and that knowing that the events occurred long ago and often in a distant city is cold comfort while witnessing the images and violence of terrorism on television.

In this chapter I will explore the relationship between witnesses and victims, simulations and images of violence, distance, and cities as theatres in a meditation on the meanings of contemporary terrorism for working people in cities. In doing so the role of the image is brought to the foreground in understanding terrorism. These four forces are examined in turn and are placed in a historical, definitional and social context. I argue that the terrorism studies literature is mostly silent in examining the impact of terrorism on working people and businesses and the relationship between these critical forces. While this literature has a role for introducing and at least partially framing these issues, I suggest that it has made little progress towards adequately exploring why terrorists target working people. This is a conspicuous gap and one that I attempt to address here.

When Terrorists Target Workers

Terrorist attacks are not random or arbitrary acts of violence as some scholars have suggested (Weinberg *et al.*, 2004: 781; Whittaker, 2007). Too often has terrorism been framed as violence that 'might break out anywhere', as 'unpredictable' and 'indiscriminate' (Whittaker, 2007: 3, 27). Terrorists are not so unpredictable. Indeed, definitional analyses of terrorism post-9/11 have found little role for describing terrorism as arbitrary, impersonal, random or indiscriminate (Weinberg *et al.*, 2004: 781).

The terrorists responsible for the attacks in New York and Washington DC on 11 September 2001 (9/11 or Ground Zero), in Madrid on 11 March 2004 (3/11), and in London on 7 July 2005 (7/7 or Underground Zero) were, in many respects, quite precise and particular about where they struck. In the cases of 9/11 and 7/7, they gave their lives for the attack and it was something they did not intend to give up needlessly. These acts of terrorism were powerful symbolic acts that targeted the cornerstones of everyday life in 'Western' and 'industrialized' nations – the city, the corporation, and the worker. If their attacks had not been symbolically significant then they would not have had such significant consequences that have extended far beyond the physical and corporeal destruction. Without symbolic significance these attacks surely would have failed as acts of terrorism. On 9/11 the 19 hijackers directed passenger airliners towards America's – and the world's – economic epicentre, its military brain, and – according to popular and academic thought – the aircraft that crash landed in Shanksville, Pennsylvania was perhaps bound for the White House or another prominent governmental target. It was a decapitation attack on three fronts – economic, military and political. This does not seem random, indiscriminate or arbitrary. In London and Madrid, the target was the public transport network at peak hour – a time when the attackers could be assured multiple casualties, a fervent media response, and a desperate fear and anxiety amongst the 'public'. Again, there is little randomness in these attacks.

Some may argue that this argument does not account for witnesses and victims perceiving that terrorism is random, arbitrary and indiscriminate. I suggest, however, that members of the 'public' are painfully aware that terrorism is not particularly random or unpredictable. I argue that terrorism is so terrifying because it is mostly predictable, yet unavoidable. This is particularly the case for working people who were the victims of the terrorist attacks in New York, Washington DC, Madrid and London. These attacks were, more than anything else, attacks against the working population. As Whittaker (2007: 12) argues of the 9/11 attacks:

> *For the victim, innocent or picked out on account of their status or position ... [f]ar more than for any onlooker or security authority, it [9/11] represents such a degree of transgression that any who survive must feel a sense of irreversible vulnerability. American commentators in 2001, following the horrific bombing of New York and Washington, have speculated that the notion of personal attack spreads far across fifty states, and beyond the bereaved relatives of the lost. In that sense, all contemporary United States citizens are victims.*

I intend to extend this logic further. It is when one considers Whittaker's (2007) proposition alongside the consequences of contemporary terrorism for working people that it becomes clear that all workers throughout the world are victims. Arbitrary distinctions between the victims and the witnesses of terrorism are revealed in their absurdity. All victims are witnesses and all witnesses are victims.

The Witness and the Victim

The figures of the witness and the victim are keys for understanding the meaning of contemporary terrorism and its impact on working people and businesses. Acts of terrorism are not aimed at those killed but at those who live to bear witness. Indeed, if there was an opportunity for terrorists to kill a large number of people that would receive no media attention, it is likely that the would-be-terrorist would not bother. Events like 9/11, the Madrid terrorist attacks and 7/7's Underground Zero were viewed in many locations large distances from New York, Washington DC, Madrid and London as images carried by the world's media.[1] Miller (2007: 79–99) argues that most activities undertaken by people in the media in reporting 'terrorism' have worked to exaggerate and sensationalize the threat that terrorism poses whilst generating justifications for the wars fought in the name of 'terrorism'. These activities and trends in reporting were among the subjects of Herman and Chomsky's (1994: 1) 'propaganda model' in their exploration of the media's role in the manufacture of consent. The propaganda model involves 'filters' that prevent accurate information reaching media audiences and consumers. These filters – size, ownership and profit orientation of the media; the advertising license; sources; flak and the flak enforcers; anticommunism (or antiterrorism in the contemporary context) as a control mechanism; and dichotomization of opinion (as in you are either with us or against us to quote a famous George W. Bush aphorism) – alter, manipulate and re-orient data and information before it reaches media audiences (Herman and Chomsky, 1994: 3–31). Despite the propaganda filters that many media producers and audiences are subject to, I would like to suggest that the media does not need to be viewed as purveyor of either truth or fiction – following Žižek (2006) I intend to argue for a third option. This option involves finding the truth that may be located within the obvious fiction of media reporting. In this way, I am not concerned with the fiction of media reporting, nor the truth that may underlie this fiction, but rather the reality within the media fiction – I argue that this reality is laid bare in images of terrorism. Images of terrorism are terrifying and powerful and produce witnesses and victims geographically and temporally distant to contemporary terrorism's flashpoint. But, as Miller (2002) and Barnett (2002: 249) have pointed out, many in close geographical proximity to terrorism also witness terrorism in images.

Many writers argue that terrorism has changed significantly throughout history in terms of methods and tactics, the targets and the victims chosen, the ideology that drives the attacks, and the way the term has been used (Rapoport, 2006; Laqueur, 1999, 2003). The nature of the witness and the victim of terrorism have also changed significantly, but some consistency nonetheless remains: the more spectacular the act the greater the audience of witnesses and victims (Rapoport, 2006). Laqueur (1999: 3) once argued that terrorism 'has been a tragedy for the victims, but seen in a historical perspective it seldom has been more than a nuisance'. It can be argued that recent events call this claim into

---

[1] The media attention that terrorism receives is the subject of many studies. See for example Miller, 2007; Nacos, 1994; 2002; 2006; Alexander and Latter, 1990; Paletz and Schmid, 1992.

question. Laqueur's argument fails to adequately account for the role of the image in generating spectacular terrorism.

The history of terrorism is rich in attempts to earn a larger audience of witnesses and victims. The 'victims' – usually a casual reference to those who perish or are injured in an act of terrorism – have been seen as instruments in achieving the greater goal of publicity: indeed, terrorism has always been theatre for the living. Groups and movements such as the *Sicarii*, the *Hashashin* and the *Thuggee* created violent imagery that instilled terror and attracted witnesses and victims both near to and far from where their attacks occurred (Laqueur, 1999). The Sicarii were an extreme Jewish faction that became active in the first century CE during the Roman occupation of Palestine. They attacked in crowds during holidays and religious festivals: their targets were mostly moneylenders, priests and other Jews that they believed were collaborating with the occupying Romans (Laqueur, 1999: 11). Their goal was to overthrow Roman rule and establish self-governance. Their terror was often combined with organized guerrilla attacks launched against strategic Roman positions from Sicarii camps and strongholds in the countryside. The crowds in which the killings took place became frenzied as news of Sicarii attacks spread. The Sicarii desired publicity for their cause and were successful in inspiring an uprising. The historian Josephus (in Rapoport, 1984: 670) wrote that the 'Sicarii committed murders in broad daylight in the heart of Jerusalem'. Their attacks occurred predominantly on holy days where the terrorists would mingle in the crowd while concealing daggers. Their violence was designed to create alarm and hysteria and news of their exploits travelled to distant places.

The Hashashin, after whom the term assassin has come into common use, were a radical Muslim sect that targeted rulers and religious leaders that they believed were corrupt. The Hashashin were responsible for the deaths of many prominent Christians and Muslims (Singh, 1977: 6, 14; Laqueur, 1999: 11). They were predominantly active between the eleventh and fourteenth centuries. In 1090, the Hashashin seized the fortress of Alamut and, several years later, completed assassinations of the Sultan of Baghdad, Nazim al Mulq, Count Raymond II of Tripoli and Marquis Conrad of Montferrat, ruler of Jerusalem (Laqueur, 1999: 11; Singh, 1977: 6, 14). They became well known in many regions for carrying out bold and brazen attacks against high-profile targets and for their supposed love of the drug hashish. It was popularly believed that the assassins would get high on the drug before embarking on a mission, although accounts on this differ. Among their chief goals was attracting witnesses and gaining publicity. Rapoport (1984: 665) argued that they did not need mass communication and media to reach witnesses and victimize people in distant locations. Their prominent 'victims' were murdered 'in venerated sites and royal courts' on holy days and during festivals to guarantee that there would be many witnesses, and that word of their actions and purpose would spread. These fanatical killers posed not only a physical threat to those believed to be targets but a threat to all who heard the tales and accepted the imagery created by the stories that emerged from their actions. Often after carrying out an assassination the Hashashin terrorist would remain and accept their inevitable fate as guards and soldiers struck them down. This defied reason for witnesses and victims and created terrifying and powerful imagery for those who heard the tale (Laqueur, 1999: 11; Singh, 1977: 6, 14). Stories of the Hashashin reached fantastic proportions. As their notoriety spread they became deeply feared.

The Thuggee first became active in the seventh century and were particularly active during the thirteenth century in what is present-day India (Rapoport, 1984: 661). They were not attempting to influence any group. Rather, they were committing murders they believed satisfied their deity: the Hindu goddess of terror, Kali (Rapoport, 1984: 660). The Thugs were not motivated by a desire to attract witnesses or gain publicity. Their acts were not carried out to achieve a greater goal: the violence was an end in itself. For this reason, Rapoport (1984: 660) argued that the Thuggee were the only true religiously motivated terrorists. As the captured Thuggee Fresingea proudly proclaimed:

Let any man taste of that goor [sugar] of the sacrifice, and he will be a Thug, though he knows all the trades and has all the wealth in the world ... I have been in high office myself and became so great a favorite wherever I went that I was sure of promotion. Yet I was always miserable when away from my gang and obliged to return to Thugee.

(in Laqueur, 1987: 14)

Where other terrorist groups have had conflated motives[2] that included acquiring and defending territory, nationalism, political ideology, and religion, the Thuggee killed for their fervent religious desires. Their violence nonetheless generated powerful terror. The Thuggee claimed many thousands of victims and stories of their exploits terrified travellers, merchants and pilgrims. News of their attacks spread far and wide and, like the Hashashin, their violence, which involved ritual desecrations of their 'victims', was perceived to be appalling and irrational. The spectacle of Thuggee terrorism generated enduring folklore and legend (Rapoport, 1984; Sleeman, 1933). These various, differing terrorist acts and agendas were indeed powerful: the fact that these groups are still discussed in journals and books today is testament to their influence. It is in this context that these historical precedents can assist in a contemporary analysis of terrorism and images and contribute to understanding the meanings and consequences of terrorism for witnesses and victims.

While only the eye-witnesses to attacks carried out by these groups viewed the violence, stories spread the message to a wider audience, creating terrifying and powerful imagery. In the twenty-first century the message remains relatively unchanged but the method of transmission has changed significantly. Internet and satellite communication allows for many more witnesses. What these key historical incidences point to is that terrorism is always for an audience, a watcher, a witness. In much of the literature examining terrorism, however, the techniques, tactics, perpetrators and their motivations are the emphasis. It is perhaps understandable to be preoccupied with the motivation of terrorists since understanding why they commit violent acts could be a pathway to preventing future attacks. But the role of the witness and victim remains critical for understanding the consequences of terrorism for working people and businesses. The comparative silence in examining the role of the witness and victim in understanding terrorism is especially evident in literature that defines terrorism.

---

2   Some have suggested that the sarin gas attacks by the Aum Shinrikyo cult was another example of religious terror. Yet this group also held millennial beliefs and desired to bring about 'World War III' and a subsequent Armageddon. See Williams (2004), *Terrorism Explained: The Facts About Terrorism and Terrorist Groups*, New Holland, Sydney, pp. 30–31.

Understanding Terrorism, Understanding Witnesses and Victims

Rapoport (1984: 660) argued that 'virtually all modern conceptions of terrorism assume that the perpetrators only mean to harm their victims incidentally. The principal object is the public, whose consciousness will be aroused by the outrage'. Yet a study by Weinberg *et al.* (2004) that examines 73 definitions of terrorism up until 2002, all of which were developed before 9/11, to assess the elements that were most frequently included shows that the witness and the victim are only occasionally considered in definitions of terrorism. The authors compared their findings with a similar earlier study from Schmid and Jongman (1988). Of the 22 elements in terrorism definitions identified by Weinberg *et al.* (2004), the role of the witness and the victim was prominent in only five. These five elements are: fear and terror outcome; psychological effects and reactions; victim/victimized distinctions; publicity; and symbolism. Interestingly the role of the witness and victim in terrorism definitions decreased significantly from 1988 to 2002. Where the 1988 survey reported 'fear and terror' appearing in 51 per cent of definitions, in the 2002 study it appeared in only 22 per cent. In 1988, 'psychological effects' appeared in 41.5 per cent of definitions – in 2002 it appeared in only 5.5 per cent. The 'victim/victimized' distinction was featured in 37.5 per cent of definitions in the 1988 study, but in only 25 per cent in the 2002 study. 'Publicity' was a feature in 21.5 per cent of definitions in the 1988 study, and 18 per cent in the 2002 study. Finally, 'symbolism' was a feature of 13.5 per cent of definitions in the 1988 study and only in 5.5 per cent in the 2002 study. The analysis of Weinberg *et al.* (2004) suggests, therefore, that the role of the witness in defining terrorism has diminished since 1988. Post-9/11 definitions, however, were not considered in Weinberg *et al.*'s (2004) study.

Alexander George (1991: 76) once described terrorism academics, journalists and government spokespeople as producing and consuming their own carefully constructed field that he called *terrorology*. In George's (1991) view this constructed discipline allowed its adherents to define and delimit the legitimate and allowable parameters of debate for discussing terrorism. The focus of the terrorologist is to confront the crimes of enemies as 'terrorism' without the burden of confronting the comparatively worse acts of their own governments and their allies with the same rigour. Edward Herman (1982: 21) – in another critique of terrorology – argued:

> 'Terror,' according to the dictionary definition, is 'a mode of governing, or of opposing government, by intimidation.' ... The 'problem' for western propaganda arises from the fact that the dictionary definition inconsiderately encompasses in the word 'terrorist' Guatemala's Garcia or Chile's Pinochet, who clearly govern by the use of intimidation.

It would appear 'utterly incomprehensible' for many citizens in the West to consider that the United States is not only a sponsor and perpetrator of terrorism, but its chief proponent (Herman [1986] in Ray and Schaap, 2003a: 40). In this view, people working in media organizations have mastered semantic manipulation by relying on specific political and academic spokespeople that perpetuate the myth that 'terrorism' is a crime that can only be committed by non-state actors (Herman [1986] in Ray and Schaap, 2003: 42–43). A useful way to disguise 'My Terror' has been to call it 'counterterrorism' (Herman [1986] in Ray and Schaap, 2003a: 45). Zinn (2002: 12) has similarly noted this problem in his discussions of the war in Afghanistan that followed the 9/11 attacks. Zinn (2002: 11) notes that this post-9/11 invasion should also rightly be considered terrorism despite the media's inattention to the detail of the invasion:

The flow of refugees started as soon as Bush promised to bomb. There are certain American promises that you can count on, and that's one of them. So, you see the pictures of these families with as many of their possessions as they can carry on their backs and wagons, trying to cross the border. We are terrorizing Afghanistan. The people who live in Kabul and other cities in Afghanistan have to live with the fear of these bombs (my emphasis).

According to Zinn (2002: 32) human beings share 'a universal instinct for compassion'. Turner (2006) has similarly described this as the human's fundamental ontological state of awareness: humans can find universality in their precariousness and vulnerability. This, for Zinn (2002: 33), is crucial for examining the role of the media in understanding how terrorism is perceived by audiences. Since death and dying in Afghanistan at the commencement of the post-9/11 war was not accompanied by the same humanizing and graphic news coverage that accompanied 9/11, television witnesses did not relate to the violence of the Afghan war in the way they could relate to 9/11 – certainly Western witnesses were not victims of this kind of terror. Yet when civilians or non-combatants die as a result of being too close to a 'vaguely defined' military target this is certainly terrorism (Zinn, 2002: 33). Choices made by the mainstream Western media to broadcast few graphic images from the wars in Afghanistan and Iraq have resulted in these wars lacking the imagery to shock and terrify witnesses and victimize television audiences.

Louis Richardson (2006) provides a definition of elements of terrorism that is useful in this context. It is contemporary and useful for describing the role of the witness and victim. While it is not particularly remarkable, it is a contemporary contribution in the tradition of describing terrorism through elements rather than one all encompassing statement (see also Paust, 1977: 18–19; Waugh, Jr., 1982: 27, 1990: 43–49). In this way it can avoid some of the shortcomings of other definitions and provide a more reliable context for understanding terrorism. Richardson (2006: 20) does not claim to formulate a definition but rather identifies 'seven crucial characteristics of the term terrorism', three of which I argue account for the role of the witness. These are: terrorism is a form of communication; terrorism has symbolism; and terrorism has victims and an audience. In relation to the first of these elements – terrorism as communication – Richardson (2006: 21) argues that terrorism is not a nihilistic pursuit where violence represents an end in itself, nor is it aimed at defeating an enemy. Violence remains instrumental but only as a message generator for an audience of witnesses. In relation to the second element – the victims and violence are symbolic – Richardson (2006: 21) argues: 'The shock value of the act is enormously enhanced by the power of the symbol that the target represents'. Terrorism works by creating a psychological impact greater than the 'actual physical act' or the risks associated with the consequences of further terrorism (Richardson, 2006: 21). As such, the witness perceives terrorism disproportionately to the danger it poses relative to other risks that contribute to human vulnerability. Horgan (2005: 3) argues that terrorism is designed to arouse witnesses to be threatened to a greater degree than the damage that the act of terrorism will likely cause. Friedland and Merari (1985) once argued that the perceptions of terrorism held by witnesses were worse than the act itself and allowed affects to be felt by people far beyond, both temporally and geographically, the initial destruction. The third of Richardson's elements – terrorism has victims and an audience of witnesses – suggests that the act of terrorism is designed to affect the behaviour of a group of people who witness the violence, not the behaviour of those who die in the attack. This formulation can enable us to begin to explore why contemporary terrorists have been so effective in reaching witnesses and victims in distant locations, especially workers: the Twin Towers and the Madrid and London rail networks were symbols of business, work and the contemporary city and their destruction produced terrifying and powerful images. This destruction was viewed by witnesses and victims in multiple configurations of time and space.

The creation of images that reach beyond the initial destruction has been the goal for contemporary terrorists (Žižek, 2002a: 11). Žižek argues that the terrorists 'did not do it primarily to provoke real material damage, but *for the spectacular effect of it*' (emphasis in original). They were able to create what Weinmann and Winn (1994) described as the theatre of terrorism. The theatre of terrorism is a place where violence is combined with images to create something greater than either the violence or image alone.

Violence and Images

Terrorism, according to Laqueur (1999: 12), was becoming a feature of politics at the turn of the twentieth century. After 1900 terrorism was increasingly described as theatre and terrorists demonstrated their media savvy in their manipulation of governments, the press, witnesses, victims and images. An examination of the historical development of terrorism is offered by Rapoport (2006: 9–13) in his 'Four Waves of Modern Terrorism' thesis. This theory is useful in demonstrating historically the increasing importance of images in reaching witnesses and audiences of terrorism. According to Rapoport (2006), the first of the four waves began in the 1880s with the anarchists who committed 'propaganda by the deed'. The second wave began shortly after World War I and was concluded with the signing of the Versailles Peace Treaty. This wave arose in response to colonial rule. The third wave was characterized by left-wing terrorism and featured the Vietnam War as a backdrop. Finally, the fourth wave is called the 'religious wave'. It commenced with the Islamic revolution in Iran and continues in the present day (Rapoport, 2006: 13).

In the first wave the most well-known terrorists were anarchists. Anarchists carried out high-profile attacks that received media attention across most of the world but particularly in Europe and America. Their terrorism combined the intent to spread a message (propaganda) through the vessel of terrorism (the deed) in their strategy of generating terrifying and powerful images and imagery. The anarchists often targeted the ruling elite but were clear in portraying the public as potential targets. As one anarchist proclaimed; 'There are no innocents' (Rauchway, 2003). The anarchists believed that dramatic and violent actions, repeated at times and places that ensured they would be noticed, would lead to a polarization of society around pro- and anti-government agendas that would lead to inevitable revolution. This quest to be noticed was assisted by rapidly changing technologies that were making mass transport and communication simpler and cheaper (Rapoport, 2002). These technologies made anarchist terrorism capable of reaching more witnesses – and therefore victims – large distances from where attacks took place. No one was innocent – this violence was targeted at anyone who watched. The more spectacular the terrorism they staged, the more likely it was that the media and the public were paying attention. The development and refinement of dynamite – a precursor to present day weapons of mass destruction – made this endeavour easier to achieve.

The second wave arose from the mandates agreed upon at the Palace of Versailles at the conclusion of World War I. The victorious nations applied the 'principle of national self-determination' in demarcating the empires of the defeated states (Rapoport, 2006: 15). Their geographical ideals undermined the victor states and many of those who were governed under mandates disagreed with how the empires had been separated. Terrorism became a successful tactic in many places as a result. These places included Ireland, Israel, Cyprus, and Algeria. However, many of the most successful campaigns of terrorism were realized 25 years after Versailles, following World War II (Rapoport, 2006: 15). The defeated in this war abandoned their occupied territories and the victors began withdrawing from their own zones of occupation. This policy of commitment to international self-determination created ambiguity in some regions which paved the way for some of the bloodiest fighting of the twentieth century, some of which endures today. Of the most notable of these enduring fights, the one that originated in Palestine/Israel following British withdrawal has had lasting effects. Both Jews and Arabs formulated radically different opinions on what withdrawal represented. Second wave terrorists and their organizations actively sought a new language for describing their violence. Where the first wave of anarchists' proudly proclaimed that they were terrorists instead of murderers, the second-wave terrorists were aware of the political liabilities that the term carried. These groups preferred instead to be described as 'freedom fighters', resistance movements and guerrillas. This wave does not lend itself to examinations of the witness or images and violence as these terrorists had strategic and militaristic goals, many of which were achieved. This included the winning of territory, the removal of a particular government, or the banishing of colonial rule. Publicity, witnesses and audiences were incidental to achieving these goals.

The third wave, often referred to as the 'new left' wave, occurred against the backdrop of the 'agonizing' war in Vietnam (Rapoport, 2006: 18). The less militarily sophisticated Viet. Cong. waged a mostly successful guerrilla campaign against the technically sophisticated military firepower of the United States. This conflict sparked hope in many parts of the world that the world's superpowers could be vulnerable to terrorist tactics. Terrorist organizations emerged, particularly in parts of the third world, in opposition to powerful state forces. In the developed world, terrorist groups formed that similarly considered themselves the 'vanguard' of impoverished third world populations (Rapoport, 2006: 18). Groups like the *Weather Underground*, the *Red Army*, and *Direct Action* carried out various attacks designed to undermine governments and draw attention to a variety of social and moral injustices.

The Vietnam War brought images of violence into the homes of people in many countries. This war continues to resonate in popular culture and fiction, and Berg (1986) argued that it characterized a generation. Images of Vietnam flooded televisions throughout the United States. The mass communication of war was not unique to the Vietnam War. World War II had been a radio war and, much like television today, radio 'brought the war home' (Berg, 1986: 96). There was one distinct difference, however – 'TV witnessed the event actually happening' (Berg, 1986: 96). As Berg (1986: 96) argued: 'The family at home watched the front ... and witnessed the fire-fights. Parents had the pleasure of seeing their children or the children of others blown away right before the weather and just after the sports round-up'. The technology used to create images of the Vietnam War created the feeling that the camera was somehow not intervening by being there, and that watching on television was like watching in person. Courtesy of television, the image is captured and is witnessed. What is more, the image is real. To argue, as Berg (1986: 96–97) did, that the images were not reality perhaps fails to adequately consider the importance of images in perception creation. These images created a violent spectacle that was witnessed by people in many places distant to Vietnam. As it is with contemporary terrorism, the violence in Vietnam combined with the image and created something more than the violence or images alone.

Rapoport's (2006) fourth and current wave is described as the religious wave. Beginning in 1979 with the rise to power of Ayatollah Khomeini in Iran this wave has endured to the present era and was intensified by the 9/11 attacks. The defeat of Russian military forces in Afghanistan by the mujahideen provided momentum to religious terrorism and it is generally believed the original motivation and organization for Al Qaeda emerged from this war. Islam was not the only religious force that led to terrorism. In 1995 a Japanese cult with state recognition as an official religion released sarin gas in the Tokyo subway, killing twelve people (Rapoport, 2006). In these attacks it was mostly working people engaging in their everyday commuting rituals that were caught up in the terror. Militant Christianity in America continues to provide concern for the US government. Indeed, the Oklahoma City bombing carried out by Timothy McVeigh in 1995 is sometimes associated with the Christian Identity movement. Radical Jewish groups and individuals sometimes carry out attacks in Israel. The most notable was the assassination of Israel's former Prime Minister Yitzhak Rabin in 1995. Some attacks since 9/11 in Madrid, Bali, and London have been attributed to groups preaching a radical version of Islam and others – such as the Beslan school and theatre sieges in Russia and bombings in Mumbai – are based predominantly on a territorial and nationalistic motivation, although religious elements overlap.

I want to suggest that the relationship between witnesses, victims, violence and images in this wave was best demonstrated on June 14, 1985. A *TransWorld Airlines* (TWA) jet carrying 150 people was hijacked by a terrorist organization calling itself *Islamic Jihad* (Lule, 1991: 30). The plane was forced to fly between Athens, Beirut and Algiers and the world's media reported the events. People tuned in daily to watch and witness the terrorism spectacle unfold. The siege lasted 17 days. Powerful images were created when a US Navy diver was killed and thrown out of the plane in full view of news cameras. The images were beamed to news affiliates throughout the world and replayed on news programmes and in journalistic spaces. The US Navy diver later became a media icon. His life story and 'ceremonial burial' were televised in a special broadcast (Lule, 1991: 31). The media was heavily criticized, especially journalists from America, for providing terrorists with a platform to communicate their message and air their grievances. Rosen (1990: 58) wrote in the *Wall Street Journal*: 'Have (US) television journalists forgotten they are American? Everyone knows that terrorists want publicity for their cause, yet no less do they want to inflate their own personal status in their communities ... Therefore, each time the media afford the right to speak, they award them a victory!' In response, the American journalist Tom Wicker (in Rosen, 1990: 58) wrote: 'It may on occasion be inconvenient, intrusive, even harmful; but if because of government censorship or network censorship the hostage crisis had not been visible, *real*, on American screens, the outrage and outcry would have been a thousand times louder...' (emphasis in original). Rosen (1990: 58) argued that the reason for the television cameras capturing those moments in Beirut echoes television's fundamental *raison d'être*: being televised is a 'condition of being'. During the 17 day standoff, 491 hostage stories were reported on American television news amounting to 12 hours of real-time coverage (Atwater, 1990: 88).

... Then There Was 9/11

In terms of this discussion, 9/11 – what Baudrillard (2002: 4) called the 'mother' of all events – generated the most powerful combination of violence and images and created something more powerful and terrifying than the violence or images alone. As Nacos (2002: 34) argues, aside from the few who were alerted by friends and family via phone calls from the planes and buildings and those on the streets below the Towers, millions witnessed 9/11 on television news, radio broadcasts, and the internet. Barnett (2002: 249) writes of learning about the attacks from the television in his New York apartment only a few miles from the World Trade Center. Prominent cultural studies academic Toby Miller (2002) turned on the television even though the Twin Towers were burning close by. He was a witness and a victim living and working in New York City yet he joined distant audiences in watching the continuous replays of the planes crashing into the Towers in the considerable media space that was devoted to 9/11. This media space was perhaps reasonable given that 9/11 was, according to Gupta (2002: 1), 'the most catastrophic terrorist attack of this sort ever witnessed'. I argue that the violence itself remains incidental when compared to the goal of capturing the media's attention and generating witnesses and victims in locations both near and far from terrorism's flashpoint. On 9/11 the calculation was perhaps simple: strike a significant psychological blow on American citizens on their homeland. But were the almost 3000 people killed needed to enforce a terror outcome?

The symbolism and the image-producing potential of the not-quite-simultaneous attacks could be viewed as devastating whether 100 or 10,000 were killed. Would 9/11 have been any less horrific if 100 people had perished? Would working people and businesses feel any less threatened? Would we not still be analyzing terrorism in the media, political debate and academic study? As Applebone (in Nacos, 1994: 3) once argued, the 'significance of international terrorism does not lie in the number of lives taken or in the amount of destruction inflicted; it lies in the number of lives threatened and in the amount of fear and terror generated'. The theatre of terrorism *targets* witnesses by creating violent images. As such the distinction between victimized and victims is problematic. Terrorism does not target the dead. I intend to suggest that some are injured and killed and others experience loss, but the distant and near-by witness is the victim. Traditional definitions of terrorism are problematized by the role of the image as it creates a world where the distinction between the victims and the victimized is unclear. The working people killed on 9/11, 3/11 and 7/7 are symbolic of the threat posed to working people in cities throughout the world.

Returning to Weinberg *et al.*'s (2004) examination of definitions, it shows that violence appears in terrorism definitions more than any other concept. It also shows that the role of the image is not accounted for. While the study of terrorism definitions by Schmid and Jongman (1988) reported 'violence' appearing in 83.5 per cent of terrorism definitions, Weinberg *et al.* (2004) reported that 'violence' appeared in 71 per cent of definitions. For Richardson (2006), in her definition of elements, violence is a central concept in the understanding of terrorism. While only two of Richardson's (2006) seven crucial characteristics relate to violence specifically, all hold violence or the threat of violence as a backdrop. Richardson (2006) argues that terrorism always involves violence or the threat of violence. Opinions on whether a threat is enough to constitute terrorism differ. Wilkinson (1974) argued, for example, that a mere threat is not terrorism and only through a proven ability to cause death and destruction can a terror outcome be realized. Thornton (in Wilkinson, 1974: 19) argued: 'The terrorist does not threaten; death or destruction is part of his (sic) programme of action'. Certainly I would argue that a threat does not produce terrifying and powerful images and is therefore not constitutive of terrorism as spectacle. Žižek (2002a: 36–37) takes this further and argues that even the carrying out of terrorism will not guarantee terrifying and powerful images. The anthrax terrorism in November 2001 is an example of this. I suggest that in a sense it was less powerful terrorism because it produced no images and no spectacle and no potential for competing with 9/11, 3/11 or 7/7. It could be argued to be a poor substitute to more terrifying terrorism. What was there for witnesses and victims to see?

Distance

Distance becomes problematic when it is the power of the image that determines the impact of terrorism. For Rapoport (1984: 660) 'there can be an inverse relationship between proximity [to terrorism] in time and distance' and proximity to terrorism 'in spirit'. Physical, temporal, electronic, digital, virtual and imaginary distance that is produced, enhanced and globally distributed, can be cold comfort for people experiencing negative effects for having witnessed destruction at the Twin Towers or the public transport networks in Madrid and London as an image event. According to Shaw (1996: 8), an act of violence in one part of the world can be felt in distant regions as psychic threats that undermine perceptions of safety and security and create fear, anxiety and alarm. As such, 'Distance, psychological and even geographical, is not therefore a straightforward question' (Shaw, 1996: 8). Distance is a complex and relational concept that needs to be constructed and reconstructed. It is an active agent that we create through a personal mechanism of distancing.

I suggest the media has constructed contemporary terrorism as close 'in spirit' (Rapoport, 1984: 660). Gupta (2002: 13) argues that media reports and accounts have 'constructed and reconstructed' terrorism through the 'tone and delivery of newsreaders', powerful lexical technologies employed by journalists, emotional eyewitness accounts from the ground, and still and moving pictures of 'traumascapes' in terror theatres across the world. They were played over and over again as reconstructions and viewers witnessed from different directions and vantage points, from close up and from a distance, and were contextualized through specialist and expert commentary and compared with before and after pictures of the New York skyline, rubble where a nightclub once stood in Bali, decimated commuter trains in Madrid, and a can-opened bus in London. It is conceivable that witnesses and victims living and working in these places would not necessarily have had a vantage point for witnessing terrorism and may have needed to refer to television for a 'better' view. Articulating this difference between the witness of terrorism inside and outside cities where terrorism has occurred is a challenge. The psychological and medical literature that spills into the terrorism studies canon argues that people in cities where terrorism has occurred are *directly* affected and witnesses and victims in other cities are *indirectly* affected. This in some respects appears congruent with the distinction between the victims and the victimized outlined in Richardson's (2006) definition of terrorism. It is to this problematic distinction that I now turn.

Indirectly Affected In Very Direct Ways

Different psychological and medical researchers have approached the concept of 'indirectly affected populations' in different ways. Sometimes it is used to describe witnesses that were not in New York on 9/11, Madrid on 3/11 and London on 7/7 – those who were simply elsewhere and watched on television. But it is also used to describe people who know someone killed or injured in terrorist attacks. Liverant et al. (2004) acknowledge both of these positions but emphasize the importance of researching populations that are geographically distant when studying the consequences of terrorism. This emphasis appears to be as much about the authors' hypothesis as anything else. Research into indirectly affected populations has strained to prove a link between increased geographical distance from a terrorist attack and decreasing effects of terrorism. Under this assumption, distance is an effective predictor of how terrorized people will be by an act of terrorism in a distant location. Working people in Sydney could have theoretically been more afraid than their colleagues in Melbourne on 9/11, so too would people in Fiji have been more afraid than people in New Zealand. I argue that it is problematic that such logic would hold in all circumstances. Indeed, the worker in New York would have experienced 9/11 differently to workers in Melbourne and London even if they were all watching the same images beamed in live from the offices of *CNN*, *Fox News* or the *ABC*. But am I to believe that the witness in Dublin is somehow more affected than I am living and working in Melbourne? That they are somehow more directly affected than me because they are geographically closer? Are we to believe that workers in Berlin now face more terrorism-related work stress than workers in Melbourne because they are geographically closer to New York, London and Madrid? It would seem to be an unlikely scenario.

Schuster et al. (2001) examined the impact of terrorism on people in an indirectly affected population. Five hundred and sixty adults in the United States were surveyed for their perceptions of terrorism and their children's perceptions. The authors presented data showing that 44 per cent of respondents reported one or more significant stress symptoms, 90 per cent had one or more stress symptom to some degree, and 34 per cent prevented their children from watching excessive amounts of television. The authors concluded that after acts of terrorism, clinicians in areas large distances from the attack should be prepared for patients exhibiting substantial stress symptoms (Schuster et al., 2001: 1507–1508). Similarly, managers and business leaders can expect increased stress and anxiety among workers large distances from where terrorism has occurred. The authors argued that perceptions of terrorism were formed through media coverage and perceived interpersonal proximity to the victims. Schuster et al. (2001) suggested that television makes witnesses feel as though they were there. The televisual images of contemporary terrorism have been 'immediate, graphic, and pervasive' (Schuster et al., 2001: 1507–1508). Witnesses clearly do not need to be close to witness: this can be done at a distance. 'Indirectly affected' also infers that special meanings and affects are attributed to terrorism when witnesses feel as though the victims – those killed or maimed – were similar to themselves. Indeed, 9/11 was described as an attack on America rather than just New York. It is not a stretch to understand the Madrid and London terrorism as attacks on Spaniards and the British. Certainly many Australians believed the attacks in Bali represented an attack on the Australian homeland and its people. Many people in the United States similarly identified with the victims and perceived the attacks to be directed generally against Americans. In this view it is clear that working people in distant cities share much of the fear and anxiety of working people in cities where terrorism has occurred. Identification with the victims was an important factor in Schuster *et al.*'s (2001) study as it resulted in a personalization of the threat that terrorism poses – victims of terrorism in distant cities may be considered close in spirit even though they are geographically distant. White (in Birmingham, 2005: 37) argues that many people hold 'a strong sense of being personally at risk from terrorists' despite terrorism directly affecting only a small percentage of the world's city-dwelling population.

Liverant *et al.* (2004) conducted a study amongst university students in Boston in the weeks following 9/11. The stress levels of 178 psychology students were measured at two time intervals: two and four months following 9/11. Liverant *et al.* (2004) conclude that despite geographical and temporal distance between the attacks and the research participants, severe psychological impacts were evident. Respondents held significantly changed perceptions of their security and threats of future harm. Others reported feeling anxiety and anger. Liverant *et al.* (2004: 136) argue that this is the result of a disruption of core beliefs and the underlying assumption of safety that people in nations such as the United States often have. These impacts, however, diminish over time. A number of negative or 'maladaptive' coping strategies were detected and deemed closely linked to anxiety caused by terrorism. These strategies include behavioural disengagement, anti-social activities and denial (Liverant *et al.*, 2004: 136). Interpersonal proximity was again an important factor in understanding the consequences of terrorism. Respondents who knew somebody injured or killed, or knew someone who had experienced loss as a result of terrorist attacks, were more likely to experience stress, anxiety and engage in maladaptive coping strategies (Liverant *et al.*, 2004: 136).

The authors of these studies argue that geographic, temporal and interpersonal proximity are key predictors of how an indirectly affected population will respond and understand terrorism. Little mention is made in these studies of electronic, digital, virtual or imaginary distance. Moreover, little comment is made about the problematic nature of distance as it is produced, enhanced and globally distributed. The authors of these studies acknowledge the role of television without critically exploring the possibility for television to reconfigure boundaries where distance is produced. It is notable that the definitional analysis of Weinberg *et al.* (2004) and Richardson's (2006) crucial elements provide no explicit explanation for the role of distance in understanding terrorism, witnesses and victims. The literature is mostly silent on the significance of the *distant* witness as – and perhaps to some degree understandably – the immediate and up-close 'victim' is given preference. Yet media images and representations provide for affects to be felt large distances from the time and space configurations in which terrorism first occurs and the victims/victimized distinction is subsequently less tenable. In short, attacks against working people and businesses in New York City, Madrid and London are easily translated by witnesses and victims to represent attacks against working people in all of the world's cities. As Jenkins (in Nacos, 2002: 75) argued 'Terrorism is aimed at the people watching, not the actual victims. Terrorism is theatre'. The witness to terrorism can be found in many places other than New York, Washington DC, Madrid and London and they are all part of the audience in the theatre of contemporary terrorism. These witnesses are the terrorists' target. How then can a target be 'indirectly' affected? For working people in distant cities the role of the image in understanding terrorism is critical. I argue that even if workers are 'indirectly affected' they remain the targets and, therefore, the victims.

Also critical in this equation is the city. In the following section, I want to argue that the city – as geographical space, symbolic space, as metaphor, as theatre – is central in understanding the consequences and meanings of terrorism for working people and businesses. Terrorism has often been temporally and geographically distant to people living in most of the world's cities. In spirit, and in the electronic, digital, virtual, and imaginary, terrorism in New York, Madrid and London still feels close for witnesses in distant cities.

Cities

Bryan Turner (2006: 26) argues 'Human beings are ontologically vulnerable and insecure, and their natural environment, doubtful'. To protect against some of the risks that people face, routine and everyday relationships and institutions are formed that come together to create what is referred to as 'society'. People gravitate to these arrangements in the urban surroundings of the city. In the city, companionships and bonds are formed, rituals are entered and adhered to, common interests and pastimes are shared, and working and political institutions are supported. These things are themselves ontologically vulnerable and insecure like the people who constitute them. The city is home to the wealthy and affluent, to industry and the worker, but it is also the home of the corrupt, the criminal and the terrorist. This uncertainty fosters common bonds to share the risks and vulnerabilities found in the city. This bonding leads to trust, empathy and sympathy. The vulnerability of people is linked closely to the vulnerabilities of institutions. Into this vulnerability terrorism is thrust as a violent event and an image. Contemporary terrorism is broadcast live into cityscapes. Whether living near or far from terrorism's flashpoint, I suggest that the possibility of terrorism is a routine and everyday part of living and working in the city.

According to Zygmunt Bauman (2005: 68), since city living is inherently insecure, complete safety and security is not possible. In the absence of total safety people have settled for the appearance of safety. In a rapidly changing urban environment increasingly characterized by insecurity people seek surety and generally 'try to calculate and minimize the risk that we personally, or those currently nearest and dearest to us, may fall victim to the uncountable and indefinable dangers which the opaque world and its uncertain future hold in store' (Bauman, 2005: 68–69). In this sense, I argue that terrorism has consequences for working people and businesses in contemporary cities via two crucial stages – terrorism as an image-event is created with the city as a theatre, and the effects of the image-event staged in one city are felt in another. For some, contemporary terrorist attacks have had special consequences due to the size, significance and the symbolic importance of the city and infrastructure targeted. Eisinger (2004: 115) argues that the attacks have lead to a fundamental shift in values, a decrease in optimism, and changes in long-held assumptions of safety. Terrorism in cities is not a recent phenomenon and attacks occurred regularly in urban theatres before 9/11 (see Coogan, 2000: 127;

Mickolus, 1979: 301; Alexander and Alexander, 2002: xiii, 9; Hocking, 2004: 83). Given these circumstances I will demonstrate that the city is the terrorists' playground: a place where the most physical, psychological and emotional damage can be inflicted.

Buzan's (2006) concept of 'macro-securitization' is a useful tool for analyzing the city as a theatre for terror. Macro-securitization is defined as securitization that is aimed at framing security discourses, agendas and issues in system-wide threats (Buzan, 2006). The Cold War provides a powerful example of Buzan's claim. The Cold War produced multiple threats through which security came to be defined through bombs *not* exploding, a polarization of people within societies, and discourses of threats to human existence. In short, the Cold War represented an almost universally perceived threat that translated into a supposedly corporeal risk that was responded to on a system wide basis through politics, militarization, and social movements and groups. Taureck's (2006) conception of securitization informs theories of macro-security by arguing that security often amounts to little more than an act of speech in situations where declaring that a threat exists can sustain belief in that threat. Many have suggested, as I do, that both contemporary terrorism and the lingering threat of further terrorism are of the same order (see Buzan, 2006; Hocking, 1993, 2004; McCulloch and Tham, 2005; Tham, 2002). By responding in a way that constructs terrorism as a universal threat, law enforcement, the government, academics, business leaders, managers, workers and the media can be viewed as active participants in the generation, construction and reconstruction of terrorism as spectacle. Witnesses and victims of terrorism are deeply encoded and active in this process. Our attraction to the images and spectacles of terrorism, our sudden interest in safety and security, the unwillingness to fly, holiday in Bali, or catch trains and the hesitation that some people experience around Muslims all infer a complicity in generating, constructing, and reconstructing contemporary terrorism and the threat of further terrorism.

The Precarious Witness in the City

People living and working in cities want to feel secure in their daily lives but this is something that the city struggles to deliver. Perhaps the best that can be offered in the face of terrorism when certainty in security proves elusive is 'pseudocertainty'. As Nohria (2006: 19) argues, doubt and uncertainty are characteristic of life in the city and the security function of government, businesses and citizens is to return certainty, predictability and control. This requires that people living and working in the city deal with dynamic uncertainty and find some comfort in the midst of ambiguity and doubt. Nohria (2006: 19) identifies this situation as pseudocertainty. Indeed, the simulation of security through creating an image of safety may seem to be the only possible outcome of securitization in the city. Total, no-gaps security is not possible and should not be considered a reachable goal. The appearance of security may prove to be the best defence against images of terrorism.

In this sense, the success of security efforts in the face of terrorism may be dependent on convincing others that security is effective. The city contains many sites where we can explore the conditions that are necessary for this to occur. Spaces where vulnerability and precariousness are routinely tolerated – exemplified by corporate and organizational spaces – would seem to be an effective starting point. The terrorism studies literature can contribute to this endeavour and I have identified three crucial city spaces where my analysis and research can begin: public transport; the built environment; and major events, sports and mass gatherings. These spaces are crucial organizational and corporate locations in which working people routinely engage in banal, routine and everyday ways.

PUBLIC TRANSPORT

According to Bergin and Yates (2006: 8–9), public transport is an attractive target for terrorists. Public transport typically has very little security and it is not feasible to carry out luggage and body searches on public transport users in ways similar to those conducted at airports. Terrorists want to create excessive alarm, they want a lot of people watching not just a lot of people dead, and attacking public transport provides terrorists with an opportunity to achieve these goals (Jenkins, 1987; Bergin and Yates, 2006). Public transport is, I argue, an ideal theatre for terrorism. In Holt's (2006) view, public transport is inherently vulnerable. It was the target for 195 terrorist attacks throughout the world from 1997 to 2000. Public transport is relied upon by large numbers of people – many without a travel alternative – and public transport organizations seek to move these people quickly and efficiently. Securitizing these networks would likely slow the movement of people, invade the privacy of travellers, and generally undermine the consumer, worker and organizational imperatives of speed and efficiency. As public transport carries people to work, school, and to the city to shop and do business, an interruption to public transport networks threatens to significantly interrupt daily life in cities (Holt, 2006: 6). Public transport spaces, especially at times such as hours of peak use and during major events, can provide terrorists an opportunity to stage terrifying and powerful image-events capable of generating spectacular terrorism.

Many vulnerable city spaces are privately owned. As Alexander (2004: 84) argues 'Without a doubt, the 9/11 attacks were the principle reasons for Corporate America's increased attention to terrorism'. Pre-9/11 terrorism was little more than an 'irritant' to business, but a 2002 survey in the United States found that terrorism was the third most significant security concern for managers in major corporations (Alexander, 2004: 84). Considerable costs are expended on corporate security in this age of terror including 'technology, security, and safety equipment; employee training; [and] modifications to logistics' (Alexander, 2004: 84). More employees are usually required at these times as well as security consultants and contractors to staff new security arrangements and monitor surveillance and checkpoint technology. As more resources are devoted to security simulations designed to create an image of safety, tensions emerge between effective security and security overkill. Counter-terrorism spending may become difficult to justify when success is measured by an absence of terror. A clear and detailed understanding of whether a security mechanism is effective will usually prove elusive. Was security successful because no terrorism occurred or was it a waste of money because terrorism is perhaps highly unlikely to begin with (Alexander, 2004: 85)? This question cannot be answered but the consequences for doing too little – or nothing at all – could be significant.

The proponent of the pseudocertainty thesis would argue that terrorism is less about physical security than it is about the appearance of security. For business leaders and managers, improving the appearance of security – making security more visible for witnesses and victims – has a number of benefits. These benefits include potential terrorist targets appearing hardened. This works to deter would-be terrorists from attempting future attacks, and generates feelings of security, safety and confidence amongst workers, customers, consumers and others who move through city and organizational spaces. Airports were once softer targets but since 9/11 they have become more fortified and subsequently a less attractive theatre for terrorism. Rail transport has proved to be a soft target due to the difficulties associated with securitizing rail transport spaces (such as stations and interchange hubs) while maintaining the openness and freedom demanded by people who use public transport (see Loukaitou-Sideris *et al.*, 2006). Loukaitou-Sideris *et al.* (2006: 733) argue that fully securitizing the rail network, whilst seemingly essential, is viewed by rail service operators as an ideal rather than something that can be attained. Security awareness campaigns are often used to improve security and create 'a *feeling* of security' in customers, employees and the general public (my emphasis). Rail operators devote considerable resources towards striking the right 'balance' between passenger convenience, cost effectiveness and security (Loukaitou-Sideris *et al.*, 2006: 735). Inherent vulnerabilities, analogous to the inherent risks to open and free cities themselves, pose barriers to security. These vulnerabilities stem from the paradox between security needs and consumer wants, and the high costs of improving security. According to Loukaitou-Sideris *et al.* (2006: 739), 'if you want to run an open mass transit system, you live with the vulnerabilities ... having a system that rapidly proves it is alright again is actually as important as establishing what has gone wrong'.

Public transport provides an ideal theatre to stage a terrorism image-event. But it is not the only one. In contemporary times terrorists have demonstrated a broad capacity to target many sites in the cityscape. One such site is the built environment.

THE BUILT ENVIRONMENT

Then and Loosemore (2006: 157) argue that the built environment is a highly attractive target for terrorists. Among the targets in the built environment are 'buildings, businesses, public spaces and public infrastructure' and the people – often workers – who occupy these spaces (Then and Loosemore, 2006: 157). These sites pose special security challenges. Many buildings are not designed to display visible signs of security as access and availability are more pressing architectural concerns. More significantly, buildings are spaces where many people will spend their working lives and where clients, customers, visitors and the general public often congregate. In some buildings the number of people that pass through can reach thousands each day. These people have specific interests and access needs and adequately securitizing these public sites will likely pose an insurmountable challenge. The built environment shares many of the inherent vulnerabilities of the contemporary city and imperatives of security can interrupt the normal use and enjoyment of the benefits that the built environment offers.

A key figure in the built environment is the skyscraper. According to Leonard Gilroy (2001) from the *Reason Foundation*,[3] the targeting and destruction of the Twin Towers left a gap in the New York skyline and an imprint on the minds of people throughout the world. Gilroy (2001) has identified something significant about the power of terrorism – the vacant space at Ground Zero is a permanent symbolic reminder of human precariousness

---

3   The Reason Foundation is a conservative US based think-tank (see Media Transparency, n.d.).

and vulnerability. This contextualizes terrorism and 9/11 in particular as the 'presence of an absence' (Fine 2002: 9). For Gilroy (2001):

> *The concrete, smoke, and grief-laden gusts that choked downtown Manhattan didn't stop in New York. They swept through the streets of Main Street U.S.A. and across the oceans to the rest of the world. We have heard numerous personal accounts of the tremendous sense of loss that people worldwide have felt when viewing the permanently altered Manhattan skyline, indicating that, in a larger sense, the terrorist attacks may be producing subtle changes in our relationship with the built environment.*

The Twin Towers clearly represented more than the steel and concrete from which they were constructed – they had a symbolic meaning that one can say was eclipsed by the symbolic meaning of their destruction (see Baudrillard, 2002; Žižek, 2002a, 2006).

Kunstler and Salingaros (2001) similarly argued that terrorism has exposed an 'underlying malaise with the built environment'. Skyscrapers 'deform the quality, the function, and the long-term health of urbanism ... by overloading the infrastructure and the public realm of the streets that contain them' (Kunstler and Salingaros, 2001). It is perhaps too risky and precarious in a time of terror for people to live and work in densely populated skyscrapers. The potential for its use as a terrorism theatre is, after 9/11, suddenly clear. Kotkin (in Gilroy, 2001) argued that 9/11 'bring[s] a new sense of dread about urban locations ... a dispersion of operations in city centres as well as suburban locales may be seen as critical both to corporate and individual security'.

MAJOR EVENTS, SPORT AND MASS GATHERINGS

Yates (2005) argues that mass gatherings like those found at major sporting and cultural events are the ultimate soft target for terrorists. While some cities have few iconic targets capable of generating powerful and terrifying images if attacked, most hold major cultural and sporting events, music festivals and concerts, and national celebrations where people congregate in large numbers (Lake, 2005; Yates, 2005). According to Toohey and Taylor (2004), major sporting events provide terrorists with 'a huge opportunity to get their message to the world'.

> *A lot of terrorism is seen as theatre, and it depends on what message the terrorists want to convey in terms of symbolic intent, and a lot of the targets that have been hit recently have represented a certain aspect of Western culture that the terrorists want to signal that they disagree with.*
>
> (Toohey and Taylor, 2004)

Terrorists have targeted sporting events on various occasions. The most prominent includes an ETA attack against a soccer stadium in Madrid, an anti-abortionist who detonated a bomb at the Atlanta Olympics, and the targeting of Israeli athletes by the Black September group at the Munich Olympics (Toohey and Taylor, 2004). In a similar vein Toohey and Taylor (2004) argue that the 2006 Melbourne Commonwealth Games would be a target for terrorists attempting to create a terrorism theatre:

terrorism isn't necessarily directed at the victims. The victims, and I don't mean that with any disrespect to people who are victims of terrorism, in the world as it is, with the global TV audience, the terrorists are seeking a larger audience than those that they actually inflict damage upon. The Commonwealth Games provide such a vehicle.

Major sporting events and the mass gatherings they necessitate are difficult to protect and a balance needs to be achieved between securitization and spectator enjoyment: '[spectators] want to be able to go there, enjoy the event, and not feel that they're constrained, but also feel like they [are] secure' (Toohey and Taylor, 2004).

Schimmel (2006: 161) argues that sport is powerfully related to the city. The sport and the city are bonded through 'material, cultural, and discursive representations of urban space' (Schimmel, 2006: 161). Sport uses large areas of city space for stadiums, image creation, and facilitating mass gatherings:

As global violence telescopes within and through local places, so now physical, social, and psychological barriers are being constructed and enacted. In the wake of 9/11, and other catastrophic terrorist attacks in the last few years, the design of buildings, the management of traffic, the physical planning of cities, migration policy, or the design of social policies for ethnically diverse cities and neighbourhoods, are being brought within the widening umbrella of 'national security'.

(Graham, 2004: 11)

Appelbaum et al. (2005: 69) argues that it is only a matter of time before a sporting facility is targeted in the present wave of terrorism. Sports venue operators and managers have since gone to great lengths to fortify their facilities but it can never be 'foolproof' (Appelbaum et al., 2005: 69).

Vulnerable sites in the contemporary city need to be fortified against terrorists seeking to create image-events (see Coaffee, 2003). However, securitization should not come at the expense of the freedom and openness that people in cities enjoy. This is most likely an unattainable goal. Instead of attempting to provide full security, most often, pseudocertainty will suffice. The appearance or image of security may be the best defence against the image-event of terrorism as spectacle.

Traumascapes

Turner (2006) argues the precariousness of the human body is reflected in the precariousness of human institutions. Bauman (2005) has similarly suggested that precariousness and vulnerability are unavoidable consequences of life in the city. The institutions and infrastructure that are found in the city environment – such as those associated with public transport, the built environment, and major events, sporting events and mass gatherings – provide a degree of security for inhabitants, but complete security is not possible. The vulnerability of the city was identified by Simmel (1971: 324) when he argued that people in the nineteenth century were increasingly 'dependent on the complementary activity of others'. Writing on the psychological life within city environments, Simmel (1971: 325) argued that these institutions, or perhaps the routines of people within these institutions, are important structural supports – both mentally and physically – of life in the city. When they are challenged, interrupted, de-routinized and violently disturbed, as they were on 9/11, 3/11 and 7/7, it poses physical, psychological and emotional challenges to the everydayness of city living.

Following Tumarkin (2005), I suggest that the contemporary city filled with vulnerable and precarious humans pursuing careers, life and leisure can be viewed as a *traumascape*. Tumarkin (2005) argues that locations and spaces that have been the site for a disaster, a tragedy or an act of destructive violence are forever imprinted with the memory of that event.

> *Traumascape is not another, catchier, word for a site of tragedy, because 'trauma' itself is not another word for tragedy or disaster. It has a distinct meaning. The word's continual misuse obscures the fact that 'traumatic' is in no way a synonym for 'unpleasant' or 'emotionally taxing' or even 'intensely painful'. One word that perhaps most closely comes to expressing its meaning is 'overwhelming'. A traumatized person cannot fully take in or comprehend what has happened to them or what they have happened to witness. They are overwhelmed by a traumatic event. So much so that the ways in which they usually experience the world and make sense of their own place in it are effectively shattered.*
>
> (Tumarkin, 2005: 11)

Described in this way, the concept of 'traumascape' can contribute to our understanding of the consequences of contemporary terrorism for working people. Tumarkin's (2005) study focuses on places that have experienced violence. Stated another way, her study focuses on the places where violence *happened* and the impact of that violence in that place across time. Yet, every explanation of traumascape that Tumarkin (2005) provides opens a space for an analysis of not only physical locations of violence but also symbolic locations of violence. For the purposes of this book, I argue that the contemporary city can be seen as one such symbolic location, 'Because trauma is contained not in an event as such but in the way this event is experienced, traumascapes become much more than physical settings of tragedies: they emerge as spaces, where events are experienced and re-experienced across time' (Tumarkin, 2005: 12). As such, traumascapes like the contemporary city – a place where the seemingly constant threat of terrorism is grappled with and negotiated in everyday and routine ways – are full of 'visual and sensory triggers' that are 'capable of eliciting a whole palette of emotions' (Tumarkin, 2005: 12). Or, stated differently, the contemporary city contains all of the actors, scenery and special effects – since the best effect is the *real* effect – for a theatre of terrorism.

As Edkins (2002: 243) argues: 'One of the most striking images of September 11 was that of people on the sidewalks in New York, their hands clasped over their mouths, transfixed in horror as they watched the impossible turning into the real in front of their eyes'. The aftermath of terrorism, according to Edkins (2002: 243) has been most characterized by silence:

> *No cry was heard. Just the silent horror, as one cartoonist portrayed it, showing Edvard Munch's 'The Scream' superimposed on the incredible landscape of the burning towers. Newspapers the following day printed nothing but pictures. And, in all the television coverage, time and time again, not a voiceover, but an image behind all the reports and discussions, as if to show, again and again, to anyone who hadn't seen it yet, that this was real.*

Contemporary terrorism has been 'unanticipated and spectacular' (Edkins, 2002: 244). It has occurred in the centre of major cities and it is traumatic for anyone who witnessed it. The Twin Towers were undoubtedly symbolic, but had they been any standardized tall building in any city in the world, the horror for those 'caught up in it' would be common: 'Those watching the collapse, speechless, were not concerned with what the buildings represented, just that there were people in there, people falling from the windows, people being burnt to death, people being ground to pulp' (Edkins, 2002: 244). The rail network in Madrid and the public transport network in London could have been any comparable network in any city throughout the world. A telling irony is that the more efficient and effective a public transport system is, perhaps the more likely it is that terrorists will have an opportunity to strike. In some cities, inconsistent services may unintentionally disrupt planning for a terrorist act. It could be argued that the freedom and speed that was afforded to travellers in the Madrid and London travel network made them especially vulnerable.

While Edkins (2002: 244–248) is careful not to equate the suffering of the 'victims' too closely with the suffering of the 'victimized', she argues that the repetitive images of terrorism, the timeless spectacle of the planes crashing into the Towers and the buildings collapsing, were witnessed by many people, some in distant locations, through live, round-the-clock coverage. Similarly, Edkins (2002) equates the suffering of New Yorkers who watched the events from a vantage point not captured in media images as more significant than the suffering of those watching on television in distant cities. Cities have never been completely safe places to live and work. But witnesses in the city have rarely seen planes fall from the sky and buildings unexpectedly collapse. These new coordinates of vulnerability and precariousness nurture a dreaded certainty that if New York can be so spectacularly targeted then why not London, Madrid, Sydney, Berlin, Paris or Melbourne? And then, if Bali, why not the Gold Coast, Majorca, Ibiza, Cancun or Miami Beach? Again, if the rail network in London and Madrid can be targeted, why not anywhere that rail, bus or tram transport can be found? If working people were the targets before, why wouldn't they be again? People can perhaps avoid injury by staying away from war-zones, but what can be done when the war zone – the strategic military target – is a civilian city?

The trauma of viewing images of terrorism can cause what Volkan (2002: 456) describes as 'regression'. Volkan (2002: 456) argues that when a threat is perceived to be significant, people sometimes regress to an earlier set of beliefs and expectations related to their security and safety that 'involves a return to some of the psychological expectations, wishes, fears, and associated mental defence mechanisms from an earlier stage of human development'. It is not necessarily good or bad to respond in this way as, in one sense, it can be seen as a Darwinian survival mechanism. But in another sense, it can lead to over-reactions that can culminate in excessive fears and anxieties, symptoms of stress and lashing out at others. Blanchot (1995: 7) more generally has described trauma as 'the disaster, unexperienced. It is what escapes the very possibility of experience – it is the limit of writing'. The standard response to this trauma has been so-called *counterterrorism*. For Eisinger (2004: 124), counter-terrorism securitization threatens the 'vitality, sense of community, and civic quality' of cities: public spaces may become closed, buildings and businesses heavily fortified like prisons, which is often accompanied by increased panoptic surveillance techniques, an increase in security screening and barriers, and fear, dread, constraint and 'foreboding' become routine. In American cities, people are often searched at mass gatherings such as football matches and the New Year's Eve celebration at Times Square, and building and business entry point screening has increased in New York City (though not in most other American cities). Perhaps because of this visibly improved security, restaurant attendance is up and people do still attend major events and gather in public places. Eisinger (2004: 125) would likely disagree as he argues that excessive securitization may threaten the apparent resiliency of people in cities. Where the actual danger posed by terrorism in cities around the world is small, the hustle of city life remains clouded by the anxieties and fears that terrorism has generated. Yet despite the various gadgets and technologies of surveillance and security employed by governments and businesses to prevent terrorism – commodities in the 'War on Terror' – Eisinger (2004: 126) argues: 'The urban streetscape has hardly become fortified'.

West and Orr (2005: 93) argue that terrorism has lead to a public 'soul searching about security' in cities. They argue that urban security and urban living is increasingly jaded by fear, anxiety, anger and mistrust and the contemporary city dweller in times of terror is receptive to new panoptic techniques. Even the value of torture routinely finds its way into the opinion columns of major newspapers. Before 9/11 Americans showed little concern about the threat of terrorism to cities. In the aftermath, it has become a 'hot-button issue' for United States' city dwellers (West and Orr, 2005: 94). If cities are to survive as open and free spaces for leisure, commerce and vulnerable and precarious bodies, simulated security must accompany urban lifestyles as a means to mitigate anxieties and fears of 9/11-, 3/11- and 7/7-style terrorism. According to Savitch (2003: 103) cities will increasingly become characterized by protection, security and public order. From the terrorists' perspective contemporary cities are both 'alarmingly powerful' and 'startlingly weak' (Savitch, 2003: 107). It is this combination of weakness and strength that provokes violence and this 'combination of a glaring threat and acute vulnerability was all too evident in the physical presence, the very symbolism, of the twin towers' (Savitch, 2003: 107). This symbolic event was broadcast throughout the world as an image that continues to have an impact across multiple configurations of time and space. For working people and businesses in cities, terrorism is real in its consequences.

Conclusion

By bringing the four themes that I have explored in this chapter closer together – the witness and the victim, simulations and images of violence, distance, and cities – we can begin to formulate a picture of working people as witnesses and victims of contemporary terrorism. The frailty of human existence is evident through the ease with which the body can be harmed. As animals that are aware of our predicament we form human bonds and institutions that sustain our existence both physically and psychologically. Terrorism undermines the stability of these institutions, perceptions of physical safety, and psychological trust and faith in the conditions that guard against our precarious existence. The city, as home and workplace for many people and home for the institutions on which people rely, shares this frailty and precariousness. Into this ontological uncertainty – this essential vulnerability – images of contemporary terrorism have been thrust. Terrorism produces images that generate a spectacle of terrorism that is witnessed by people living and working in cities the world over. This was the terrorists' goal (Žižek, 2002a: 11). They wanted a lot of people watching, not just a lot of people dead. As Baudrillard (2002:

27) argued: 'Among the other weapons of the system which they turned around against it, the terrorists exploited the "real-time" of images'. Images are transmitted instantly around the world even as events are occurring. Images hold the event up for close scrutiny through pristine production quality yet simultaneously hold the event hostage in a world of replay and re-transmission. In this way images of terrorism reproduce and restrict meanings. The image-event is consumed, absorbed and offered again for consumption (Baudrillard, 2002: 27). The image gives terrorism a spectacular impact, but an impact trapped in an image-event.

A clear separation between directly and indirectly affected witnesses and victims living and working in cities would seem problematic when bringing the role of the image to the foreground in understanding the meanings and consequences of terrorism. Geographic and temporal parameters seem out of place in such a discussion since images transcend time and space. Terrorism is not aimed at those killed in an attack – it is aimed at the witness wherever they watch. The witnesses watching television in distant cities do not experience terrorism in the same way that people living and working in New York, Madrid or London did, yet witnesses in all cities are the targets and the victims. Is it not then inconsistent to talk about an indirectly affected target or an indirectly affected victim? As targets, city dwellers and workers should expect terrorism to impact on their lives whenever they witness spectacular terrorism. Not all terrorism however will be spectacular in the way that recent acts of terrorism have been but all subsequent acts of terrorism are understood through the re-animation of the devastating attacks in New York, Washington DC, Madrid and London. This account of terrorism seeks to understand the relationship between the witness and victim, simulations and images of violence, distance, and the city. Through this relationship the cityscape is illuminated as the terrorists' visual playground possessing all the necessary elements for the terrorism theatre – the stage, the players, the audience. Terrorism as spectacle creates powerful and terrifying images that are witnessed throughout the world – contemporary terrorists count on it.

CHAPTER 3
The Consequences and Meanings of Terrorism for Businesses

Introduction: Businesses in a Time of Terror

In the previous chapter I set out the conditions for being a witness and a victim of contemporary terrorism in places both near and far from terrorism's 'flashpoint'. It may be that these four coordinates – witnesses and victims, simulations and images of violence, distance, and cities – go some way to explaining the targets that terrorists choose, the goals of their political message, and what it means to live and work in the city in a time of terror. Building on these coordinates, my intention in this chapter is to lay out the coordinates for understanding businesses and organizations in a time of terror and pave the way for the outcomes of research that I present in Chapters 4–6. The coordinates for businesses and organizations represent *intersecting narratives*. The narratives represent the intersections between *international terrorism, workers*, and *management and security*.

These narratives broadly correspond with how terrorism emerges as a threat to business – international terrorism is the *problem*; all workers (including managers and business leaders) bear the *consequences*; and the role of managers and security managers is to organize and deliver the *responses*.

Working people and businesses are at home in the city. The city is a place to which people flock to benefit from the social, cultural and employment opportunities that organizations in cities provide. In this chapter I explore the consequences and meanings of terrorism for businesses, organizations and workers. I take some lead in this endeavour from the limited existing literature that examines the business consequences of terrorism. This literature, a large segment of which was prepared by leading scholars in the terrorism studies cannon but whom are painfully unaware of a variety of crucial managerial and business concerns, is useful for its insight into potentially fruitful areas for research and analysis. Yet this literature is little more than a glimpse – a tiny and fragmentary acknowledgement of a multi-layered problem that promises enormous consequences yet lacks an analytical and critical depth of understanding. I do not dispute the consequences but I seek to address the lack of critical depth in this chapter.

A number of studies have explored the meanings and consequences of terrorism from the perspective of the city and urban landscape (as explored in Chapter 2). Other studies have attempted to deploy 'disaster management' models for understanding terrorism and work (Fischer III, 2002, 1998a, b; Mankin and Perry, 2004). Research that explores the consequences of terrorism for businesses and workers remains desperately lacking. This existing research is also deficient for its lack of interest in the human consequences of terrorism. The emotional and psychological costs to working people, who are the terrorists' chosen witnesses and victims, can be demoralizing. It is my contention in this chapter that visible signs of security improvement – whether simulated or fortress building – can be vital for maintaining security for those who work and live in the city. While some authors who explore the meanings of terrorism for businesses devote some attention to the emotional and psychological consequences of terrorism for working people (Alexander and Alexander, 2002; Alexander, 2004; Alexander and Kilmarx, 1979; Ackerman, 2008; Committee on Government Reform, 2006), for the most part these authors are preoccupied with questions of security cost, business continuity and maintaining productivity during times of terror (ironically with little thought to how workers may contribute to this goal). Sometimes these same authors see working people as a hindrance to high-quality security rather than a vital ally in times of terror. I suggest that any change or improvement to business counter-terrorism preparedness can only be successful if it is integrated into the day-to-day routine and even banal habits of workers, managers and business leaders. Counter-terrorism should not be treated as something separate to core business, a nuisance or an unnecessary burden – to respond to terrorism in this way may lead to disaster. I suggest that counter-terrorism should be seen by business leaders and managers as part of everyday functioning and good corporate citizenship.

Narratives of International Terrorism

The best reason for thinking that a nuclear terrorist attack won't happen is that it hasn't happened yet, and that is terrible logic. The problem is not that we are not doing enough. It is that there may be no such thing as enough.

Senior writer for *Times* magazine, Bill Keller

Since 9/11 people have been given different versions, different realities, and different explanations for why it occurred, what we should do and how we should live. As I sketched out in the introductory chapter of this book, the terrorism of 9/11, 3/11 and 7/7 has had extraordinary consequences throughout the world that have ranged from international war, torture, the curbing of civil liberties and populations of witnesses and victims living in fear and terror. In the post-9/11 world, it is perhaps difficult to not think about the worst-case scenarios. Witnesses and victims are only too aware that the terrorism in New York, Washington DC, Madrid and London may only be the beginning of a much broader terrorist campaign that will see cities throughout the world targeted again and again. For people who run, manage, and work in businesses and organizations that make their home in the city, this awareness takes on different dimensions. For these people terrorism is not only an attack on democracy or freedom as former US President George W. Bush believed. It is also an attack on the everyday life of the worker. The following headlines in newspapers in the US immediately following 9/11 illustrates what terrorism means for some people in business:

- Business Grinds to a Near-Halt After Terrorist Attacks.
- Does a Disaster Await Markets?
- Attacks Trigger Nationwide Office Evacuations.
- Attacks Cast Shadow over Boardrooms.

- World Bank, IMF May Cancel Meetings.
- Overseas Stocks Plunge.
- Wall Street Comes to a Halt.
- Fed Ready to Support Banks.
- Exxon, Chevron Freeze Gas Prices.
- Wall Street Fears for Employees.
- Telecom Networks Stressed, but Operating (Alexander and Alexander, 2002: xvii).

Encoded within these media headlines is a broad-spectrum account of the consequences and meanings of terrorism for businesses and workers. These consequences and meanings relate to business continuity, the attitudes and behaviours of stakeholders, the attitudes and behaviours of employees and managers and the emotional and physical well-being of workers, customers and visitors in city spaces. The problem, according to Marren (2002: 20), is that the way we all viewed the world on 10 September 2001 was not the way we viewed the world on 11 September 2001. Our ability to think about the unthinkable and confront danger and risk in everyday ways emerges directly from how we view our world. But throwing out old ways of thinking and ushering in the new is never easy and it may be especially difficult for 'business strategists' who must convince employees and managers, customers, shareholders, law-makers, regulators and a host of other stakeholders that the most productive steps are being taken and that the appropriate balance between security and conducting business will be reached. This task requires careful planning, imagination, calm and unhysterical analysis and, most importantly, the best information about the meaning of terrorism and its consequences.

But this section is not designed to detail the history of when terrorists have targeted workers and businesses. Rather, I intend to demonstrate how three particular acts of contemporary terror – 9/11, 3/11 and 7/7 – hold special significance for working people and businesses in a world that can be indefinitely defined as 'post-9/11'. I do not mean to suggest that the targeting of businesses, organizations and their workers by terrorists is something new or recent. But to properly account for the complexities of the problem of terrorism for businesses my analysis must extend beyond a mere history of times when terrorists successfully carried out attacks against business interests. This is because the threat posed by terrorism to businesses is not limited to explosions, devastation and death. I argue that in the course of everyday life and work in the city, terrorism is most felt *when nothing explodes*.

To explain what I mean by this, we need to examine the multiple meanings of the word 'terrorism'. In one sense, terrorism is a violent political tactic designed to influence governments, persuade populations and disseminate – usually through the mass media – a political message through violent symbolic and attention-seeking attacks (Laqueur, 1999, 2003; Whitaker, 2007; Williams, 2004). In another sense, terrorism is an emotional response to shocking and horrific events – events that defy belief, calculation and understanding (Horgan, 2005; Riech, 1998; Baudrillard, 2002; Žižek, 2002). These different perspectives share one crucial characteristic – terrorism exists wherever *terror* is felt. Understanding this distinction – or perhaps this is best described as a *continuum* between different terrorisms – is crucial for knowing how to respond to terrorism as both a political tactic and an emotion. These differing conceptions of terrorism have radically different meanings and consequences. If terrorism is defined as a political tactic, then it is best understood by exploring what happens when bombs are detonated, infrastructure is destroyed and when people are maimed and killed. If terrorism is defined as an emotion, then it is best understood by exploring what happens when bombs are *not* detonated, when infrastructure is *not* destroyed and when people are *not* killed, but when people live with the possibility of devastating violence changing their lives at any moment and without warning.

Overwhelmingly, businesses have responded to only one kind of terrorism – the type that emphasizes physical acts of political violence. This response has often resulted in the emotional and psychological consequences of terrorism being mostly ignored or treated as a secondary concern. The impact of terrorism on businesses was the focus of two books written after 9/11. In Dean Alexander and Yonah Alexander's (2002) *Terrorism and Business: The Impact of September 11, 2001* the authors examine the impact of 9/11 on the economic functioning of businesses. Alexander and Alexander (2002: 123–152) spend one chapter examining the impact on 'US Labor'. For the most part, however, this book fails to account for the human consequences of terrorism focusing instead on a variety of strategic and functional dilemmas that have emerged from the economic consequences of the attacks. As the authors argue:

> *The attacks damaged confidence and lessened demand, leading companies to reduce production, eliminate business units, freeze investments, and dismiss workers. Furthermore, concerns about the speed of economic recovery, catastrophic terrorist events, anthrax attacks, employee safety, the effectiveness of U.S. military actions in Afghanistan, and confusion on the scope and length of the U.S. war on terrorism also negatively influenced the U.S. economy.*
> (Alexander and Alexander, 2002: 18–19)

Alexander and Alexander (2002: 23–24) note that unemployment sharply rose following 9/11. It was estimated that between 11 September and 7 November 2001 around 250,000 jobs were cut by prominent US companies. In some sectors, including hospitality and tourism, many businesses went into short-run economic shutdown.

Similarly, in Dean Alexander's (2004) *Business Confronts Terrorism: Risks and Responses*, the focus remains on the economic and financial systems and networks in the aftermath of 9/11. Alexander (2004: 145) writes of the initial consequences of catastrophic terrorism: 'The initial economic impact of the 9/11 attacks was acute and negative, exemplified by: substantial declines in stock markets and, thereby, the value of public companies (e.g. airlines, travel businesses, and insurance); and closure of stock and bond markets for several days due to damage near those locations'.

As I discuss in greater depth later in this chapter, in focusing on the economic consequences of only one type of terrorism – the type that relates to political violence – the emotional and psychological consequences for workers are treated as secondary consequences of terrorism. I argue, however, that emotional and psychological consequences should be brought to the foreground in understanding terrorism because without precarious and vulnerable witnesses and victims, terrorism would not be very successful in inspiring fear in a targeted population. More attention needs to be focused on terrorism as something that inspires fear and anxiety and a variety of other psychological and emotional responses.

The different conceptions of the meaning of terrorism that I have outlined require very different responses. Responding to terrorism as a violent act can best be accomplished by improving the physical parameters of security through increasing the numbers and quality of security staff, improving entry-point security for organizational and public spaces, training people in security awareness and facilitating movement towards fortification of business and city spaces. Responding in this way to the emotion 'terror', however, would most likely make the problem worse. Fortifying organizational and city spaces may generate more alarm, more fear and anxiety, and more terror. It is more appropriate to mitigate the consequences of the emotion 'terror' by managing the well-being of workers and managers through counselling, emotional and psychological support, and flexible working environments. Yet, these responses will do little – or, more likely, nothing – to prevent physical violence, crime and political terrorism. Responding to only one type of terrorism leaves working people and businesses vulnerable to terrorism's other consequences.

In this way, I argue that terrorism can be understood as a 'contranym'. A contranym is a word that is encoded with opposing meanings – its existence embodies a contradiction. Terrorism is a word that signifies both violence and the absence of violence. By only responding to terrorism as violence more terror, anxiety and fear may result. By only responding to terrorism as an emotion, psychological management strategies and complacency may detract from efforts to physically improve security and fortify organizational and city spaces. Finding some sort of imaginary equilibrium that balances emotional and psychological needs with security needs may not be a useful response. This may merely result in an ineffective response to both types of terrorism. Contemporary acts of spectacular terrorism embody the problem of terrorism as contranym. The attacks on 9/11, 3/11 and 7/7 were not only devastatingly violent. They have also generated a lasting fear, anxiety and dread throughout the world. The simulations and images of spectacular terrorism captured by global media organizations on these dates combine with the violence of terrorism to create something more powerful than the violence or images alone.

These three attacks – 9/11, 3/11 and 7/7 – are the most successful attacks carried out by terrorists seeking to directly target working people and businesses. It is within the context of these attacks that I loosely refer to as the 'Big Three',[1] that an analysis of the meanings and consequences of terrorism for working people and businesses can occur.

9/11

The 11 September 2001 attacks in New York, Washington DC and Shanksville, Pennsylvania have become popularly known as '9/11'. It has been described, inaccurately for some, as the worst terrorist attack ever and for the United States a 'Second Pearl Harbor' (Whitaker, 2007: 27). The links forged between 9/11 and the attack on Hawaii during WWII is perhaps testament to the symbolic power of both of these events. In Manhattan, the hole in the ground where the Twin Towers once stood is known as 'Ground Zero', and it was the epicentre for this historic day. These attacks were not only the most devastating of the three targets on 9/11 but also the most visible. Cameras were already pointing at the World Trade Center Towers when passenger airliners were ploughed into their upper floors resulting in the collapse of the buildings and the deaths of almost 3000 people.

---

[1] These attacks were not as significant as many instances of state terror for example, especially in terms of casualties.

Many of the 'victims' in or underneath the Twin Towers at the time of the attacks worked at the many companies housed in the World Trade Center. These buildings symbolized the economic heart of the planet. International and domestic companies from most sectors of the economy, including governmental and non-governmental organizations, endured the deaths of managers, business leaders, employees, clients and visitors. About 2000 people working in the financial industry alone died in the attacks (Alexander and Alexander, 2002: 124). Some companies, including Cantor Fitzgerald/eSpeed, the New York City Fire Department, Marsh and McLellan Co. and Aon Corp lost substantial segments of their workforce (Alexander and Alexander, 2002: 124). The destruction was not confined to just World Trade Plaza: in total 23 buildings in and around the World Trade Center were destroyed or damaged. As Baudrillard (2002: 4) argued, it was the 'mother' of all events.

9/11 is a location and date. Its everyday and even mundane usage conveys far more than simply one terrorist attack – it conveys disaster, suffering, precariousness and vulnerability, shock and awe, the fantasyscape of Hollywood disaster movies, the wars fought in its name, the freedom sacrificed for its posthumous prevention, the conspiracy theorists that argue that the US government staged these attacks in a war against the American people, the fracturing of hegemonic power, the malaise of the city as a safe and secure space, and dread and fear of an enemy who hides in plain sight. As Whitaker (2007: 27) argues:

> *Dates for most of us are fixtures pointing to the inescapable importance of meetings, assignments, financial obligations and pleasurable occasions. Dates such as 11 September 2001, 11 March 2004, and 7 July 2005, though, have a salience that is steeped in horror, death and indiscriminate injury for people in the United State, Spain and Britain. These were the dates when, out of the blue, terrorists savagely attacked a number of great cities.*

These time and space coordinates represent moments when working people became witnesses and victims of international terrorism. Those killed on these dates in four cities of global significance are only part of the story. Terrorism, by its very nature, transcends the time and space coordinates in which it occurs. The attacks created not only witnesses and victims in these four major cities, but in all cities throughout the world. I suggest that anyone with a television is a witness and a victim of terrorism. Yet working people were especially identified as worthy targets on these dates. Far from these attacks occurring 'out of the blue', they were meticulously organized and coordinated to kill people at work or travelling to work. They are representative of a terrorist policy to generate terrifying and symbolic violence with working people as a material focus of their message.

Spain's 9/11

The terrorist attacks in Madrid on 11 March 2004 resulted in the deaths of 191 travellers and injured around 1900 during peak hour on the city's rail network. Ten bombs were delivered to the scene in rucksacks and detonated. Four trains were destroyed. The targets were commuters en route to the city for work, school and leisure. The views of one train commuter in Madrid perhaps highlights both the greatest strength and greatest weakness of precarious and vulnerable witnesses and victims: 'If people really want to cause another bloodbath, eventually they will find a way. What can you do? Certainly not lock yourself up forever' (Adler, 2004).

Whitaker (2007: 30), in an almost condescending tone, suggests that the terrorist attacks in Madrid can be viewed as 'Spain's 9/11' – an event that was 'different' and 'smaller' in comparison to 9/11 but 'quite horrendous to Spaniards'. Spaniards have considerable experience with terrorism. The Basque separatist group, Euzkadi ta Askatasuna (ETA) have carried out a protracted campaign in Spain and France. Initially, some law enforcement officials were quick to presume that ETA were behind the 3/11 attacks even as it was becoming increasingly likely that al-Qaeda inspired extremists were responsible.

The targets were not random, and not incidental. They were hand chosen for their spectacular value. The Madrid terrorist attacks represented another site where working people became the currency of international politics and violence. Not surprisingly the 3/11 attacks 'dramatically brought people's memories back' to 9/11 (Moreno, 2005: 65). As Virilio (2002: 82) has argued, 9/11 has continued to explode in the minds of witnesses throughout the world. The Madrid attacks worked to reinforce the fear, anxiety and uncertainty felt on 11 September 2001. The attacks also had a number of social, cultural and political consequences. According to Moreno (2005: 66) in the minds of many Spaniards these attacks would not have happened if the Spanish Prime Minister José María Anzar's party had not been such a staunch supporter of George W. Bush and Tony Blair and their policies in dealing with Iraq. A general election in Spain on 14 March 2004 ousted the ruling conservative party and installed a leftist-socialist party that immediately announced the removal of combat troops from Iraq. In a nation haunted by Basque separatist terrorism – a spectre drawn on by Anzar with his insistence that ETA were responsible for the attacks even as it became apparent that they were not – the attacks allowed people throughout Spain to draw on the pain and anger fostered in another time and space.

7/7

On 7 July 2005, 52 people were killed and around 700 were injured when coordinated suicide bombers targeted the London public transport network. Three bombs were detonated in trains just outside Liverpool Street and Edgware Road stations and another travelling between Kings Cross and Russell Square. Around an hour later, a bomb can-opened a double-decker bus in Tavistock Square (Whitaker, 2007: 34). Images of this mangled bus have become a timeless icon of the 7/7 attacks.

This attack was not contained within the date coordinates of '7/7'. To disconnect the attacks of 7/7 from the attempted attacks on 21 July 2005 and the killing of innocent civilian Jean Charles de Menezes the following day is to misunderstand the meaning and consequences of terrorism. The attempted attacks on 21 July profoundly undermined any hope of a speedy return to feelings of security and safety for witnesses and victims in the city: 'On July 8, it was possible for survivors to think that we had missed the city's big bad luck. On July 22 [an unfortunately choice of date], the sense was not of somber gratitude for escape but grim acceptance of the possible beginning of a pattern' (Lawson in Tulloch, 2006: 71). This pattern, I argue, had already been well established on 9/11 and 3/11. The worker, the city, the business was once again the 'target'. The damage that terrorists can cause is exemplified by the unscrupulous killing of an innocent man on the London rail network on 22 July 2005. Initially this killing was lauded as a successful execution of counter-terrorism policing (see Tulloch, 2006: 81). It was soon revealed to be 'collateral damage' in the so-called 'War on Terror' (McNab in Tulloch, 2006: 81).

The 7/7 attacks shattered a number of myths about terrorists and terrorism. First, the idea that terrorists were somehow jealous of Western ideas and values became unsustainable – if it was ever sustainable – on 7/7. It was homegrown Britons who carried out these bombings to devastating effect. Second, 7/7 showed that closing the borders through excessive policing of immigrants or refugees would do little to prevent terrorism. More generally, targeting people who appeared 'foreign' in counter-terrorism operations is an unreliable form of profiling. It is likely that 'twenty-two-year-old, college-educated, cricket-playing, Mercedes-driving young Briton(s)... from Leeds' would rarely be considered the source of international terrorism (Richardson, 2006: 91). Indeed, such people would be considered by criminologists to be among the least likely. On 7/7, however, they joined the chorus of international terrorism.

The Big Three

The significance of these attacks for working people in cities throughout the world is difficult to overstate. Yet, these so-called 'Big Three' have taken place in a broad historical context where working people and businesses have often been the targets of terrorism. The IRA targeted business interests in the UK for many years. Timothy McVeigh destroyed a government building in Oklahoma City killing 168 and injuring 674 (Alexander and Alexander, 2002: 6). In 1995 the Tokyo subway was targeted by the Aum Shinrikyo religious sect killing 12. The contemporary terrorist attacks on 9/11, 3/11 and 7/7 I have identified as especially significant not because they are necessarily the most deadly attacks – although the attacks in New York and Madrid were among the most deadly – or because they caused the most disruption. Events such as the bombing of Hiroshima and Nagasaki at the end of WWII should place the three major acts of terrorism in some context. This context, however, does not diminish the power of the 9/11, 3/11 and 7/7 attacks to cause terror and this power should be located in the symbolism of the targets – a symbolism that was beamed instantly throughout the world through a variety of traditional and new media even as the events were occurring. These were symbols of Western prosperity, capitalism, and work. At the beginning of the twenty-first century attacks against hegemonic Western cities should be an unlikely occurrence. Yet, cities, businesses and workers are the preferred targets. Surely large-scale violence against workers, businesses and capital interests should have disappeared with the Cold War. But perhaps this is the beginning.

As I have already argued, not enough attention is paid to the workers who are witnesses and victims of terrorism. In the next section I explore the post-9/11 narratives of the worker.

Narratives of the Worker

This study of the consequences of terrorism for businesses places the vulnerability and precariousness of working people at the centre of an understanding of contemporary terrorism. It employs the notion of working people as witnesses and victims of terrorism.

Their vulnerability is tied to a powerful commercial logic that creates the space for the emergence of sometimes conflicting and paradoxical situated knowledges, the violent language of terrorism, and a conceptualization of the business, the organization, and the corporation as a location for developing counter-terrorism responses. As Turner (2006: 26) argues 'Human beings are ontologically vulnerable and insecure, and their natural environment, doubtful'. Yet these ontologies of insecurity are not static or stagnant. They are fluid, flexible and emergent and point to a world that can be universally characterized in indefinite ways as 'post-9/11'. The institutions, routines and rituals that people enter in response to their precariousness and vulnerability are, in turn, insecure. These institutions are often centered in organizations, businesses, and work, the foundations of which 'rest in common experience of vulnerability and precariousness' (Turner, 2006: 27). It is the people who inhabit these spaces constituting organizations, businesses, and work and the associated institutions, routines, and rituals that were the targets of terrorism in New York, Washington DC, Madrid and London at the beginning of the twenty-first century. Being a worker, a witness and a victim in the city is an unavoidable part of life for millions of city-dwelling workers, an 'inevitable contingency of human existence' and makes 'emplacement ... crucial to our sense of identity, security, and continuity' (Turner, 2006: 27).

Contemporary terrorists understand these contingencies well. The contemporary city houses millions of workers and organizations. The city is home to the affluent, the prosperous and the worker. It is also home to the criminal and the terrorist. I argue that the city is the terrorists' playground and the worker is the target of their violence. It is through these contingencies that conceptualizations of terrorism that accentuate its supposed arbitrary and random nature are revealed for their absurdity. Whitaker (2007: 27) has described the terrorism that targeted New York, Washington DC, Madrid and London as attacks 'out of the blue' targeting 'a number of great cities'. Whitaker (2007: 34) suggests in reference to the Madrid attacks that such 'unpredictable, random violence' ensures that the city's population 'will never be quite the same again' no matter how much security is improved and hardened. Perhaps by treating terrorist violence as arbitrary and indiscriminate the inevitable confrontation with terrorism's root causes can be postponed and eventually avoided.

It is these three acts of contemporary terrorism that capture what it means for working people to be victims and witnesses of terrorism – the 9/11 attacks or 'Ground Zero'; the Madrid attacks in 2004, sometimes referred to as 'Spain's 9/11' by at least one American writer (Whitaker, 2007: 30); and the London 7/7 attacks, otherwise known as 'Underground Zero' (Tulloch, 2006: 5). These were certainly far from the first acts of terrorism to strike at the lives of working people. At a conference held at the Georgetown University Center for Strategic and International Studies in 1977, many consequences of terrorists targeting businesses and working people were explored (Alexander and Kilmarx, 1979). The organizing theme for this conference was:

The facilities, personnel, and operations of the business community at home and abroad are becoming increasingly vulnerable to threats and acts of terrorism, including bombing, kidnapping, hijacking, maiming and assassination. During 1970–1978, this form of violence was directed against business targets in 2,427 cases out of a total of 5,529 terrorist incidents during the period.

(Cline, 1979: v)

It is perhaps astounding that this problem, stated so aptly in 1977, was virtually ignored until nearly 3,000 workers were killed in the Twin Towers – a centre for the capitalist and working elite. Even when the Twin Towers were first targeted by international terrorists in 1993, little was said about these buildings as an epicentre for routine working and business lifestyles. The publications from the conference focused on a myriad of business and terrorism concepts and concerns, yet few focused on the targeting of working people. Naturally, the chief concern of this conference was the communist threat and left-wing terror groups. While once the ideology of such groups necessitated targeting societies consisting of 'the contradiction between the wealth and power of the "haves" (big business coupled with ruling oligarchies) and the greatest numbers but impotence of the "have-nots"' (Miller and Russell, 1979: 56), the change in terrorist ideology in contemporary times has not been accompanied by a change in targets. The equation for the terrorist is relatively simple – find a location where many people will be killed and injured and the region will be brought to a stand-still. It does not take a terrorism expert or a risk analyst to quickly identify tall buildings and public transport in major cities as terrorist targets *par excellence*.

Miller and Russell (1979: 60) made a particularly noteworthy observation as part of their exploration of a crucial 'dilemma' in counter-terrorism security for business in the publication from this conference. Businesses, by their nature, are open and designed to be freely accessed by the public. Businesses in designing their offices, their workforce and management structure, at least partly if not substantially, seek to create 'favorable, receptive images before the consumer' (Miller and Russell, 1979: 60). Naturally, threats to this corporate image can only be countered by more positive corporate images. An over-fortified building, a heavily-secured workplace, multiple security vetting and checking procedures, and invasive prying into the lives of customers and employees in the name of security will not only be counter-terrorist, but counter-productivity, counter-profitability and counter-well-being for those most closely associated with the organization.

This was a crucial dilemma that people in businesses faced before and after 9/11. This, I argue, is why a bomb was passed through security checks and found its way onto a commercial plane that exploded over Lockerbie in Scotland killing 270 in December 1985. It is also why knapsacks loaded with powerful explosives were carried onto the Madrid and London public transport networks and detonated. It is why risk managers will be hopelessly unable to predict the consequences and the likelihood of the next attack. It is why people in businesses and counter-terrorism professionals will learn much about the attackers from closed circuit television (CCTV) footage following the next attack on working people, but nothing before.

More than anything, an effective organizational response to terrorism must account for the precarious and vulnerable human body – the worker, the witness and the victim. People occupy various spaces within the cityscape. Chief among these spaces is the workplace, public transport networks and locations of major events. The workplace is a particularly crucial location for managing and organizing human behaviour, attitudes, opinions, riskiness and danger, and efficient and effective production, and is therefore a place where the effects of terrorism can be resisted. In this way 'management' plays a vital role in maintaining worker morale, motivation and well-being during times of terror. As Parker (2002: 2–3) argues management has become a precondition for an organized and functioning society:

Management protects us against chaos and inefficiency, management guarantees that organizations, people and machines do what they claim to do. Management is both a civilizing process and a new civic religion. Even if we don't share the faith in today's management, we often seem to believe that the answer is 'better' management, and not something else altogether.

Management and organizations provide regular people with the means to become masters of a risky and unpredictable world. Although progress towards a better understanding of the consequences of terrorism has been slow, the need to understand these consequences has changed little since 9/11.

Terrorism and the Worker

Of the small number of studies available that have investigated the impact of terrorism on workers, few have substantially contributed to our understanding of the meanings and consequences of terrorism for workers. According to Alexander (2004: 124) – a contribution that does significantly advance this exploration – 'Any prospective terrorist attacks in the United States or abroad will victimize labor'. In particular, he argues, the 9/11 terrorists were successful in creating an environment where it seemed that another terrorist attack was likely and this has resulted in a variety of negative consequences for the health and well being of people at work. These effects can take months to years to subside and have a significant impact on satisfaction and productivity at work. In the time following an act of terrorism workers are more likely to change organizations and professions, move house, and reprioritize life goals to place less importance on work and more on family and leisure. Others will continue to work through and may be asked to perform to a higher level to return operations to a pre-terrorism threat state. These people experience high levels of stress and anxiety that may manifest as depression and other mental illnesses, the most damaging of which is Post Traumatic Stress Disorder. In the months following the Oklahoma City bombing, Alexander (2004: 128) argues, people were absent frequently, took leave as soon as it accrued, left their jobs, and engaged in reckless behaviours such as alcohol and narcotic abuse and excessive smoking. Reports from organizations affected on 9/11 tell of similar experiences. Other affects include a desire to join social organizations such as trade unions, lower demand for high-profile positions in prestigious organizations especially when they are housed in large cities and job insecurity as economic impacts are felt. When this happened it created significant workplace relations management problems – these potential consequences are known to significantly inhibit an organization's performance. Alexander (2004) also indirectly refers to occupational health and safety considerations, business continuity issues, culture and managing diversity. This study, however, does little more than identify a series of problems that may occur and provides little evidence to support these claims. Moreover, despite Alexander's reliance on short comments from interviews conducted with company executives and security managers, there is a sense that these important workplace concerns are 'played down' and treated as insignificant. Despite Alexander's acknowledgment that any act of terrorism will likely victimize labour, the author furthers the cause of those writers and researchers that seek to make the concerns and dangers faced by workers in a time of terror secondary.

Czinkota *et al.* (2005) similarly explore some of the consequences of terrorism for organizations and management yet, like most of the limited literature that explores terrorism and business, the human element is seemingly stripped from the equation. People will feel the terror, and their response and coping strategies will determine the future of an organization. 'Terrorism' makes no sense without people. For Czinkota *et al.* (2005: 581) terrorism 'poses both direct and indirect threats to the operations of the firm'. The authors argue for an emergent understanding of the consequences of terrorism for businesses and working people that includes strategic considerations of the threat terrorism poses. Where the authors err is in their assessment of direct and indirect consequences. As I have argued in Chapter 2, working people are in no way 'indirectly' affected by terrorism. Working people are the intended targets – they are the witnesses and the victims of contemporary terrorism. Czinkota *et al.* (2005) stumble upon a key problem that they do not fully develop in their research – businesses will make decisions that ensure the profitable, efficient and effective operation of the firm, not decisions that will necessarily provide complete counter-terrorism security. In some businesses, counter-terrorism will only be considered an important issue so long as it contributes to the so-called bottom-line.

Another study conducted by Mainiero and Gibson (2003) in December 2001 vastly improved our knowledge of the social and psychological impacts of terrorism on workers. The authors analysed survey data collected from 5860 respondents that explored the 'emotional fallout from 9-11'. Mainiero and Gibson (2003) argue that 'The terrorism of September 11th, 2001, unleashed primal emotions in the minds and hearts working in corporations all across America. The magnitude of the violence and the relative randomness of those who were affected left us feeling traumatized and horrified'. Mainiero and Gibson (2003) conclude that workers throughout the United States experienced trauma as a result of the attacks – not only those in New York and Washington DC. Three primary emotional responses were exhibited by respondents in this study – fear, denial and anger. Many reported profound fear and described themselves as 'dumbfounded and scared' when at work. Others were said to be in a state of 'denial'. This often manifested as some workers being dismissive of co-workers who claimed that they were traumatized by 9/11 and believed that it 'should not affect' their working life. Others were angry and directed their rage towards co-workers and their employers who they believed were unsympathetic to their pain and anguish. These behaviours often led to conflict and a breakdown of workplace relationships which in turn led to decreased satisfaction and increased stress. When this occurred the result was often higher absenteeism, turnover and lower productivity. The authors additionally conclude that proximity of workplaces to the World Trade Towers was a factor. Oddly, the authors also conclude that women were found to be more susceptible to the emotional and psychological consequences of terrorism, and both genders were more likely to be affected if they were married or/and had children. It may be, they conclude, that women are more willing to express feelings and people with families are more likely to reprioritize the importance of work and be more sensitive to risk.

While formal research is limited the same cannot be said for the anecdotal and journalistic commentary that flowed following 9/11. These reports were often based on simple interviews and observation and were largely speculative and told from an American perspective. Yet they may serve to direct more rigorous academic endeavours that seek to understand the meaning of terrorism for business. Some of the broad themes from this commentary are identified and presented here.

PSYCHOLOGICAL IMPACTS

The potential for negative psychological impacts in American workplaces following 9/11 have been broadly examined in research and anecdotal literature alike. Chief among these impacts were feelings of vulnerability and anxiety leading to higher levels of occupational stress and lower job satisfaction (Summers, 2001). This has had a number of flow-on effects in workplaces and has caused disruptions to organizational culture, harmony, productivity, and triggered interpersonal and industrial disputes, absenteeism and turnover. Sullivan and Anderson (2004) identify five specific fears that employees experienced after 9/11: working in tall or symbolic structures, business air travel, working in industries or regions perceived as vulnerable, being subjected to 'graphic news coverage', and a heightened awareness of mortality leading to a reassessment of priorities away from work to family and leisure. Poe (2001: 46) similarly notes that the attacks on the World Trade Towers were particularly fearsome because office workers were not incidental victims but were targets by design. Office workers all over America have likely felt vulnerable in the post-9/11 world – seeing people in suits leap to their deaths from burning office buildings perhaps made this almost inevitable.

TECHNOLOGICAL CHANGE

It has been suggested that some organizations may adopt technology quicker to limit the need for commuting, business travel, and boardroom style meetings. It is estimated that there was a 50 per cent increase in the use of electronic conferencing in the United States after 9/11 in companies where employees are required to frequently travel (Summers, 2001). According to interviews conducted by Summers (2001), '… 58 percent of travel managers surveyed said that company trips will be curtailed over the next several months and only 19 percent said that business travel would proceed as planned … these findings reveal a future workplace with much heavier reliance on the flows of digital information'. Mahmud (2003) believes that email, video conferencing, and 'telecommuting' – where work communities operate almost entirely in an online format – would increasingly be used in preference to face to face meetings, staff exporting and business travel. According to Mahmud (2003), working in times of terror is a matter of 'working smarter, not harder'.

CULTURAL CHANGE

Organizations that have improved security at vulnerable locations may also need to consider how these changes interact with organization culture. Improved physical security that is not accompanied by improved security awareness among workers may not make businesses more secure. People should be encouraged to willingly participate in security procedures, be aware and alert to strange behaviour and to report anything unusual, and to receive security training mainly in using security equipment. Often, security personnel will be hired to perform these tasks. Improved physical security is often implemented sceptically by employers to fulfill occupational health and safety obligations and to make employees feel safer. Some have suggested that no real improvement can be realized in these situations. St. John (1991) argued that in some airports security upgrades were understaffed by underpaid and untrained workers. Other technological upgrades may lead to greater surveillance of workers. Many employers are hesitant to implement such measures for fear of the legal ramifications for privacy breaches but MacDonald (2004: 34) argues 'The law creates few barriers for employers installing video cameras for surveillance in the workplace'. Perhaps a greater concern would be undermining an employee's trust and creating authoritarian management control methods.

WORKPLACE DIVERSITY: CONFLICT AND MANAGEMENT

Workplace diversity management has proved difficult since 9/11. Racist sentiments, misunderstandings, rage and suspicion aimed at Muslim co-workers have been reported, mostly in America, that has upset workplace dynamics and caused alienation and a number of other emotional consequences. Investigations by Mourtada (2004: 24–6) and Healey (2004: 25–7) have discovered when this occurs mistrust, bigotry and violence, discrimination, workplace bullying, a collapse of work teams, low motivation, high absenteeism and turnover, low morale and decreased satisfaction and productivity is the result. Failure to prevent discriminatory behaviour can have significant legal consequences. Sixel (2003) reports on an Egyptian worker who successfully sued for unfair dismissal from an up-market restaurant in the United States when he discovered that managers had attributed bad performance post-9/11 to having a Muslim employee. The Equal Employment Opportunity Commission won $1.4 million USD in the two years following 9/11 from employers on behalf of employees for similar cases involving discrimination.

OCCUPATIONAL HEALTH AND SAFETY

Protecting workplaces from terrorism is considered by some firms to be an occupational health and safety responsibility (Conlin *et al.* 2001: 38; Nighswonger, 2002: 24–27). After 9/11 some organizations are considering the safety of its people in ways that had previously not been considered. The increased responsibility for firms has led to improved access, production, and process security, increases in disaster and emergency response training, first aid training and increases in emergency response drills (Nighswonger, 2002: 25).

LEADERSHIP

Kennedy (2001: 18–19) and Argenti (2002: 103–109) argue that effective leadership in times of a heightened terrorist threat helps organizations maintain strong workplace relations. Argenti (2002: 104) argues that the threat of terrorism creates low morale and a workforce desiring up-to-date information. As such, leaders must maintain a visible presence and maintain effective communication channels in the workplace. Healthy dialogue may help employees deal with their emotions and socialization at work can be a uniting influence when many might feel safer at home.

WORKPLACE SPIRITUALITY

Spirituality in the workplace is a phenomenon that is gaining in popularity (Robbins et al., 2003: 60). According to Robbins et al. (2003: 60) it recognizes that people are 'nourished by meaningful work that takes place in the context of a community'. Stewart (2002: 92) argues that when facing the threat of terrorism workplace spirituality offers a 'safe harbour' and a meaning to life and work. 'An emerging spiritual renaissance in the workplace' keeps people attending work and can lead to economic recovery (Stewart, 2002: 92). According to survey research conducted in firms in California, 55 per cent of respondents claimed that spirituality plays a part in their working lives and 34 per cent of those believe that this role has increased since 9/11 (Stewart, 2002: 92).

Among these speculative narratives of the worker in times of terror there may be some truths. It is unlikely that all, or even some of these, will be present in any one organization at any one time. However, these narratives speak of a need for further research and analysis – it is a need that I hope to confront in this book and in the data chapters that follow. In confronting the problem in this way it may be necessary to think about terrorism as a problem with consequences that may never be fully understood. But when businesses take steps to respond to terrorism, each organization will become a testing ground – a type of counter-terrorism laboratory – for understanding the meanings and consequences of terrorism, and a clinic for experimentation and formulation of business strategies for mitigating terrorism's impact.

Workers as Targets

In order to understand the meaning and consequences of terrorism for workers it is important that I address what it means for the worker to be a target of international terrorism. I ask the question, why wouldn't workers be considered ideal targets for terrorism? According to Ward Churchill (2003), the 9/11 attacks were a case of the 'chickens coming home to roost'. Churchill (2003) asks what was illegitimate about the targets of the 9/11 terrorist attacks, as most authors claim. The Pentagon was a military target – most would agree with this assessment. But Churchill (2003) controversially contends that the American working people that were killed and maimed on 9/11 were members of a 'Perpetrator Population' and if 'good Germans' following WWII were held responsible for the actions of a government they vicariously condoned, then why should 'good Americans' be exempt from being similarly accountable? Moreover, Churchill (2003) argues that the merchant bankers and financiers that inhabited the Twin Towers were hardly innocent civilians. Workers in the Twin Towers were on the front-line of international speculation that can draw extraordinary wealth to the investor at the expense of an unknown, exploited overseas community. Indeed, this would not be the first time that the corporate world has been made the scapegoat for the world's ills. As controversial as Churchill's views may be, he undoubtedly taps into a groundswell of popular belief that extends through many parts of the world and manifests as what some might call 'anti-Americanism' (see Rubin and Rubin, 2004).

With their proven desire and capability for mass murder – exemplified by 9/11, 3/11 and 7/7 – the contemporary terrorist poses a diabolical threat to the everyday and routine operation of the corporate world. But we are all complicit in the consequences of terrorism because terrorists are most damaging when they inspire fear, anxiety and overreaction. Before I can proceed in earnest down this line of reasoning with an exploration of corporate counter-terrorism it is important to critically consider the meaning of 'counter(-)terrorism'[2] and its significance for understanding the diabolical nature of the threat of terrorism. In politics, the term 'counterterrorism' has been used as a 'vehicle' for oppressive policy and violent governmental reprisals against people deemed to be 'terrorists' (Simpson [1996] in Ray and Schaap, 2003: 75). It is a cornerstone of terrorism theory that oppressive responses to terrorist violence can in turn generate more fierce and determined responses from terrorists. As such counterterrorism can be counterproductive. Managers through their corporate counter-terrorism policies and practices need to be wary of creating more terror. Managerial and security narratives become crucial for articulating the threat of terrorism for workers, providing the appropriate conditions for effectively confronting the threat, and allowing the corporate counter-terrorism laboratory to generate emergent, creative and situated solutions. Turning workplaces into fortresses will likely cause more fear and anxiety amongst workers and may do little to prevent a determined suicide bomber or car bomber detonating their device in the crowds that congregate outside organizational spaces or on the public transport networks that bring an organization's workforce to the city. More than anything, overreacting to terrorism can create workplace stress and anxiety, be detrimental to perceptions of security and safety which can in turn decrease motivation, productivity, and efficiency and subsequently hand terrorists an unnecessary victory. Managerial and security narratives must stand not only on the frontline of counter-terrorism response, but they must also form a rear-guard defense against over-reactions, politicized hyperbole and paranoid suspicions that threaten to undermine the post-9/11 business world.

Narratives of management and security

I have, up until this point, focused most of my attention towards the *problem* of terrorism and its *consequences* – consequences that I argue are most felt by precarious and vulnerable workers. I now turn my attention towards *responses* to terrorism. I argue that these responses are framed within management and security narratives that interpret, define and contextualize terrorism whilst developing the techniques, practices and methods to prevent and mitigate its occurrence and impact. Building on my argument that terrorism should be understood as a contranym, it is important for managers and business leaders to respond to terrorism as both a destructive and deadly act of political violence *and* as an emotion.

In a time of terror and a world popularly characterized as post-9/11, businesses play an important role in a nation's counter-terrorism efforts. Not only does this role extend to closing the gaps in security in city spaces by maintaining security in stores, public spaces, and office buildings, but also to supporting the social and cultural lives of workers by providing a livelihood, social networks and emotional support. In doing so, businesses can play a role in fighting both terrorism as political violence, and terrorism as an emotion. I suggest that organizations have become a space for understanding the

---

2 I use the hyphenated 'counter-terrorism' to represent a critical approach to the concept. The non-hyphenated 'counterterrorism' represents its uncritical usage in governmental and legal discourse.

meanings and consequences of terrorism and a place where counter-terrorism efforts can begin. Some of the actions that managers and business leaders can take are discussed in this section and in Chapter 6.

The many ways that managers can respond to terrorism represents a growing range of managerial roles that include the management of risk and security and worker well-being. These roles sometimes compete for prominence. Some business leaders and managers will work to fight terrorism through efforts to improve physical security by hiring more security staff, purchasing security technologies such as surveillance equipment, bomb and metal detectors, enhancing security at entry points to buildings and stores, and training existing staff in security awareness. Others will spend millions of dollars outsourcing the 'risk' of terrorism to firms that specialize in disaster management and the threat of terrorism. These firms represent a booming industry and some have seen the War on Terror as an opportunity to capitalize on the fear and anxiety of witnesses and victims. These firms offer a range of products ranging from gas masks and decontamination equipment to under-the-desk parachutes that can allow workers in high-rise buildings to supposedly leap to safety from burning buildings (Alexander, 2002; Alexander and Alexander, 2004).

Resolving the workplace consequences generated and sustained by terrorism poses considerable challenges to working people and organizational decision-makers. Any response to terrorism will have both intended and unintended outcomes. Some of these will be positive and some will be negative. Often, deciding which outcomes are positive and which are negative will be difficult. To make such decisions, managers and business leaders will rely heavily on methods for measuring risk and understanding its consequences. Regardless of the methods used to understand the threat of terrorism, responses must be situated within the nuances and routines of each organization in ways that are appropriate, manageable and that calmly integrate the possibility of terrorism into the everydayness of organizational life. Before I turn to how this integration might be accomplished, it is necessary that I spend some time explaining the nature of 'risk' and its shortcomings as a device for understanding the problem of terrorism, its consequences and how managers and business leaders should formulate responses.

Risk

Risk has quickly become the dominant ideology for understanding the post-9/11 world. While a wide variety of studies have employed diverse perspectives on 'risk', theories of risk have been dominated by the work of Ulrich Beck (1999) and Anthony Giddens (1991). Beck and Giddens have explored the societies of risk – characterized by the presence of so-called 'high-consequence risks' (Peterson, 1997: 190) – and their interrelationship with industrial and global capital, the movements that arise to oppose capital, and people seeking selfhood, identity and a 'personal sense of security' (Peterson, 1997: 190):

> In a context of heightened concerns the work of both writers [Beck and Giddens] would seem to have found a ready audience among those seeking to make some sense of the global context of risk and establish some basis for personal decision-making in the face of apparent increasing uncertainty.
>
> (Peterson, 1997: 190)

Yet neither writer explores the underlying assumption of risk theory – the assumption that people are autonomous rational actors capable of assessing risk and making appropriate judgments to avoid dangers. The threat of terrorism is often formulated within this theoretical construct of Beck's (1999) 'risk society'. Coaffee's (2003) exploration of terrorism, risk and the city for example, details many of these theoretical dimensions as they relate to the city in times of terror. For Coaffee (2003: 6) 'the potential threat of urban terrorism' has generated a counter-effort to 'design out' risk through security advancements that must improve quicker than terrorist innovation. Failure to do so, according to Coaffee, can create heightened perceptions of being at risk from terrorism and a significant decline in consumer and business confidence. In short, the urban landscape is 'materially and symbolically' undermined by the risks associated with terrorism (Coaffee, 2003: 7).

Much of this rests on the underlying assumption that regular people are able to calculate risks as they go about their everyday lives. However, some argue that people are not designed to adequately calculate the risk of dreaded events such as terrorism. As Žižek (2002: 248) argues, 'this theory of the risk society falls short' because it places 'common subjects' into an 'irrational predicament'.

> *We are again and again compelled to decide, although we are well aware that we are in no position to decide, that our decisions will be arbitrary. Ulrich Beck and his followers refer to the democratic discussion of all options and consensus building. However, this does not resolve the immobilizing dilemma: Why should the democratic discussion in which the majority participates lead to better results, when, cognitively, the ignorance of the majority remains?*

Žižek's explanation of Beck's 'risk society' highlights an important paradox within risk frameworks – measuring 'risk' is dependent on how people perceive their precariousness and vulnerability regardless of whether their perceptions are reasonable/accurate/well-informed. It may be that some corporate 'risk analysis' does little more than audit the fears and anxieties harboured by business leaders, managers and workers. I argue that this paradox is especially problematic for managers and business leaders that base many of their decisions on the outcomes of risk analysis. The outcome of any risk analysis is, naturally, only as reliable as the information – the inputs – that form the foundation of the analysis. Information, data and inputs that illuminate the possibility and threat of terrorism are hard to come by. Risk managers are most comfortable when predicting business trends, economic and financial swings, and national and local growth and employment figures. When planning for terrorism, risk managers are forced to rely on anecdotal intelligence analysis, all-disaster trends, and business continuity plans. This will help little when planning for scenarios where the corporate offices of an organization are destroyed or where half the workforce is killed in a terrorist attack. Yet these were the realities that some managers and business leaders faced after 9/11, 3/11 and 7/7.

Perhaps this is why the 'Armaggedon complex' (Haraway, 2000) is so prevalent in corporate and security culture and why the worst-case scenarios are so easy to imagine. I argue that this is where a distinction can be drawn between *risk* and *dread*. These two concepts are linked and should be viewed, for the purposes of this discussion, as two sides of the same coin. Risk – on one side of the coin – is a mythic universe of calculations, probabilities, inputs, facts and figures. It embodies the need to know when what can be known is perhaps nothing at all (at the very least most will acknowledge that it involves a lot of guess work). Some have been more scathing than others in describing risk in this way. Mueller (2006) argues that due to this lack of understanding of terrorism and the threat it poses it has been consistently and irrationally 'overblown'. He argues that politicians and the terrorism industry – the terrorologists – work hard to accentuate and inflate perceptions of terrorism. Mueller (2006: 1) seeks to engage with a key question for understanding terrorism – 'Which is the greater threat: terrorism, or our reaction against it?'

> *That the costs of terrorism chiefly arise from fear and from overwrought responses holds even for the tragic events of 11 September 2001, which constituted by far the most destructive set of terrorist acts in history and resulted in the deaths of nearly 3,000 people. The economic costs of reaction have been much higher than those inflicted by the terrorists even in that record-shattering episode, and considerably more than 3,000 Americans have died since 9/11 because, out of fear, they drove their cars rather than flew in airplanes, or because they were swept into wars made politically possible by the terrorist events.*
>
> (Mueller, 2006: 3)

I do not intend, however, to rely on numbers games such as this to determine what business leaders and managers should do in responding to terrorism. The numbers of people killed or the financial costs of terrorism events are only a small part of the story. These figures do not tell us, for example, how terrorists might choose their targets or how people will behave when forced to confront the threat of terrorism. Perhaps the most important thing we need to know about terrorism – a threat that cannot really be calculated – is that it is not something that is likely to occur, but when it next occurs it will probably cause significant damage and kill either a few people or a great many people. When Michael Moore in an interview on the US *60 Minutes* current affairs programme said that terrorism remains a highly unlikely occurrence, interviewer Bob Simon replied 'But no one sees the world like that'. Bob Simon is right. He is right because terrorism causes *terror*. So while I do not believe that the emotion terror can be alleviated by an appeal to numbers that suggest it is a highly unlikely occurrence, I do believe that terrorism must rank lower than other threats and risks. It is perhaps more likely that someone will be killed as a passenger in a motor vehicle or even struck by lightning, but these more likely dangers can perhaps be more easily avoided. We don't have to get into cars and we don't have to stand in fields during storms. But how does one remain safe from terrorism? How do we manage its risk? I suppose we could stay at home and not go to work. For many, this is not a decision that can be made. Mortgages must be paid, bills continue to accrue and the kids must be sent through schools and universities. Moreover, if people stopped attending work, societies would have to radically change. Few would be prepared to overreact in such a way. So people continue to work in cities and travel on public transport networks. We all, in one way or another, deal with the post-9/11 threat of terrorism as part of our working lives – it is a threat that has become a routine and everyday part of living and working in cities.

Žižek (2002: 248) takes this argument against 'risk' a little further. He argues that risk invokes 'political frustrations' among people who are called upon to 'decide' the conditions of dangerousness and risk while being reminded that they are 'in no position' to decide or 'objectively weigh the pros and cons'. Resorting to conspiracy theories can be viewed as a desperate attempt to resolve this risk paradox. These conspiracy theories are not solely the domain of left-wing political radicals and anti-Semitic ideologues. Some of the chief conspiracy theorists are drawn from the world of counterterrorism and business.

I have sat through endless counterterrorism conferences listening to fantastic possibilities of terrorists who want to somehow 'turn our cities into deserts' by detonating a nuclear warhead or releasing biological, chemical, or radiological material on an unsuspecting population in a major global – always Western – city.

On the other side of the coin is dread. Dread in this context represents the impossibility of the order of risk. When the calculation of risk and danger is not possible, the inability to calculate – and, therefore, understand – the threat of terrorism reduces once rational and confident city-dwellers into stressed-out and anxious witnesses and victims of terrorism. When there is nothing to flee from, one cannot flee. In contemporary times significant acts of terrorism have occurred in New York, Washington DC, Madrid and London. Then why do people in other cities throughout the world fear the possibility of terrorism? Even many people living and working in cities targeted by terrorists did not witness terrorism first hand. Much like people in distant cities throughout the world they watched the terrorist events unfold on television, in newspapers and listened in on the radio. To avoid crime one can avoid high-crime suburbs. But how is terrorism to be avoided when it seems to be everywhere and nowhere at once? How does one understand the terrorist when they hide in plain sight, when they are one of *us* as they were on 7/7? The dreaded *possibility* of terrorism can be said to lurk in every corner of every city. If 9/11, 3/11 and 7/7 had not generated this fear and dread in cities throughout the world then we surely would not have described them as acts of *terror*.

I weigh in here with Kierkegaard (1957) and his distinction between fear, an emotion bound in events and occurrences that we know and understand, and dread, a fear of the events and occurrences we cannot yet fathom. As Kierkegaard (1957: 38) wrote: 'I must … call attention to the fact that it [dread] is different from fear and similar concepts which refer to something definite, whereas dread is freedom's reality as possibility for possibility'. Kierkegaard (1957) used biblical references to Adam and Eve to illustrate this distinction. As God hands to Adam prohibitions he also hands the consequences of disobeying: 'Thou shalt surely die'. Death, of course, is devoid of meaning to the first person. For Kierkegaard the emotion that this strikes is dread, or a fear of nothing. Perhaps New Yorkers can choose to avoid airplanes, tall buildings and the inner city areas, and Londoners can choose to not use public transport. What should workers in distant cities avoid in order to feel safe from terrorism (moreover, when Londoners avoid public transport or New Yorkers avoid airplanes and tall buildings they may not be more safe at all!)? One could argue through the concept of dread that the fear of terrorism for witnesses and victims is a fear of something unreal, unfathomable – it is a fear of something that defies explanation and our ability to take steps to protect ourselves without overreacting.

The power of terrorism stems partly from the fact that it can have an impact in places where devastating terrorism has never occurred. In the immediate vicinity of an act of terrorism some will be killed and injured and buildings may be destroyed. The families of the victims will feel trauma, as will those who live and work in the targeted city. Terrorism, however, can have meaning and consequences for people in cities throughout the world as I seek to demonstrate in this book. Even if terrorism does not occur on the streets of Melbourne – my home town – terrorism still has very real meanings and consequences. The meanings and consequences of terrorism in Australian cities are well documented. Michaelsen (2005: 330) argues that Australians hold a 'general assumption' that terrorists are trying to carry out an attack in Australia. A poll conducted in the *Sydney Morning Herald* found that 68 per cent of respondents believed that terrorists would strike in Australia before too long (Michaelsen, 2005: 330). In a study conducted by *The Lowy Institute* (Cook, 2005), 'international terrorism' is viewed as the third most worrying outside threat behind nuclear proliferation, and global warming and ranking ahead of international disease, population growth and the growth of China.

The question should not be who is right and who is wrong, or who has a right to be legitimately afraid of terrorism and who is afraid of nothing. But it is my argument that 'risk management' will only account for part of the problem that terrorism poses. The standard categorization of terrorism under risk management models as 'low probability, high consequence' says little about the threat of terrorism, the damage it causes, and how an effective response can be developed.

I return now to the practical responses that managers and business leaders can be developed to respond to terrorism, prevent its occurrence and mitigate its consequences, and how these responses can be integrated into the day-to-day routines of business. I have organized my discussion of these responses under two headings that represent key goals for post-9/11 business security – *corporate counter-terrorism* and *simulating security*. I argue that these key goals are linked by the need to incorporate counter-terrorism security into the routine, banal and everyday practice of business and management.

Corporate Counter-Terrorism

The destruction wrought on the Pentagon was of little consequence; what exploded in people's minds was the World Trade Center, leaving America out for the count. The business of America being business – and, principally, world business – it is in fact the apparent economy of the planet which finds itself lastingly affected here by the dystopia of its own system (emphasis in original).

(Virilio, 2002: 82)

Some would have spent squillions. Others would not have spent a cent. Well, nothing happened. Interesting isn't it?

(Owen, 13 December 2005)

I have presented several papers in which I have tried to outline the important role that businesses can play in the 'War on Terror'. One such paper I presented at the *Recent Advances in Security Technology Conference* at Melbourne University in 2007 – this was a conference that was well attended by academics, business managers and leaders, and security professionals. When I had finished my presentation, the inevitable questions were asked – how do we improve our counter-terrorism security? What specific things can we do to protect our businesses and workplaces? Can we realistically do anything to prevent terrorism? There were also other questions – when is terrorism most likely to occur? What damage is it likely to cause? How do we continue with 'business as usual' after terrorism? I had some answers to these questions (and the research informants that are the focus of Chapter 6 do as well), but counter-terrorism efforts should perhaps not be universally prescribed. While there are broad tactics and techniques that business leaders and managers can adopt to improve their counter-terrorism security, there are also many significant *situated* factors where an organization's environment, operating practices, culture, personnel, design, managerial methods and a host of other contextual and operational features will act as *filters* for implementing counter-terrorism security.

I also presented another paper dealing with these issues at *The Australian Sociological Association* (TASA) conference at the University of Auckland in 2007. The concerns and questions of this audience of scholars and academics with sociology and social science backgrounds were quite different – this audience of scholars and academics who were free of the burdens of running a post-9/11 organization were most concerned for the emotional, psychological, and everyday well-being of precarious and vulnerable workers. Their questions included: How do workers feel about working in times of terror? How will organizations protect their workers? What can workers do to decrease their likelihood of being caught up in an act of terrorism? Does the threat of terrorism cause added stress, fear and anxiety? Will people work in cities in the future?

I am eager to share with you, the reader, everything I know about what practical steps business leaders and managers should take to protect their organizations from terrorism and the threat it poses. But to do so would be problematic. If you are a security manager at a major international airport or a nuclear power facility then the more security the better – upgrade the skills of security guards, purchase the latest, cutting-edge technology for biodetection, metal and bomb residue detection, and gain access to the best trained air marshalls and security sniffer dogs. Indeed, if you are a manager at one of these locations, or other locations requiring the highest levels of security, then I imagine the existing literature on the impact of terrorism on business would provide you with a host of ideas and methods for protecting your organization against terrorist violence. It is perhaps appropriate in high-security environments for the workers to take second place to physical security imperatives. I would still suggest that the workers should be the chief concern of managers in high-security situations, but I also acknowledge that there are times when workers will need to be willing to deal with rigorous and strict security. If you are a business leader and manager in a city-dwelling organization – and the city where your organization is located is not in a war-zone – then I imagine that the sort of security I referred to above would be wildly inappropriate and damaging to workplace cohesion, bottom-line productivity and worker well-being. In such situations extreme security such as the kind you would find at airports and nuclear facilities should be avoided at all costs.

This, of course, makes my task in this section a difficult one. I do not want to provide a 'shopping list' of counter-terrorism gadgets of high expense and moderate value, nor do I want to provide an all-purpose 'recipe' for good business counter-terrorism. But what I can do is provide a *map* of how business leaders and managers can prevent terrorism by improving security, managing worker well-being, and integrating the post-9/11 threat of terrorism into the everydayness, routines and rituals of everyday business life.

The two very different audiences in Melbourne and Auckland asked two very different types of questions. It is perhaps to be expected that business leaders and security managers would be preoccupied with how terrorism might affect the everyday operations, functions, viability and continuity of their businesses. It is perhaps equally predictable that academic sociologists and social scientists would be preoccupied with their concerns for the precarious and vulnerable citizens of cities. These different sets of questions are illustrative of what business leaders and managers should aim for in protecting their businesses from the consequences of terrorism – protect the office buildings, stores and locations where businesses are housed, and protect the physical, emotional and psychological well-being of precarious and vulnerable workers. It is the latter aim that I argue is the most important. If business leaders and managers protect the physical, emotional and psychological well-being of workers – their physical safety through security improvements, and their emotional and psychological well-being through mitigating their feelings of fear, stress and anxiety – then all other aspects of business counter-terrorism security will more easily fall into place.

Despite the obvious importance of the worker in any business plan to prevent and mitigate terrorism – the worker's consent to security changes, training and procedures, their know-how, and their vulnerability and precariousness – most of the literature that explores the meaning and consequences of terrorism gives less regard to the security of workers than to the security of the buildings where organizations are housed. This problem arises from how we view terrorism and how it is delivered through the mass media – we concentrate on terrorism where things *explode*, not where *terror* is felt. Because of this, the information that witnesses and victims rely upon for understanding terrorism is reactionary – always bound to the most recent terror attack that has been splashed across the front pages of major newspapers. It is to the problem of *reactionary security* that I now turn.

Reactionary Security

Business leaders and managers should rely on the best available information about terrorism to formulate their responses, but sometimes there is little useful information available. Naturally, much of the information that is available is drawn from the most recent high-profile terrorist attacks. However, focusing on these most visible and recent attacks – as many law enforcement agencies, governmental departments and businesses have been accused of doing – has sparked a series of *reactionary* responses. After 9/11, airports and aircrafts received renewed attention and soon these once so-called 'soft targets' had been significantly fortified to the point where many experts suggest that it is highly unlikely that passenger aircraft will be targeted in such a way again. This naturally does not diminish the number of terrorists that the world faces. There is a displacement effect where would-be terrorists begin to seek softer targets with less security protocols and a greater likelihood for a successful attack. It should not have been a surprise that rail commuters and networks became targets. In response, considerable energy and resources have since been expended to battle terrorism in the theatre of public transport. But what will be the consequences of this displacement effect? Much has been documented about the continued vulnerability of rail and public transport networks yet if I were to think like a terrorist – and as I have already suggested, they are not as arbitrary and unpredictable as some have argued – I would be looking for other softer targets.

> *I think after 9/11, the focus in this country [Australia], like the United States, was mainly around aviation security, and it's only more recently that we've picked up on maritime and port security. But surface transport security is something we're only now really grappling with and as events in London have demonstrated, it's mass transit systems that are clearly the most vulnerable, where you have large concentrations of people, where the system by its very nature is open, where it's obviously impractical to do mass screening as you would for aviation, where, with aviation, you've got a record of bookings obviously security can't be checked through*

bookings on mass transit trains. So certainly, mass transit, certainly surface transportation generally is an area that we need to focus more on.

(Bergin, 2005)

It may be reasonable to insist that security at airports take on a fortressed quality and that everyone who boards a passenger aircraft be screened by highly-trained security staff using bomb and metal detection equipment. The need for such measures is clear given the long history of terrorists' willingness to target airports and planes. But it would not be desirable to use the same methods to protect rail and bus transport – the consequences of airport-style security screening for other transport services would most likely outweigh the benefits. There would be better physical security perhaps (I say 'perhaps' because rigorous security did not prevent 9/11 and a host of other terrorist attacks launched from airports), but it would be at the expense of the free and open use of public transport services. It is clear that counter-terrorism security needs to be implemented with a broad consideration of the situational factors inherent to any particular organization's internal and external environments. For this reason counter-terrorism security needs to be part of strategic business planning and not merely part of a security manager's delegated authority.

Yet, even if managers and business leaders spent years strategically planning for terrorism, it remains likely that business responses to terrorism would be *reactive*. This word holds negative connotations. To be reactive in a time of terror suggests that too little is being done, that plans are being implemented to prevent threats from the past but not the future, and it implies that international terrorists are always one step ahead. The terrorist attacks of 9/11, 3/11 and 7/7 sparked a whole range of reactionary security responses. These responses stretched well beyond the world of work. International war, discriminatory and violent reprisals carried out against Muslims living in Western cities, draconian counterterrorism legislation, and behavioural responses characterized by fear, stress and anxiety are all side-effects of ill-considered and poorly planned reactions to terrorism. So too, the business responses to 9/11 were in many instances reactive, dramatic, overzealous and overblown. John Mueller (2006) has argued against overreacting to terrorism in his exploration of what he calls the 'Limited Destructiveness of Terrorism'. He argues that despite the high levels of anxiety, fear and danger usually associated with terrorism, it remains that the likelihood of dying in an act of terrorism is 'microscopic' (Mueller, 2006: 13). Relevant here are the comments of one of the business managers that I interviewed as part of the broader research project that has resulted in this book. He believed that the 'Y2K bug' threat was analogous to the threat of terrorism: 'Some would have spent squillions. Others would not have spent a cent. Well, nothing happened. Interesting isn't it?' (Owen, December 13, 2005). It may be that in some instances the best thing to do in response to terrorism is nothing especially when visual and physical improvements to security may create more fear and alarm amongst workers.

However, doing nothing will rarely be an option. If a future act of terrorism was to damage an organization's built environment or kill its workers, the fact that a strategic 'nothing' was done to prevent terrorism may result in significant legal and social consequences. As such, following a major act of terrorism it will be natural for managers and business leaders to rigorously explore ways of improving physical security in the stores, offices and buildings where their organizations are located and, in the process, an overreaction might sometimes be the result. This is because, as Alexander and Alexander (2002: 52) argue, the way we think about the nature of corporate 'risk' dramatically changed on 9/11. Organizations in locations considered vulnerable and precarious – such as those in or below tall and prominent buildings, prominent retail districts, and public transport networks – rushed to improve security. Others, Alexander and Alexander (2002: 55) argue, 'have likened investment on security measures to funds allocated to reducing pollution in that they are both socially helpful but economically unproductive'. This is a dangerous assumption. The 9/11 hijackers were able to exploit lax security at airports to carry out their acts of terrorism. The commercial air travel sector has subsequently devoted considerable time and money towards improving security through physical security upgrades and fostering security awareness among workers. Surveillance technology and monitoring has also been deployed to improve security and assist in the development of security-oriented cultures in the airport/airline industry.

Businesses in all sectors, Alexander and Alexander (2002: 52–53) suggest, can reduce the possibility of terrorism by 'adding new security guards, purchasing surveillance equipment, acquiring metal and bomb detection equipment, buying chemical and biological agent detectors, acquiring machines that can irradiate mail, and training security and office employees'. Alexander and Alexander (2002: 52) argue that business managers that act quickly and become the first to adopt more stringent security may gain a competitive advantage. However, the consequences of more stringent, more visible security can be detrimental to corporate performance – higher costs, shrinking profit margins, and interruptions to the flow of inventory and services, and a failure to manage the security perceptions of employees, clients, customers and other people who frequent the various locations that a business may occupy may become serious business problems.

Finding the balance between responding too little or too much to terrorism has kept security professionals, terrorism experts and business leaders guessing. I have sat through many debates at national and international security conferences where participants have rambled on about worst-case scenarios and the elaborate security methods and products that will prevent them. These methods and products run the continuum from the slightly silly to the entirely ludicrous. What if a nuclear weapon was detonated in the middle of Sydney Harbour and took out the army, the police and the fire brigade, and two million people are dead? – one breathless security 'expert' once shrieked. What if a nuclear weapon was detonated in the Pacific Ocean and kills millions of people in Australian and US coastal cities? Would people in middle-Australia and middle-America know what to do? Do people working above the thirteenth floor in Australia's high-rise buildings have parachutes? Do people have their pre-arranged 'Go bags' complete with toilet paper? They don't? God help us all!

The funny thing about this Armageddon complex – or as Haraway (2000) describes it, our 'endangered species discourse'[3] – is that by focusing on these ludicrous scenarios, many will ignore the more important, yet seemingly less significant, aspects of business and city security that can be reorganized and reoriented to improve preparedness for terrorism and the threat it poses and, most importantly, improve *feelings and perceptions of terrorism and security* among employees, clients, customers and all people who live and work in the city. This, I argue, should be considered the front line for the so-called 'War on Terror' and a location where leaders and managers in businesses and organizations can most contribute to the prevention and mitigation of terrorism. By tackling the anxieties

---

3   Haraway (2000) added: 'The line between crisis and apocalypse is a very thin one'.

and fears of precarious and vulnerable working people – people who are the chosen targets of contemporary terrorism – managers and business leaders can do more than most to prevent and mitigate the impact of terrorism.

As I have already suggested earlier in this book, there is a contradiction between the imperative for maintaining a free and open workplace for consumers, clients and workers and the need to close off and secure workplaces from terrorism for these very same people. Naturally this is a complex dilemma and ideally a balance will be found between freedom, openness and security. I suggest that this dilemma is crucial for understanding contemporary terrorism as it affects working people. As general secretary of the rail workers' union in Britain argued following the 7/7 bombings: 'Where you've got … six exits … It's not like where people single-queue and put their bags through. The actual stations are massive open spaces' (in Tulloch, 2005: 169). The suggestion here is that perhaps little can be done by way of security to prevent attacks such as 7/7 from occurring. This problem was similarly explored by Holt (2006) who suggests that public transport is particularly vulnerable to terrorism. A successful attack against the public transport networks – as witnesses and victims have seen firsthand – kills many people sitting and standing in enclosed environments, severely inhibits access to the city, interrupts flows of products, inventory and people travelling for work and leisure, and, most importantly from the perspective of contemporary terrorists, these networks occupy sites that are exceedingly difficult and undesirable to secure. Indeed, no competitive corporation would be willing to significantly disrupt travel flows, people movement, and freedom and openness in the name of security. Even if restrictive security measures could be justified and accepted by the broader public, it would be an 'own goal' of sorts. Terrorists hope that witnesses and victims will change in response to their violence. Implementing restrictive and oppressive security that diminishes the freedom of movement and thought would surely award terrorists an unnecessary victory.

From this, a further difficulty becomes evident. Perhaps in New York, Washington DC, Madrid and London organizations may feasibly enforce extraordinary security measures to mitigate and prevent terrorism at the expense of openness and freedom for workers, clients and customers. Perhaps organizations in these cities can justify the deployment of excessive security on the basis that terrorism has happened here before and may again – chances, perhaps, cannot be taken. What of the many other cities around the world housing witnesses and victims of terrorism? Surely excessive security could not be tolerated in a place where devastating terrorism has never occurred?

Reactionary responses carry a number of burdens. Such responses embody a continuing unwillingness to confront terrorism's root causes – an ongoing area of considerable academic endeavour that is beyond the scope of these pages and far beyond the scope of any business concern. But reactionary responses point to a deeper problem that should be a primary concern for business leaders, managers and working people – only treating the symptoms will often lead to a recurrence of the problem. As Haraway (2000) has argued, 'We know how to win the last war but don't have a clue what is going on now'. Business managers, workers, witnesses and victims of terrorism respond in such a way. In many respects we all come together to form 'a broad, illiterate population' (Haraway, 2000) in our fight against terrorism.

I have already identified in this chapter some of the research and literature that has contributed to our understanding of the meanings and consequences of terrorism for business. This literature also makes some strong cases for specific and practical actions that business leaders and managers can take in responding to terrorism. I have summarized the best of these in the following section as a way of moving forward and setting the stage for the emergence of what I argue is the best way to respond to terrorism as an act of violence and an emotion – what I call *simulating security*.

COUNTER-TERRORISM IN PRACTICE: TECHNOLOGY, PLANNING, CULTURE AND TELECOMMUTING

At the 'Terrorism and US Business' conference held at Georgetown University in 1977, Robert Kupperman (1979: 97) argued that technological change could form an important part of business counter-terrorism, but he warned:

> *Technology is but one means of countering terrorism – it is not offered here as a panacea for an advanced society lacking the commitment to remain vigilant in its own defense. Counterterrorism must necessarily use intelligence, police, and military operations, as well as psychological, medical, and behavioral science techniques before, during, and after threatened or actual incidents. Technology has a role to play in support of these efforts.*

To best understand how technology may be used in support of business security efforts, Kupperman (1979: 97–98) suggested that counter-terrorism should be understood as a 'functional task' that must account for 'various scenarios'. Counter-terrorism, in this view, should be a task undertaken as part of the everyday and routine task of conducting business. He suggested that the business counter-terrorism function consists of four parts: prevention, control, containment, restoration.

To *prevent* terrorism business leaders and managers need to deny access to would-be terrorists, maintain high security at high-profile locations, and work towards 'deterring' incidents through 'a combination of denial and protection'. To *control* terrorism, plans and mechanisms should be set in place to facilitate decision making and coordination with policing organizations in order to 'seize the initiative from the terrorists'. Terrorism can be *contained* by limiting the physical damage that terrorism can cause through security improvements, the design of work stations, and organizational layout, and working to 'decouple' the psychological impacts of terrorism from its intended political consequences by providing workers and managers with 'emergency health care' after an attack. Finally, organizations can be *restored* quickly after terrorism through deliberate and careful planning for not only business continuity, but operational continuity that will provide the basis for returning to 'normal and routine' work and business (Kupperman, 1979: 97–98).

Kupperman's model for responding to terrorism is relevant and useful for responding to contemporary terrorism that has targeted working people. However, this model is also susceptible to some of the pitfalls of other authors and theorists that have developed methods for protecting businesses from terrorism. As is common in this type of literature Kupperman predominantly focused on the physical violence of terrorism and gave little regard to terrorism as an emotion. When Kupperman argued that providing health care after an attack could form part of containing terrorism, it is noteworthy that he did not suggest providing counselling or other emotional and psychological care. Perhaps as a consequence of Kupperman's bias for responding to terrorism as violence but not the emotion 'terror' he has seemingly ignored the importance of responding to terrorism by prioritizing the role and care of precarious and vulnerable workers. If business leaders and managers hope to implement a terrorism response model such as the one suggested by Kupperman, workers would play a significant role in preparation and planning, and through their willingness and desire to return to work following an act, or threatened act, of terrorism.

Alexander and Alexander's (2002) and Alexander's (2004) studies of the impacts of terrorism on business produced – among other things – many suggestions for managers and business leaders charged with establishing counter-terrorism plans for their organizations. These suggestions ranged from the purchasing of security equipment and the hiring of highly-trained security staff that should be rotated on short shifts (the shorter the better), to moving operations and encouraging all staff to work from home and 'telecommute' (more on this to come). The most useful contribution that these studies have made to our understanding of the practical steps that business leaders and managers should take in a time of terror can be found in the logic and motives that underpin their suggestions for deploying spectacular security technology. More than anything, I believe the authors are arguing for the fostering of a securitized culture and the incorporation of the threat of terrorism into the everyday routines of business (Alexander and Alexander, 2002: 54–56, 93–101; Alexander, 2004: 12, 84–103). These authors make a strong case for counter-terrorism security as something that must not be considered a hindrance or an annoyance – rather, counter-terrorism should form part of the everyday functionality of doing business. Alexander and Alexander (2002) argue that post-9/11 business security must be accompanied by a security-centric logic for all aspects of day-to-day business functions. Examples of this logic in practice may include the dispersal of employees across multiple locations instead of in the one workplace, 'forbidding workers from wearing or using company logos while traveling overseas' (p. 55), directing employees to work from home during times of heightened terrorism threats, 'raising the training and skills of security officers' (p. 55), and improving security at connection and adjacent sites to the workplace such as foyers, public transport networks, and shopping malls.

These practices can accompany physical security improvements that may include 'Biometric Devices' (p. 93), 'cutting-edge' bomb, chemical, metal, x-ray and biometric detection equipment, video cameras, CCTV, 'Video-Chip Technology' (p. 96), document authentication equipment, software to defend against cyberterrorism, and firearms. Alexander (2004: 12) argues:

> *companies must comprehend ... that in the post-9/11 era security is a component of corporate citizenship ... the advantages of establishing a corporate security program are manifold: protecting assets (human, physical, technological, and financial), ensuring business continuity, reducing litigation risks, lowering insurance costs, and reducing dangers to customers and employees.*

In addition, businesses 'serve roles in addition to providing a job and wage. After 9/11, labor may view the employer as playing a semi-paternalistic/quasi-government role: provide physical security, emotional assistance, and guidance in times of catastrophe' (Alexander, 2004: 135).

Whilst the fostering of a securitized culture in conjunction with some of the fairly dramatic suggestions for security improvement that these authors suggest may indeed provide considerably better and more complete physical security, such a culture may generate more problems than it mitigates. Consider some of the suggestions of security expert and editor of *Chief Security Officer* magazine, Mike Ackerman, for corporate counterterrorism: 'Investigate thoroughly key employees, distributors, vendors, jointventure partners, and domestics. You will have your hands full with external forces and you don't need problems inside your tent'; 'Train personnel bound for high-risk areas in protective tactics'; 'Armored cars ... though a useful part of a security program, should not be considered impenetrable cocoons'; 'Well trained bodyguards have a role to play'; 'it is often best to stay put instead of heading for the exits in the immediate aftermath of a coup or a uprising' (Ackerman, 2008).

Any improvement to security will prove expensive. For this reason – and many others – it is unlikely that any business not being deployed to a war-zone would adopt many, if any, of these security measures nor would such measures be necessary for most organizations. Moreover, these suggestions would likely have a demoralizing impact on employee morale, satisfaction and well-being. It would be difficult to feel safe in such an environment. To be fair to Ackerman, it is likely that he is imagining organizations located in war zones and countries that experience civil unrest. But this in turn points to another limitation of his counterterrorism measures – he assumes that terrorism is something that occurs *over there* in exotic and war-torn foreign lands but not *over here*, in Western nations and cities. But this example of security run amok should not detract from the importance of nurturing organizational culture in responding to terrorism. For organizations in the post-9/11 city, terrorism *is* part of culture. On this point there is perhaps no decision to be made.

Another novel, potentially cost-effective and alarmingly popular method for preventing terrorism and mitigating its impacts on workers is telecommuting. Proponents of telecommuting rely on the belief that people who rarely leave their homes will be safe from terrorism – on this point, the proponents of telecommuting are most likely correct. However, to date there has been little consideration of the social, cultural and emotional ramifications of allowing the threat of terrorism to turn people living in cities into organizational 'shut-ins' so afraid to step onto public transport and sit in high-rise offices that we would rather work, shop, form relationships and be entertained in the safety of our homes.

The massive psychological and emotional consequences of significantly reducing human interaction in city spaces and at work – consequences that every manager would be deeply aware of and concerned about – are treated as trivial in Alexander and Alexander's (2002: 54) study:

> *If employees are dispersed in the name of reduced centrality, with little damage resulting if one of several sites is attacked, there exists a downside – though minor – of reduced company cohesion. After all, daily human contact among peers tends to nurture cooperation among workers that videoconferences, e-mail, and other technological advances cannot completely replicate.*

The United States' Congress in 2006 hosted a hearing for the 'Subcommittee on the Federal Workforce and Agency Organization' entitled 'Telecommuting: A 21st Century Solution to Traffic Jams and Terrorism' (Committee on Government Reform, 2006: i). In his introductory address to the hearing, Jon Porter argued that 'With an increase in traffic congestion, fuel prices, time away from one's family, and terrorist and pandemic threats, the time is right for the subcommittee to examine the Federal Government's use of telecommuting for our Federal employees' (Committee on Government Reform, 2006: 1). The consensus reached by the politicians, the industry spokespeople and public sector experts that participated in the hearing was that 'Telework is a prudent response to probability' (Committee on Government Reform, 2006: 7). Amid the sometimes hysterical promotion of telecommuting as the way of the future, there was no critical debate on the consequences of teleworking on employees – aside from the all blinding benefits of reduced pollution, improved productivity, enhanced 'family life and morale' (pp. 7–8), greater autonomy over work, a more 'balanced' lifestyle (p. 22), no longer needing to battle traffic (p. 39), and a quick return to work following a major disaster and accident (p. 64) there was still – perplexingly for most at the hearing – resistance and unwillingness from both employees and managers to purge the worker from the workplace.

> *I fully understand that every employee is not eligible for telecommuting. But the truth is that there are many employees in a given office setting who are perfectly suited to be telecommuters, yet agencies are not currently taking advantage of it. This may be due to management fears, cultural change, or perhaps lack of awareness of the available technology or even a lack of central leadership pushing agencies and managers to the many advantages of telecommuting.*
> (Jon Porter, Committee on Government Reform, 2006: 3)

I believe the answers for this resistance lie elsewhere. I find it incomprehensible that no consideration was given to the emotional, social and cultural needs of the precarious and vulnerable humans that occupy workspaces throughout the world. These are people who set their alarms, take the kids to school, go to work, drink their morning coffees, socialize and network, have lunches and breaks with colleagues and friends, and then return home eagerly to their families and friends at night – telecommuting takes much of this routine and ritual away and renders physical human interaction a security threat, unproductive and illogical. It is yet another example of bright ideas that improve security at the expense of the worker – the witness and victim of terrorism.

However, this argument should not render all telecommuting technologies and techniques disastrous for workers' well-being. On the contrary, some may jump at the opportunity to telecommute some, if not all, of the time. Others, as Alexander and Alexander (2002: 108–109) point out, use telecommuting to replace unnecessary business travel:

> *In their post-September 11 mindset, many business travelers may avoid travel. Several companies provid[e] videoconferencing, teleconferencing, and Internet-based collaboration tools … While all face-to-face business meetings and events cannot be replaced by videocameras and Internet chats, executives across many industries are cognizant of the factors weighing against frequent business travel: time, expense, and with the specter of terrorism, safety. Fortunately, technological advances will enable individuals worldwide to meet regularly and inexpensively.*
> (Alexander and Alexander, 2002: 108–109)

But technologies for telecommuting should not be viewed as a security panacea – they may be useful supplements that bring a whole variety of benefits to organizations and employees, but there are also significant consequences. Aside from providing the possibility to purge the workplace of workers and eliminate many opportunities for human interaction, they may fatally disrupt what it means to be in an organization. How, for example, would a manager develop and nurture trust, maintain control, reward employees, socialize and network, define acceptable organizational behaviour and establish group norms without employees present? Would we still call the teleworking employee an employee and would we still call their employer an organization? These are perhaps questions beyond the scope of this book but they remain serious concerns as we leap toward countering terrorism and creating safer workplaces.

This discussion has been designed to lead to the following section and a discussion of what I call *simulated security*. Simulated security may provide the best hope for business leaders and managers responding to terrorism in a cost-effective and sensible way and provide a way for business counter-terrorism to become part of the everyday and routine function of business and a facet of good corporate citizenship. It may be, I suggest, our best weapon in the war on terror.

Simulations of Security

According to Zedner (2003: 154–155), security is 'a slippery concept', with multiple meanings that contain little clarity but can nonetheless loosely be defined as a subjective condition that incorporates a combination of 'feeling safe' and having 'freedom from anxiety'. Security professionals and security studies scholars have long agreed that security can rarely be entirely impenetrable and 100 per cent reliable (Wood and Dupont, 2006; Zedner, 2003). The word 'security' is associated with a certain degree of incompleteness and vulnerability and it is generally acknowledged that complete, no-gaps security cannot be guaranteed. However, not all managers that are required to play a role in counter-terrorism are security managers, and the idea that security is insecure may not be as clear to some as it is to others. Non-security managers – managers for whom security is not their primary function – struggle with securitizing their businesses from risks, threats and potential disasters because these managers do not share the luxury of announcing that security cannot be guaranteed – their stakeholders do not have the same appreciation for the realities of security management. Customers, clients, workers and members of the public want to be able to believe that an organization's security is complete and without gaps.

It is here that I argue we can uncover another contranym that sits alongside the contranym of terrorism – the contranym of security. The word 'security' embodies a certain incompleteness. In one sense, 'security' represents the regulation of disorder (Agamben, 2001). It is the act of physically and psychologically protecting people, places and assets and generating perceptions of safety and certainty. 'Security', however, will often fall short of these ideals. Despite massive efforts being devoted to security, breaches regularly occur. People break security barriers and cordons. People commit crimes, acts of violence and terrorism. When this occurs, it undermines the perceptions of security, safety and certainty held by those who were supposedly protected and secure. It is at these moments that seemingly secure people know that 'security' is not 'secure'. Recalling for a moment Larry Daley's realization in *Night at the Museum* (2006) that I introduced in Chapter 1 – now that I think of it, I never thought it was!

This insecure nature of security was illustrated in a popular television program in Australia called *The Chaser's War on Everything*. Affectionately known simply as 'The Chasers', this group of young men comedically criticize many aspects of Australian political and social life. In what is now the group's most renowned stunt, they turned their comedic eye to the Australia-Pacific Economic Cooperation Summit (APEC) that was attended by many world leaders including the then United States President, George W. Bush. The Chasers organized a motorcade of shiny black vehicles, flanked by jogging men in black suits and black sunglasses – they appeared to be 'secret service' agents and who would have had reason to doubt them? The black vehicles were all adorned with Canadian flags – a nation that The Chasers believed would not cause suspicion.

With the cameras rolling, this fictitious Canadian diplomatic motorcade – a nation not represented at APEC – rolled past several security cordons, at times being directed and guided by federal police officers, before The Chasers decided that the joke had gone too far. The Chasers pulled their motorcade to a halt out in front of the hotel where President Bush was staying and one of the crew leaped from the car wearing an Osama bin Laden costume. Amidst the outcries from police and the government in the aftermath of The Chasers' stunt, security professionals, academics and business security experts asked the awkward questions about how one of Australia's largest security operations – at a cost of $250 million – was so easily breached (Watson, 2007). Indeed, Australian security and law-enforcement agencies may consider themselves lucky that terrorists chose not to strike at the APEC summit. Among the props in this farcical security scenario were identification badges that were labelled with the word 'Insecurity', and the APEC security stickers on the vehicles read: 'This vehicle belongs to a member of *The Chaser's War on Everything*. This dude likes trees and poetry and certain types of carnivorous plants excite him' (Braithwaite and Petrie, 2007). In their defence The Chasers issued a statement that they never intended to breach any security cordons and they were shocked the prank was so successful. Despite Australia's then Foreign Minister Alexander Downer deflecting the security gap as unproblematic since The Chasers were not intent on physical harm, it remains a day of infamy in Australia when a comedy team were ushered past snipers, federal police, and intelligence and security agents supposedly during a time of intense and spectacular security. As an epilogue that would be funny if it had not demonstrated how ineffective security can be, the charges against The Chasers were ultimately thrown out of court because police and security forces had given 'tacit permission' for the comedy crew to enter the high-security zone near President Bush's hotel.

What I intend to suggest with this story is that establishing high-quality security is exceedingly difficult. At best, security to prevent terrorism is problematic, at its worst it can be viewed as a futile exercise in attempts to prevent terrorism. This story serves as a metaphor for counter-terrorism efforts throughout the world's cities. It shows that we all play a role in our insecurity. We are the police officers waving the terrorists through. Our security is a revolving doorway through which terrorists travel. We are precarious and vulnerable witnesses and victims, complicit in the terrorism we are subjected to. Traditional notions of corporate security and risk management are unreliable resources in the so called 'War on Terror' and I argue that a new, alternative and emergent method for preventing terrorism is needed.

The contranym of security is paradoxically clear. 'Security' has oppositional meanings. In one sense, security is being secure. In another sense, security is deeply insecure. By corporeally and physically enhancing security, we can become more secure. By enhancing the visible aspects of security, people who rely on this security can feel and believe that security is secure. One meaning requires a response that physically improves security, the other requires a response that improves perceptions of certainty and safety that security can – and perhaps should – deliver. By physically improving security it is reasonable to assume that people will feel more secure. The opposite will also hold – doing little to physically improve security will generate both a physical and emotional vulnerability. However, by visibly improving security – perhaps with little corporeal or actual improvement to security – it is similarly reasonable to assume that people will feel more secure. Moreover, I suggest that focusing on the visible aspects of security as a way of fighting terrorism is far less arduous and costly than vainly attempting to close all security gaps (most likely without success). Making security truly secure will likely always be an ideal rather than a realistic goal. Instead of hiring expensive specialist security guards, minimum-wage security guards may suffice in generating visibly improved security. Monitoring and maintaining security cameras can be costly. Perhaps the presence of security cameras – even if they are not regularly monitored and operational – will be enough to deter would-be terrorists and criminals and generate perceptions of safety. Believing security is effective may be more important to consumers, customers, clients, workers and managers than complete, fortressed, no-gaps security. *Deterring* terrorism – as violence and as an emotion – will likely be more effective than overwhelming and overblown security. I call this *simulating security* through generating an *image of safety*.

This is loosely related to what Coaffee (2003: 160) has described as an inside and outside discourse of security. In Coaffee's view there are key groups that can influence security outcomes for businesses and organizations in cities. The pro-security inside discourses are fostered and maintained by 'urban managers', 'political authorities' and corporations (Coaffee, 2003: 160). The 'outside discourse' is embodied in civil liberties groups and other community interest groups. I agree with Coaffee's (2003) contention that there is more-or-less a general consensus among urban populations that security should be improved – even if this improvement is only a visible improvement – yet this improvement does not necessarily need to embody the militarist ideology of urban fortification. I suggest that simulated security can achieve many of these goals and can do so without creating a 'fortress city'. In Chapter 6 I return to the meaning and development of simulated security as described by the city-dwelling business leaders and managers that I interviewed for this book.

Wilson (2007) argues that 'The best security measures are sometimes simple and cheap. They're usually low-tech, physical and human. Some of the most advanced systems, on the other hand, are brittle and insecure'. Georgio Agamben (2001) wrote shortly after 9/11 that we face 'extreme and most dangerous developments in the thought of security' and while discipline produces order, security seeks to regulate disorder. I argue that this type of security was once the domain of the state but now operates from decentralized stages in cities where organizations are asked to close the gaps in security to play their part in counter-terrorism. Organizations are not well placed to provide this security. Corporate logics, the need to maintain a profitable enterprise and the limitations of risk management techniques means that good decisions will not always be made. As Davis (in Wilson, 2007) points out, whilst billions continues to be spent on high-tech counter-terrorism equipment and training to prevent fantastic possibilities of biological, chemical, radiological or nuclear attacks, the unsophisticated car-bomb continues to be a potent terrorist weapon. Something similar can be said of the suicide bomber. Suicide bombers are thinking, improvising, organic, killing machines. If a would-be suicide bomber plans to target a densely populated location but discovers that location to be fortified and securitized, they can simply go somewhere else to complete their attack. In Israel it is believed that terrorists seeking to target shopping malls often find them to be protected by security guards. The terrorists simply move their bomb to another populated area – often in the middle of a crosswalk as people are crossing the road. A 'guns, guards and gates' approach to security will likely not stop a car or suicide bomber (Wilson, 2007):

> Since September 11, Australia has spent twenty billion dollars on the war on terror. Despite this dizzying figure, Australians are, according to ASIO [the Australian Security Intelligence Organization], still no safer from the threat of terrorism. Five, six years later – longer than the First World War – and we're no more secure.

Conclusion: The Counter-terrorism Laboratory

These intersecting narratives that I have explored in this chapter are not mutually exclusive and cannot be clearly distinguished. The problem of business counter-terrorism is one characterized by these narratives when understood in relation to the four coordinates for understanding contemporary terrorism that I identified in Chapter 2. At the beginning of the twenty-first century, business leaders and managers face the complex threat of terrorism in their everyday business. It is a problem involving witnesses and victims, simulations and images of violence, distance and cities, politics and ideology, locations, histories, the global news media, and intersecting narratives of international terrorism, workers, and management and security responses. These variables, factors and contexts form a narrative – a narrative that is at times disorienting, incongruent, and paradoxical. These narratives involve some mythical creatures of the complex twenty-first century where corporate logics of risk meet international terrorism and, as they so often have been, working people are the collateral damage. In this process I am a witness on two fronts – both an insider and an outsider. I am a worker in the contemporary city and therefore a subject of this book. I can at any moment become a target, like millions of working people in cities throughout the world. Yet I am also a researcher, a writer and an academic. I control narratives and discourses and in the coming chapters I speak on behalf of other targets, witnesses and victims that I interviewed for this book.

Much like the exploration of terrorism's meanings and the consequences for witnesses and victims that was the subject of the previous chapter, I find the literature that explores the consequences and meanings of terrorism for business and management to be lacking in its failure to account for a number of crucial dimensions for understanding contemporary terrorism and its impact on working people. There can be little doubt that businesses and working people have been the target of choice for contemporary terrorists. The 9/11, 3/11 and 7/7 attacks have served as profound symbolic targets that accentuated the vulnerability and precariousness of working people in city-dwelling organizations. This is a crucial contemporary problem for business leaders and managers, and the corporate counter-terrorism response should be considered a vital part of strategic organizational planning. Yet I do not base this argument on the assumption that terrorists pose a clear and present danger to organizational or worker survival. Rather, I suggest that it is the power of terrorism to generate witnesses and victims small and large distances from terrorism's flashpoint that requires swift and decisive corporate responses. In this way, corporate counter-terrorism can be viewed as primarily a task of mitigating, preventing and protecting against *terror* rather than militarily defending organizational spaces from unrelenting terrorists who we are told are inspired by a fundamentalist world-view and who may or may not be hiding in caves in the borderlands separating Afghanistan and Pakistan. I do not want to frame the problem of terrorism and the consequences for working people and businesses only in terms of the threat posed by al-Qaeda or the so-called 'Global War on Terror'. I suggest that terrorism works best when nothing explodes. Terrorism is most felt by the people who live to bear witness. The witnesses are the victims – these are the true terrorism experts.

CHAPTER 4
Terror and the Mediated City

> *Los Angeles certainly looks, sounds and smells familiar, with its wattle, bottlebrush and gum trees lining the freeways, but now that the barbarians are at the gates, the wheels are really falling off Tinsel Town. Post-September 11, the happy pills aren't working, the table-thumping televangelists are being taken seriously, the fearful are fleeing to Lake Tahoe, and the driving wounded are looking shell-shocked and exposed, as if a golden horde of Mongols had just galloped through their Bircher-muesli breakfasts.*
>
> (Hirst, 2003: 9–10)

Introduction

In the post-9/11 world, Los Angeles (LA) and Melbourne are not so different. What is more, it is likely that LA and Melbourne are not the only cities filled with people enduring the threat of terrorism. It is perhaps easy to understand the heightened threat of terrorism in New York, Washington DC, Madrid and London but it is less clear why distant cities such as LA and Melbourne experience such significant consequences as a result of terrorism. The city represents a central location, a social and cultural interface, and a workers' oasis that emerges on the skyline during the morning commute that millions undertake each day. The 9/11 terrorist attacks on the Twin Towers and the Pentagon, the 3/11 attacks on the Madrid rail network and the 7/7 attacks on the public transport network in London put people living and working in cities throughout the world on notice. But perhaps those LA folk could be equally justified in their fears and anxieties – it was believed on 9/11 that a plane was en route to LA and the city was also the focus for a planned attack that never took place on the millennium New Year's Eve. But don't try telling some Melburnians that terrorism is less likely in Melbourne than it is in LA. Whilst many Melburnians would perhaps agree with this threat assessment, I suggest that people worried about terrorism don't think in terms of probabilities.

In this chapter I situate, locate and emplace the threat of terrorism and its consequences for working people and businesses in the city of Melbourne. I locate Melbourne as a city like any other around the world and despite Melbourne never being a theatre for devastating act of terrorism, nor is Melbourne close to any city or region that has, its inhabitants hold a 'general assumption' that terrorism will occur before too long (Michaelsen, 2005: 330). Following even a casual examination of the Australian media, it is not difficult to see why. In particular, the Melbourne media during times of terror accentuated the threat of terrorism by delivering a heady blend of 'opiniotainment' and exaggerated danger. It is this media and the city-dwellers that bear witness that are the subjects of this chapter. I argue that Melbourne can be viewed as a metaphor and analogy for understanding the consequences of terrorism for working people and businesses in all cities. The city of Melbourne and the businesses that are housed there are the laboratories where terrorism can be better understood and the clinics where counter-terrorism responses can be formulated. Much like people living and working in New York, Madrid, LA and London, working people in Melbourne perceive terrorism to be a significant threat that poses a clear and present danger to everyday life in the city.

The distinctive demeanour of terrorism as spectacle, when compared to the spectacles examined by Debord (1983), carry unique affects. Where traditional spectacles represented convergent points of consumption and alienation, the contemporary terrorism spectacle is giddily superficial and banal and reaches witnesses as an image in many locations both near and distant to where terrorist violence has occurred. Witnesses and victims of the spectacle of terrorism are influenced in many ways. This spectacle captures the gaze and navigates the consciousness as it arrives in a steady flow of images and imagery. Terrorism as spectacle relies on witnesses being unable to look away.

Terrorvision

Debord (1983: §1) argued that society was little more than an accumulation of spectacles. Spectacular images in the media have a powerful impact on media audiences. Pickering's (2005: 52) study of refugees similarly examines the spectacularization of supposed refugee deviancy in Australia's print media. She argues that refugees have been continuously depicted in the Australian media as illegitimate, illegal, shady and violent and framed in a media discourse of criminality. Pickering (2005: 53) argues that 'the incessant hum of refugee deviancy has primarily been the business of the mundane and increasingly everyday reporting of refugee issues'. Much like 'refugee deviancy' for Pickering, I argue that terrorism is reported in the press incessantly, particularly following critical moments when reporting of terrorism fills journalistic spaces and is 'produced and reproduced as an event, a scene, a spectacle' (Pickering, 2005: 53). The Australian print media formed an important part of the context in which research with working people in Melbourne took place. Many informants discussed the world's media at length.

Business leaders and managers should be concerned with the media images that working people are exposed to. Simulations of hyperreal terrorism saturate media and popular culture, and images of terrorism since 9/11 have been unavoidable. In an article from the Melbourne daily newspaper, *The Age*, the headline read: 'Threat of Terror Keeps Us Tuned In' (Ziffer, 2006: 8). Ziffer's (2006: 8) article examines the popularity of counter-terrorism themed reality television that depicts real and everyday moments of securing the nation and protecting the community. Ziffer (2006: 8) begins his article: 'Welcome to Fear TV'. Indeed, welcome – although you were likely already there. In this article Ziffer (2006: 8) argues that: 'In an uncertain time, Channel Seven's *Border Security* is Australia's most popular show'. *Border Security* is reality television for the post-9/11 consumer. The programme trades on the fascination with homeland security and terrorism and banks on the desire of people to *see* how the Global War on Terror is going in a local and familiar setting. The programme presents the everyday operations of border security professionals in Australia's airports, mailing centres and in coastal waters. At the time of writing *Border*

Security is in its fourth season with a fifth season planned. It is frequently viewed by more than two million people nationally and it was the most viewed programme in Melbourne in the period for recording ratings in late 2006 (Ziffer, 2006). For Australians wondering if they will be the next target of terrorism, programs such as *Border Security* satisfy the need to see and know. I argue that this show plays an important role for witnesses and victims dealing with the threat that terrorism poses to everyday life in a time of terror. In this sense, it can be argued that counter-terrorism television, reality or otherwise, resonates 'with viewers shell-shocked by violence and terrorism in far-off lands – and the threat of it arriving here' (Allen in Ziffer, 2006: 8). Contemporary terrorism strikes this resonance for working people in all cities. Indeed this terrorism as spectacle feels closer than its geographical proximity would sometimes suggest. This is because the spectacular image works to problematize traditional perceptions of time and space. It is the world's (tele)vision of global events that impact locally. As Debord (1983: §3) argued: 'The spectacle cannot be understood as an abuse of the world of vision, as a product of the techniques of mass dissemination of images. It is, rather, a *Weltanschauung* [world view] which has become actual, materially translated. It is a world vision which has become objectified'.

Working People and Media Exposure

Alexander (2004: 124) argues 'Any prospective terrorist attack in the United States or abroad will victimize labor: whether they are at work or wherever they find themselves – at the wrong place, at the wrong time'. The media play a significant role in this victimization – without the media, terrorists would have no way to generate spectacular images of violence and counter-terrorism operations and image-management techniques would not be necessary (see Miller, 2007: 74–111; Herman, 1982; Herman and Chomsky, 1994).

> *Since 9/11 the near daily barrage of terrorist threats has frayed on the raw nerves of employees. Multiple terror attacks worldwide against numerous sectors, and the broad array of modus operandi used, particularly suicide bombings, has exposed the public to the risks that exist.*
> (Alexander, 2004: 129)

The values and quality of the media can differ considerably across the world. According to Miller (2007: 74) the US media can be characterized through its 'hyperemotionalism and mythic folksiness' that is deployed as a substitute for critical journalism and reporting. As such, the US audience of terrorism has been witness to heart-wrenching accounts from eye-witnesses at Ground Zero and emotional and furious outbursts from many Americans, both near and distant, to the violence of terrorism. US audiences hear little, however, about why terrorism occurs and the vicious US military response that resulted in far more carnage than 'terrorists' have generated.

Tulloch's (2006) witnessing of London's Underground Zero was initially from the perspective of a 'victim' in that he was severely injured at the Edgware Road explosion. Soon Tulloch's (2006: 41) perspective changed as he began to see his image being used in the media. Tulloch (2006) critically evaluates how his image as a bloodied victim of terrorism was used to justify oppressive counterterrorism legislation and continued involvement of the British government in the wars in Iraq and Afghanistan. The prevailing trend in British reporting of the 7/7 attacks – and the failed attacks of July 21 – communicated a clear message to all witnesses and victims – another 'terrorist attack was inevitable in London – not if, but when' (Tulloch, 2006: 49).

In LA, the threat of terrorism had particularly damaging effects immediately following 9/11 and dramatic shifts in Californian lifestyle can be found in the account of *Midnight Oil* drummer, Rob Hirst, during the band's US tour in an 'Age of Terror', immediately following 9/11. Hirst (2003: 11) describes the once childhood Mecca (although Hirst cautions against this word in post-9/11 USA) of Disneyland as 'Fort Mickey':

> *Disneyland ... has become a high-security zone. Today it's virtually deserted, the much-loved old theme park looking less like a fun place for kids ... As soon as our minibus breaches the military cordon, a uniformed posse of goons go to work on it, crawling underneath with flashlights, prodding inside the engine bay with bomb detectors, and dusting (presumably) for any trace of weapons-grade plutonium.*

The band were dumbfounded that Mickey Mouse or Donald Duck were considered terrorist targets or that one of Australia's most well-known rock bands would be the conduits for the global war waged by a network of al-Qaeda terrorists. But this example may be illustrative of the mindset of many shortly after 9/11. Counterterrorist business security reduced a popular tourist attraction to virtual desertion in the name of security. Few business leaders, managers and working people would be willing to tolerate this tragic own-goal victory delivered to international terrorism, especially when the nearest terrorist atrocity had occurred such large distances away.

The images of contemporary terrorism, where terrorism entered perception through televisual reality, have been powerful and terrifying. These images of violence have also arrived through written media. Where images of terrorism can be captured and witnessed as the events are taking place, not all terrorism is captured in televisual images. I argue that imagery of contemporary terrorism has often been invoked to provide context and meaning to terror reporting post-9/11. As a referent for all subsequent terrorism 9/11, 3/11 and 7/7 – and events like the Bali bombings – enter the news media as an 'incessant hum' (Pickering, 2005: 52–54) of terrorism reporting. In this sense the mundane reporting of terrorist events as routine and everyday is a production that seeks to substitute real images and imagery for real events. McHoul and Miller (1998: ix–x) argued that an 'everyday event ... becomes *spectacular*' by becoming part of a collective memory of constructed meanings. As terrorism's witnesses and victims go about their working lives in cities, terrorism routinely and mundanely reappears through media reporting of the latest terror scare. In these times and spaces we enter, or are invited into, a journalistic museum of terrorism where the artefacts come to life – as they did in *Night at the Museum* – to tell us that they are not violence, only imitations of violence – what is colloquially known as *terror*. It is a place where every new terror scare is juxtaposed to what it can never be: a spectacular and pristine image-event like 9/11, 3/11 and 7/7. In this place that I call a 'black museum of journalism' the banal and mundane is intensely scrutinized (Virilio 2002: 23). I intend to suggest that closer inspection may reveal that there is nothing more to see.

The City

Melbourne is a prosperous city located in South-Eastern Australia. The city has a population of around 3.7 million and is considered a cultural and sporting epicentre. Melbourne is home, workplace and leisure centre to culturally diverse and prosperous communities. The city houses people from more than 140 countries who arrived in Melbourne displacing indigenous communities via four main waves of migration. The first wave of immigrants who came in the 1830s were English and Irish. These immigrants were responsible for the first disruption of the indigenous Kulin people. The second arrived during the 1850s gold rush and included significant numbers of Chinese immigrants. This caused further displacement of indigenous populations. The third came following WWII when people arrived from Europe. This wave of immigration had been encouraged to boost Australia's small population. The fourth wave originated from Vietnam and Cambodia. New Zealanders and people from the UK are the most represented in the immigrant population. Melbourne annually holds major cultural and sporting events including the *Melbourne Cup* horseracing event; the *Australian Open* tennis; international cricket; the Australian Rules football league Grand Final which is attended by over 90,000 people each September; and the motorcycle and formula one Grands Prix. Melbourne hosted the 1956 Olympic Games and the 2006 Commonwealth Games. The city hosts various social and cultural festivals including the *Moomba Waterfest*, food and wine festivals, the *International Comedy Festival*, the *Fringe Festival*, and the *International Arts Festival*. The *Melbourne Arts Centre* regularly holds operas and performances of international significance (City of Melbourne, 2006; Australian Bureau of Statistics, 2005). Encoded in these events and in witnesses in this city distant to contemporary terrorism are a variety of images – images of religion, society and culture, images of Selves and Others, and images of media and televisual culture. Like all major cities I argue it can be understood as a 'desert of the real' (Žižek, 2002a: 15), and is characterized by uncertainty, precariousness and vulnerability, and the attempts to manage and regulate these conditions.

In this often dynamic and vibrant locale, city dwellers go about their daily lives. In dealing with the everydayness of vulnerability and precariousness in their city – which is built into the physical, visual, and knowledge spaces and institutions – they confront anxieties and fears, bodies and places, images and imagery. I live and work in Melbourne and I conducted research with people who work in organizations that are housed in the city. During interviews I explored with informants the meanings and consequences of terrorism for working people and businesses. The city, I have argued, is the terrorist's visual playground. It is a mediated location where spectacular images of terrorism can be theatrically produced – as they were on 9/11, 3/11 and 7/7. Melbourne has never been the theatre for spectacular terrorism – nor has many other cities across the globe – but it is a city with a fearful population. People living and working in Melbourne witnessed and are victims of contemporary terrorism even as terrorist events were occurring live on television. I was watching the popular television program *The West Wing* that depicts everyday life in the Whitehouse when the alarming and surreal reports from New York began to filter in. Melburnians were appalled by these attacks and were again when the resort island of Bali in Indonesia was targeted on 12 October 2002 killing 202 people – 88 of whom were Australian holiday-makers. The Australian Federal Police (n.d.) described this attack as 'one of the most horrific acts of terrorism that has come *close* to Australian shores' (my emphasis). Melburnians again watched and witnessed as Madrid's public transport network was devastated by a series of bombings that killed 191 people.

Two thousand and five proved to be a shocking and demoralizing year for an already fearful population of witnesses and victims in Melbourne. There were three terrorist events that filled journalistic spaces and plunged the city into terror. The first half of 2005 was relatively uneventful – I conducted a series of interviews during this time. Then, shortly after the beginning of the new financial year on 7 July the London public transport network was targeted, killing 52 people including one Australian – a former Monash University student and employee, 28 year-old Sam Ly (AAP, 2005). Many Australians had friends and family living in London and, as such, many have stories of jumping on the phone and email to ensure that loved ones had not been caught up in the terror. To say that London is geographically distant to Melbourne is to miss the point. I knew of two friends who were travelling in London at the time of the bombing – one had missed one of the trains where a bomb was detonated. When I tell this story I am often accused of contributing to a popular urban legend. On 1 October of the same year, Bali was targeted for a second time. Twenty-three people were killed when popular restaurant districts were targeted. The recovering Balinese tourist industry was again crushed by this attack so soon after the first Bali bombing. In late 2005, terrorism seemingly arrived in Sydney and Melbourne. In November, following a lengthy period of intelligence gathering, operatives from Australia's various policing and intelligence agencies swooped on houses in Sydney and Melbourne in dawn raids. Eighteen men were arrested and detained because they were supposedly on the verge of committing a terrorist atrocity.

Witnessing is Always From a Distance

Tulloch's (2006) perspective as a witness and victim of contemporary terrorism is different to that of people in Melbourne but it shares many similarities. John Tulloch was an Australian academic living and working in the UK – a common and routine scenario. He was severely injured in the 7/7 bombings while travelling to work. In fact, John Tulloch was sitting a few feet from one of the Edgware Road suicide bombers with his briefcase at his feet – a routine and banal move that saved his legs (Tulloch, 2006: 16). While witnessing terrorism for most people in cities throughout the world occurs at a distance, for others this distance is only a few feet. But Tulloch's (2006) situated knowledge of terrorism – much like the situated knowledges for working people in Melbourne – was one bound in mediated images. Tulloch's (2006) slow recovery from his injuries was accompanied by a rediscovery and re-creation of the events through media images. His role as a victim of terrorism soon gave way to be being a witness to simulated media imagery:

> *On Saturday, 9 July, and Sunday 10 July ... I saw for the first time what the newspapers were doing with the terror attack. My concussion meant that I couldn't read much – at most the odd paragraph beside a picture to begin with. I could, though, and did, look closely and lengthily at the photographs, like the ones of me ... emerging from Edgware Road. I began to perceive the way in which these images were already becoming iconic in representing the terrorist attacks.*
> (Tulloch, 2006: 41)

Tulloch's (2006) account of the 7/7 attacks powerfully embodies what it means to be a worker, a witness and a victim. It demonstrates the many subtle and unsubtle literary techniques and technologies employed in journalistic spaces in a time of terror. In particular, his account explores the mediated images of terror – and their mis- and re-appropriation that paints a contradictory picture – a paradox of the terrorized city. Londoners were portrayed with images of 'helplessness, confusion and displacement' but also defiance, pride and courage that re-animated Britain's 'Blitz resistance' mentality (Tulloch, 2006: 42-43).

Tulloch (2006: 43) argues that an editorial in the *Sun* on 9 July captured the typical mood of British newspaper reporting. Entitled 'True Brit Grit', this article was a space for broad connections to be drawn between the resistance of the British to Nazism and their new resistance to terror – 'Men, women and children from every walk of life – not just the military – worked fearlessly and tirelessly to crush Hitler's tyranny ... Today Britain calls upon a new generation of heroes to fight an enemy every bit as sinister' (Tulloch, 2006: 43). The cover of the *Sun* on 9 July showed pictures of a bloodied John Tulloch and the 'can-opened bus' at Tavistock Square accompanying the headline '53 Dead in London Terror Attacks. Our Spirit Will Never Be'. In the *Daily Mirror* the headline read, '37 Dead, 700 Injured in London Suicide Terror. Blair Vows: Britain Will NOT Be Intimidated' (in Tulloch, 2006: 45). The implication here is clear – injured but not beaten in the War on Terror; a war fought by soldiers and city-dwelling civilians alike. The message in Australia during times of terror was quite different.

In Australia, like many countries throughout the world, we have no experience with devastating, large-scale terrorism. Some may point out that I am being glib in this assessment. Australians have experienced what could be defined as terrorism. In 1978 the Hilton Hotel in Sydney was bombed during the Commonwealth Heads of Government Meeting (CHOGM) killing three people. Militant groups associated with war and violence in the former Yugoslavia have carried out acts of violence within their communities in Australia. If the critical eye was to be turned upon the European heritage of many Australians, that is if we call a spade a spade even if only for a moment, then the closest thing to devastating terrorism that Australians have witnessed on Australian soil is the murder and displacement of Aboriginal communities from the time of European settlement. Terrorism like 9/11, 3/11 and 7/7 has never been seen in Australian cities – indeed Australia has nothing to which a catchy date-slogan could be attached. The Hilton bombing is not known as '13/2'. It sounds rather lame to attribute the symbolic date technique to this less insignificant act.

I am not suggesting that Australians are not witnesses and victims of terrorism, however. Indeed, I am suggesting quite the opposite. Australians and Australian workers are among the best placed witnesses in the world. We had front-row seats on 9/11, 3/11 and 7/7 and continue to have the perfect mediated and simulated view whenever the latest terror scare hits media spaces. Australians experienced their own terror scares in 2005 and I document their reporting in the media here. I use this reporting to reaffirm my belief that terrorism is most effective and most damaging when *nothing explodes*.

Terror Scares and Newspapers

As terror events pass into history the image and simulation reappears time and time again in different configurations of time and space. The 'unconscious movement of time', as Debord (1983: §125) described it, prevents the event from being seen again as anything other than an image. This, I argue, is not the end of the story. The possibility remains for events that pass into history to re-emerge, to be re-born, in other guises. The terror events that occurred, around a month apart, late in 2005 represent terrorism's power across different configurations of time and space. I suggest that as terrorism passes further into the past, its re-animation – re-manifestation, re-emergence, re-constitution, re-occurrence – through terrifying and powerful images and imagery of non-9/11, 3/11 and 7/7 terrorist events continue to terrify people who live and work in the city. Debord (1983: §125–129) argued that this production and reproduction of events through media spectacles gives events a circular quality where events can be witnessed again and again. I argue that working people may be grounded in time and space in particular organizations in particular cities but they are destined to witness and re-witness terrorism in various guises again and again.

I argue that this is what occurred following two major terror scares that affected people working and living in Melbourne – the 1 October 2005 Bali bombings, and the 8 November 2005 anti-terror raids. The first of these terror scares was the second time that Bali had been targeted since 9/11. On both occasions Australians were killed – 88 on 12 October 2002 when the first bombing occurred and four on 1 October 2005 – and these attacks have left a lasting impression on Australian witnesses and victims. The terrorists were strapped into suicide-bombing vests that were detonated in crowded restaurant districts in Kuta and Jimbaran Bay. Graphic amateur video footage captured the moment when one of the suicide bombers entered a restaurant and detonated the backpack that he was wearing. The terrorists were discovered to be Muslim extremists, most likely linked to the regional terrorist group *Jemaah Islamiya* who are accused of having links with al-Qaeda. According to Aglionby and Ressa (2005), the attacks were masterminded by two of South East Asia's most wanted men – Malaysian citizens Azahari bin Husin and Noordin Mohamed Top. Husin and Top were believed to have fled from Malaysia to Indonesia following security operations instigated after 9/11.

The second terror scare that I explore is that of the anti-terror raids of 8 November 2005 which began when federal policing and security agencies raided the homes of terror suspects in Melbourne and Sydney at dawn. The arrests were declared later that day to be a momentous event in Australian history (Moran and Drummond, 2005: 5). Sections of the media had been informed where and when the raids were to occur and were able to capture on film the moments in which they took place. Charges were laid against 16 men in Sydney and Melbourne for crimes relating to the preparation for carrying out an act of terrorism in an Australian city. Discovered in the anti-terror raids were a 'shopping list' of chemicals used to make bombs, a handgun, and a map of a government building in inner city Melbourne (Moran and Drummond, 2005: 5). The group was believed to be part of a global network of terrorists that quietly go about their lives as sleeper cells while preparing to carry out acts of terror. In a report in *Terrorism Monitor*, Stanley (2005) argues that the anti-terror raids occurred in an environment where Australians have been warned that 'an attack on Australian soil by al-Qaeda or its allies is probable, if not inevitable'. The threat posed by the men arrested in Sydney and Melbourne was, according to Stanley (2005), 'very real' despite scepticism amongst many Australians about whether terrorism posed a serious threat in Australia. The leader of this so-called cell was 45 year-old Abdul Nacer Benbrika. All of the men arrested were reported to be devout Muslims and many attended a mosque in Brunswick, an ethnically diverse inner-Melbourne suburb, where Benbrika preached. Stanley (2005) argues that the terror suspects arrested in these anti-terror raids in Melbourne and Sydney were part of an international trend towards the development of mostly 'home-grown' terrorist organizations. A prosecutor at the committal hearing on 9 November 2005 in the Melbourne Magistrates Court argued that the terror suspects were 'committed to a jihad' and obsessed with becoming martyrs (Australian Broadcasting Corporation, 2005).

I witnessed the stream of opinion columns, journalistic articles and letters to the editor that appeared in major newspapers both in Australia and worldwide following 9/11. The opinion-editorials and letters to the editor seemed to peak along with the journalistic articles following incidences of terrorism that received media coverage in Australia. When the resort island of Bali was targeted by terrorists for a second time on 1 October 2005 and when anti-terror raids were carried out in Melbourne and Sydney on 8 November 2005 there was an intense response from the journalistic communities and particularly from opinion writers. It sparked several concurrent debates about terrorism; some debating the threat that terrorism posed to Melbourne and how we should respond as a community. Since many key informants in the research that I conducted listed newspapers as one of their most frequently-used media sources, an analysis of Australia's major newspapers provides an important context for their responses.

The Bali bombings and the anti-terror raids were reported incessantly in the days that followed these terror scares, and re-emerged from time to time for several months after the events. It was Australia's major newspapers that were among the first to break these events as news stories, and these major newspapers are the focus of the content analysis presented in this chapter. In my content analysis I have focused on the *Herald Sun* and *The Age*, both of which are daily newspapers in Melbourne; *The Australian*, Australia's nationally-focused major daily newspaper; and *The Sydney Morning Herald* which is based in Sydney but widely read throughout Australia. The *Herald Sun* is Australia's most read daily newspaper with over 554,000 copies sold each day to a readership of 1.5 million people (The Herald and Weekly Times Pty Ltd, n.d), and is owned by Rupert Murdoch's *News Corporation*. It is presented in tabloid format and has larger advertising, sport, entertainment and opinion sections than other major Australian newspapers. The broadsheet *The Australian* is also owned by Rupert Murdoch's *News Corporation*. It is Australia's best-selling national daily newspaper yet attracts only a comparatively small readership of around 130,000 per weekday with the weekend edition attracting around 195,000 readers. The *Herald Sun* and *The Australian* are in competition with the *Fairfax* owned *The Age* and *The Sydney Morning Herald*. *The Age* is a Melbourne daily newspaper that is read daily by over 202,000 people, by over 302,000 readers on Saturdays, and by over 220,000 readers on Sunday (*The Age* – Corporate Information, 2007). *The Age* is a broadsheet newspaper and is colloquially seen as a non-tabloid, more legitimate and even 'highbrow' alternative to the *Herald Sun*. *The Sydney Morning Herald* is Australia's oldest newspaper (Isaacs and Kirkpatrick, n.d: 22). It is read by 882,000 people each weekday and on Saturdays it is read by over 1.1 million people. The *Herald Sun* and *The Australian* are considered, by some, to support conservative political values. Such views have been expressed on talkback radio and in weblogs by both members of the public and political and expert commentators (see for example Myriad Mint, 2005). *The Age* and *The Sydney Morning Herald* are sometimes accused in these same forums of being left-wing (see for example Jackson, 2007). A fifth major Australian newspaper that makes a brief appearance in this content analysis is the *Financial Review*. It has a smaller readership when compared to other major Australian newspapers – its circulation still reaches over 85,000 people each day. It considers itself the most important business-oriented newspaper in Australia (*Australian Financial Review*, n.d). From time to time the *Financial Review* participates in these crucial moments of terrorism reporting.

While some will watch the evening news on television for information about their city and their world, others will read reports, opinions and letters contained in major newspapers. Others write for newspapers as journalists and opinion writers, and still others write letters that actively create the spectacle that they consume. The stories, opinions, and letters produced and printed in these major Australian newspapers use 9/11 as the 'mother' of all events through which all previous and subsequent terrorism events are analyzed. I argue that these stories, opinions and letters contribute to terrorism as spectacle, but they are far from spectacular. These stories, opinions and letters are mundane, banal, everyday and routine. The fact that these comparatively minor terror scares received so much attention – in some respects more attention than more deadly attacks such as 3/11 and 7/7, undoubtedly due to the personal feel of these late-2005 attacks to Australians – is testament to how everyday and routine the threat of terrorism had become. The second Bali bombing and the anti-terror raids were constantly reported – whether there was anything to report or not – because it made a nation unmolested by terrorism feel as though we were as endangered as any New Yorker, Londoner, Spaniard or Californian.

The Blasts Were in Bali but they Ring in the Ears of Melbourne

The second Bali bombing occurred late on Saturday night 1 October 2005. This timing meant that there was minimal reporting in the Sunday editions of Australia's major newspapers. In the *Sunday Age* on 2 October, however, there was one news article that reported that there were blasts in Bali on the previous night and that they were 'clearly the work of terrorists' (Mbai in Forbes *et al*., 2005: 1). On 3 October there were detailed news articles, opinion pieces, editorials and letters to the editor in Australia's major newspapers. Pages 1–15 of the *Herald Sun* for example, contained articles about the Bali bombings that were accompanied by colour pictures of wreckage, victims and faces frozen in expressions of trauma and fear. On page four there was a map of Bali and highlighted on this map were the locations where the attacks occurred. On page four the reader was directed to pages 20 and 21 where opinion editorials about the Bali bombings were published. On pages eight and nine a timeline of terror was offered that reinforced the impact of contemporary terrorism on people who live and work in cities far from terror's flashpoints. In this timeline – which was headlined 'Trail of Destruction' – the starting point is 9/11 (*Herald Sun*, 2005a: 8–9). Here 9/11 is immediately a reference point and it is given special emphasis. The timeline continues by highlighting several other attacks that have impacted on Australian interests. These include the first Bali bombing in October 2002, the bombing in front of the Australian Embassy in Jakarta in September 2004 and the October 2005 Bali bombing. They are juxtaposed with other acts of contemporary terrorism, and the fact of their comparative insignificance in terms of buildings destroyed and people killed underlies the journalistic discourse of the October Bali bombings and the terrorism reporting in the days that followed.

Page 15 of the October 3 edition of the *Herald Sun* features an interview with Jason McCartney, a former professional Australian Rules footballer and a survivor of the 2002 Bali bombing. This provided the *Herald Sun* with a unique opportunity to combine spectacular issues in one news article. Jason McCartney was already a well-known celebrity in Melbourne before the first Bali bombing. He was an AFL footballer with three clubs – Collingwood Magpies, Adelaide Crows and North Melbourne Kangaroos – and had played 181 games before being severely injured in the terrorist attacks at nightclubs in Bali in October 2002. In a triumphant comeback game in which he wore bandages to protect his burns and a jumper with two numbers – 88 for the number of Australians who died in the first Bali bombings and 202 for the total number who died – he influenced his team's victory and, in a post-match interview announced his retirement to the crowd live on television. He has since written a book about his experiences in Bali (McCartney, 2003). His advice following the second Bali bombing was that the resort-island was, as a consequence, too dangerous to visit (Nolan, 2005: 15). In the 'Your Say' section he again expressed his 'concern' that 'It's happened in New York, Bali, Madrid, London – it's getting close' (*Herald Sun*, 2005b: 18). His comments reanimated contemporary acts of terrorism as a reference point for understanding all terrorism.

The attacks occurred in the midst of an ongoing debate in Australia regarding the need for strict anti-terrorism legislation, and the debate intensified in the week following the 1 October Bali bombings. *The Age* presented an appraisal of these laws and the media's reaction. The laws as they were proposed at the time would allow for the 'tagging' of terrorism suspects by the federal police: powers to detain people as young as 16 for long periods; the creation of a new offence for inciting violence; and the searching and questioning of people at major sporting events and mass gatherings (Haywood, 2005: 8). The laws had been opposed in some sections of Australian society but Attorney-General Philip Ruddock (in Haywood, 2005: 8) advised 'The discomfort involved in restrictions of this nature imposed upon an individual is nothing compared to the lifetime of pain and suffering for the innocent survivor of a terrorist attack'. An editorial in *The Age*, 24 September 2005 argued, with direct reference to 9/11, that it had been four years since 'the world changed' (Editor – *The Age*, 2005: 10). The editorial called for vigilance in confronting terrorism and denounced heavy-handed legal responses. Some would say that this was a predictable response from *The Age* as it is often identified as being politically left-wing (see for example Cornish *et al.*, 1996: 495).

An opinion-editorial (op-ed) in the *Herald Sun* on October 3 by Ian Shaw (2005: 21), a postgraduate student from the University of New South Wales, discussed the terrorist group believed to be responsible for the Bali attacks, *Jemaah Islamiya*, and their choice of 'soft targets'. He offered a general warning that venues such as 'open-fronted restaurants and bars and alfresco eateries' are attractive targets (Shaw, 2005: 21). I suggest the vagueness and obviousness of such a statement underlies the mundane and everydayness of terrorism reporting. It is a tautological statement, which amounts to something of the order that 'terrorists choose targets that cause terror'. But it once again points to the attractiveness of working people and businesses as targets of terrorism. Another op-ed by Paul Gray (2005: 21) discussed whether proposed anti-terror laws are needed. He described the laws as 'hysterical' and responsive to 'non-existent' terrorism. He questioned whether restricting civil liberties was really the best way to fight terrorism. Gray (2005: 21) argued that terrorism is not a domestic problem for Australia: it happens overseas in New York, Madrid, London and Bali. He considers the 34 pieces of anti-terrorism legislation in Australia 'since September 11' to be clear evidence of an overreaction (Gray, 2005: 21).

I have included here a discussion of the 'Vox Pop' section. It is a daily feature of the *Herald Sun* that asks members of the public their opinion on an issue that affects Melbourne, and it appears in the same section as the op-eds. It is perhaps not best placed in the opinion editorial section of my content analysis since op-eds are most often reserved for experts and established commentators, but since the *Herald Sun* has chosen to compare expert and public opinion in this way I have decided to embrace their technique and similarly explore the Vox Pops in the same space that I explore the op-eds. The Vox Pop for this day asked 'Do you support the proposed new anti-terrorist laws such as the power to detain people without charge for 14 days?' (*Herald Sun*, 2005b: 18). The result was a resounding four out of five in favour of the proposed legislation. Vox Pops and letters to the editor allowed witnesses to actively create their spectacles and articulate their own personal terrorism imagery following the 1 October Bali Bombings. Baudrillard (1988: 30) has argued that 'The need to speak, even if one has nothing to say, becomes more pressing when one has nothing to say'. I want to suggest that Vox Pops and letters to the editor are examples of the need to speak when we have nothing to say in response to images of terrorism. In this way witnesses and victims can be seen participating actively in the creation of a theatre of terrorism.

A Matter of 'When' Not 'If'

In an interview in the *Herald Sun*, Victoria's assistant police commissioner Simon Overland argued that 'it was only a matter of time before terrorists struck on Australian soil' (Mickelburough, 2005: 9). According to Overland (in Mickelburough, 2005: 9):

> I think it is inevitable that, at some stage, we will have an attack here ... This is an incredibly difficult thing to stop. They [terrorists] use everyday common sort of items: backpacks, packages, shopping bags. It could be anything and that's one of the challenges we face.

In the same *Herald Sun* news article Victorian Premier Steve Bracks confirmed that terrorism might occur in Melbourne: 'That's the assumption that we've had for some time now, of course, since September 11, since London and Madrid and, of course, the dreadful events in Bali' (Mickelburough, 2005: 9). Premier Bracks believed the main targets may be transport networks and anywhere people gather for major events, but he also offered calming words: 'I think the evidence at the moment is that it [Jemaah Islamiya] doesn't have a base here and it doesn't have a big supporter base here' (Mickelburough, 2005: 9).

Another former Australian Rules footballer, Dermot Brereton, offered his views on the latest Bali violence and his pending surfing trip to Indonesia in the *Herald Sun* on October 4: 'I view it not as much as an attack on Australians this time, I think it is more of a concerted effort to destroy the financial structure of Bali' (in Dunn, 2005: 8). Brereton is determined not to let the terrorists win 'and his group will go ahead with their trip' (Dunn, 2005: 8). It is possible to suggest that this is mundane terrorism reporting at its most banal. What gives a former Australian Rules footballer and football commentator the capacity to comment on the 'financial structure of Bali'? It is perhaps surprising that this item appeared in a news articles section of the *Herald Sun* and not in the opinion pages. It is possible that this article provided some solace for readers, for encoded in Brereton's comments was defiance. Brereton could do what many Melburnians would perhaps have liked to do: be defiant as terrorism threatened. Another news article three pages after Brereton's advice discussed what it meant to witness the terrorism in Bali. Witnessing terrorism in Bali, according to Robinson and Whinnett (2005: 11), has made many people question whether they should continue visiting Bali. Many holidaymakers left immediately following the bombing and others stayed 'defying warnings to leave Bali, saying it would hand a victory to the terrorists' (Robinson and Whinnett, 2005: 11).

On page twelve of the same issue of the *Herald Sun* the story of a young train enthusiast is featured. He was banned from taking photos of trains by a Melbourne rail company (Edmund, 2005: 12). Twelve-year-old Jason Blackman was told he had to fill out a form declaring his intention to photograph trains at Melbourne's Flinders Street Station. He and his father duly complied only to be told that their plans of taking photographs during 'school holidays and occasional weekends' were not stated specifically enough (Edmund, 2005: 12). Jason's father argued 'I can't see the harm. We're not going to blow anyone up. We're not terrorists. We're just normal people' (Edmund, 2005: 12). A spokesperson for the company replied to this suggestion by claiming that: 'It's unfortunate but in today's climate and with the security conditions we need to enforce, we ask amateur photographers to give us some prior warning ... Even in the case of a 12-year-old boy we don't make assumptions about who is or isn't a risk' (Edmund, 2005: 12). It would seem that a routine leisure activity enjoyed by many children was a security risk. The fact that it was reported as a news item is banal and adds to the incessant hum of terrorism reporting.

Controversial Melbourne-based law academic Mirko Bagaric also contributed an op-ed – it appeared on the same page as my own. Bagaric is perhaps best known for his views regarding the morality of torture – he has argued that the 'reflex rejection of torture needs to be replaced by recognition that it can be a moral means of saving life' (Bagaric, 2005a: 13). He began his op-ed published in the *Herald Sun* on October 4: 'The latest Bali bombings, so close to Australian shores, highlight the catastrophic consequences that stem from a terrorist attack' (Bagaric, 2005b: 21). Bagaric (2005b) argued that the attacks should put the new anti-terror laws into perspective and affirm their necessity. He accused opponents of the anti-terror laws of lacking 'imagination' and maintained that terrorism poses a risk that must be taken seriously. Bagaric (2005b) argued that the securitization of society must be undertaken with a full appreciation of the risk that is faced. He argued that whilst we were not 'in a war' we are also not in a traditional risk framework: 'Depending on who you ask, the risk is anywhere between remote to a near certainty. If we split the difference it's a sure bet that there is a real risk that terrorists will launch an attack on Australian soil in the foreseeable future'.

In the editors remarks in the 4 October edition of the *Herald Sun* the readers were reminded that terrorists are set to target Western interests in general, 'and Australia and Melbourne in particular' (Editor – Herald Sun, 2005: 20). The editor reiterated the comments made by the Police Assistant Commissioner that an attack in Australia was inevitable and that 'common sense dictates' that the Melbourne Commonwealth Games could be the likely target (Editor – *Herald Sun*, 2005: 20). The editor of the *Herald Sun* cited a statement issued on behalf of civil liberties organization *Liberty Victoria*. This statement argued that the new anti-terror laws are a greater threat to our way of life than terrorism. The editor responded that this statement was 'Dangerous, deluded stuff!' (Editor – *Herald Sun*, 2005: 20).

In *The Australian* on 5 October West and Stein (2005: 15) drew comparisons between 9/11 and the Bali bombings. Citing Susan Sontag's comments after 9/11 that the terrorists were not cowards as a general example of free speech being exercised, they wrote that debate and discussion must not be stifled in the aftermath of the Bali attacks. Another example of this appeared in *The Age* where a manager at Melbourne's international airport argued that a travel slump comparable to that after 9/11 is expected after the Bali bombings (Jackson, 2005: 4). In *The Australian*, Victorian Police Chief Commissioner Christine Nixon argued that an attack at the Melbourne Commonwealth Games 'cannot be ruled out' as it is 'the first major public event (in Melbourne) since 9/11' (in Kerin, 2005: 8). In an article by Macnamara (2005: 7) in the same issue of *The Australian*, academic Joseph Siracusa warned that Australia is a 'terrorist's delight' and added that since 9/11 there had been few steps taken to protect Australian cities.

Bolt (2005a) in the *Herald Sun* of 5 October speculated in general about the risks he believed terrorism posed to people living and working in the city, using statements from accused terrorists to support his arguments. I was most alarmed by Bolt's general references to Muslims and Islam as perpetrators of terrorism. While he intended most likely to criticize only Islamic extremists, he allowed his language to occasionally drift into general criticisms of Muslims and Islam: 'Islamic fascists', 'That's how Islam's death cult has spread', 'new Islamist cult of death', 'And should Muslims use nuclear weapons against us?' (Bolt, 2005a: 23). It is not my intention to take these quotes out of context to demonize Andrew Bolt – as a conservative commentator he is often demonized – but rather point to how casual language and generalized statements can become part of the consequences of terrorism. In these particular cases the consequences are overreaction, hyperbole and the demonizing of innocent people. Were Bolt's words to result in negative attitudes towards Muslims – or rather people who appear to be Muslim – it would be an alarming consequence of media reporting of terrorism in Bali.

On 6 October – five days after the Bali bombings – the incessant hum of terrorism reporting that reanimates other acts of contemporary terrorism became more gentle and nuanced as brash and dramatic pictorial reporting made way for more analytical accounts from journalists and opinion writers. In a news article by Meade (2005: 17) in *The Australian* it is argued that the media and its response to terrorism has been fine tuned since 9/11: 'Terrorist attacks have become more commonplace since September 11, 2001, and newsrooms are much quicker to respond when disaster strikes'. Meade (2005) explained that news of the Bali bombings was received at around 10.15pm on 1 October in Sydney and several journalists had already been booked on flights to Bali by 11pm. According to one news director, 'I remember after September 11 it took us almost 24 hours to realise what had happened … Now … it has become such big news, we react straightaway' (Meade, 2005: 17).

Also in this edition of *The Australian*, Kissane (2005: 10) reported that some people in Indonesia believed that terrorism is a product of a Western conspiracy against Islam. Kissane (2005: 10) continued the trend of reanimating contemporary terrorism in the journalistic spaces devoted to the Bali bombings. Kissane (2005: 10) argued that some

Indonesians see Osama bin Laden as a hero, and believed that he was not behind recent acts of terrorism. Conspiracy theories relating to 9/11 are mentioned specifically on three occasions in Kissane's article about the Bali bombings. News articles about the Bali bombings in the 6 October edition of the *Herald Sun* were pushed almost entirely from the front page. A small banner across the bottom of the front page stated: 'World Police Team Up To Hunt Bali Bombers' (*Herald Sun*, 2005c: 1).

The most substantial coverage of Bali bombings in the *Herald Sun* took place in the opinion pages, in an op-ed by Neil Mitchell (2005a: 23) – the host of a popular talkback radio program on Melbourne radio station 3AW on weekday mornings. Mitchell (2005a: 23) argued that 'The unthinkable is now considered inevitable' and people living and working in Melbourne should start planning for the day that terrorists attack in their city. Mitchell (2005a) argued that there are several deficiencies in Melbourne's preparedness for the worst case terrorism scenario: scenarios such as 9/11, 3/11 and 7/7. He argued that the hospitals are under-prepared, that there may be a lack of coordination between doctors and nurses in the event of a terrorist attack, and that the readiness of current and former police and fire-fighters was questionable. Mitchell (2005a: 23) asked:

> *Has the kid in the divvy van in Fitzroy been told what to do if the MCG is attacked? Has he been trained in how to cope with massive casualties and mass hysteria? He'll try, of course, but is he ready? How many retired police or firefighters would be sitting at home counting flowers on the wallpaper while this unfolded? They would want to help and could be used in traffic control or on the phones. Has anybody asked them?*

This was not just a problem for emergency workers in Mitchell's (2005a) view. Tow-truck drivers would also want to help clear debris and damaged or destroyed vehicles. Bus drivers, who are trained to watch out for suspicious packages, would be particularly on edge during a terrorist scare. In short, how could the employed population – the victims and targets of terrorism – participate in the response to terrorism? Mitchell (2005a: 23) asked: Would their training in identifying the suspicious extend to acting on their observations? Would train drivers know not to pull into a station if they believed there was a bomb on board? Would they be willing to risk their own safety to preserve the lives of many others? Mitchell (2005a) provided an example of the emergency response to a chemical fire at Coode Island in 1991 in an outer suburb of Melbourne. A fire broke out at a chemical treatment plant near Melbourne and radio and television reports warned people to stay indoors until further notice. Mitchell (2005a: 23) noted, however, that 'After reporting the fire I drove cautiously into the city. Life was normal. People were shopping, chatting and commuting as the smoke threatened. The warnings had been unheard or ignored'.

By 7 October there was little interest in the Bali bombings but there remained significant interest in terrorism and the likelihood of it occurring in Melbourne. On 7 October it was six days since the Bali bombings that targeted a popular restaurant district and only five months before the city hosted the 2006 Commonwealth Games. That day's edition of the *Herald Sun* reported on page three that 'High Flyers Can Go Jump' (Kelly, 2005: 3). A subheading explained: 'Former police chief Kel Glare wants parachutes for people who work or live above the 13th floor' for the next time terrorists attack tall buildings as they did on 9/11 (Kelly, 2005: 3). Reactions to the story were mixed among people that were interviewed by Kelly (2005), and who lived or worked above the thirteenth floor. An occupant of a building in inner city Melbourne who worked a kilometre from the World Trade Center in New York on 9/11 commented that they had no lingering fears and would not be buying a parachute. Another occupant, who lived in a city high-rise apartment block, believed the suggestion was 'absolutely laughable' (in Kelly, 2005: 3). Others, however, thought it was a great idea, despite the $250 price tag being a barrier (*Herald Sun*, 2005d: 3). Some experts felt the suggestion was impractical. Assistant Chief Fire Officer Greg Bawden argued that 'You couldn't do it in Melbourne. Where would you land?' (Bawden in Kelly, 2005: 3). Unsurprisingly perhaps, a parachute manufacturer thought it was a good idea.

I suggest that this week of reporting in Australia's major newspapers that reanimated other acts of contemporary terrorism represented a commodification of terrorism. In this sense the terror parachute is an example of an escalation of this commodification. Unsurprisingly, this news story was reported like any other. It was mundane, routine, everyday and banal. I suggest that the terror bombardment that readers of Australia's major newspapers were subjected to following the Bali bombings created the space for this ridiculous suggestion to be incorporated into banal terror news.

By Saturday 8 October 2005 there was little discussion and reporting on the Bali bombings. In the *Herald Sun*, stories about the Bali bombings were relegated to page 13. Seven days after the Bali bombings and a week-long media hum of terrorism reporting, the journalistic spaces fall mostly silent on terrorism. Page 13 described an Anglican Archdeacon in Geelong who called for prayers not just for victims but for terrorists too (Houlihan, 2005: 13). On the same page was the story of little 'Victory' whose father had died in the first Bali bombing, in October 2002, before he was born: it was suggested that he will always be a testament of what terrorism can never destroy (Whinnett, 2005: 13). Page 19 contained two news items that again demonstrated the everydayness and banality of terrorism reporting. A *Rolling Stones* concert at the University of Virginia in Charlottesville in the United States was stopped for ten minutes to allow bomb sniffer dogs access to the stage (*Herald Sun*, 2005e: 19); and United States soldiers in Iraq discovered what they believed to be plans to blow up the New York subway (Associated Press et al., 2005: 19). In response, a 'security blanket' was thrown over New York's subway system with police searching 'bags, briefcases, strollers and other luggage' (Associated Press et al., 2005: 19). Everyday situations and rituals – going to concerts, travelling to work and around the city – were made to seem potentially risky and precarious.

Letter Writing in an Age of Terror

The letters to the editor in the week following the 1 October Bali bombings are illustrative of how terrorism spectacles are generated and received by media audiences. There were a number of letters to the editor published on 3 October that related to the bombings. One was displayed prominently in bold font. It asked the Victorian Premier Steve Bracks: 'Mr Bracks, will you have enough security at the Commonwealth Games next year?' (*Herald Sun*, 2005b: 18). The bold font stands out and catches the eye when page 18 is opened. This letter placed the Bali bombings in a Melbourne context by forging a link with a major sporting and cultural event that was to be held in Melbourne in March 2006 – the Commonwealth Games. Major cultural and sporting events are critical components of everyday life in the city of Melbourne. Close to the central business district of the city there are two large sporting stadiums. One – the Melbourne Cricket Ground (MCG) – is a world-renowned venue with the capacity to seat around 100,000 spectators, the other – the Telstra Dome – is smaller but still enormous with a capacity for around 50,000 spectators. The Telstra Dome is located just behind the newly refurbished Southern Cross Station (formerly Spencer Street Station) which was renovated in time for the Commonwealth Games and has taken its place as one of Melbourne's most prominent locations from which to travel on the vulnerable rail network. Southern Cross and the 'Dome represent key coordinates in a theatre of terrorism. A bomb detonated in this region of Melbourne would kill and terrify many people living and working in Melbourne. The possibility of this occurring kills no one, but terrifies many.

In *The Age*, Ray Brindle wondered what 'the real risk' was (*The Age*, 2005a: 12). He argued that more people die on US roads in a month than died in the 9/11 attacks. Colin Hughes wondered why Jemaah Islamiya's spiritual leader, Abu Bakar Bashir, was never arrested on one of his many visits to Australia. After all, 'It is unlikely he came for the footy' (The Age, 2005a: 12). Paul Rozental also in a letter to *The Age* argued that terrorism is nothing new and our only options are to fight or do nothing. He pointed out that there was terrorism *even before 9/11*.

In a letter to the *Herald Sun's* 'Your Say' section, Dale Hughes took aim at an op-ed by Paul Gray from 3 October: 'Paul Gray seems to underestimate the threat of terrorism in Australia' (*Herald Sun*, 2005b: 18). Hughes argued that the terrorism in New York, Madrid, London and Bali meant that terrorism in Australia was 'almost inevitable'. His solution was tough terror laws that he argued would restrict our freedoms far less than terrorism would.

The result of a reader poll was reported in the *Herald Sun* on 5 October. The poll had asked: 'Is Australia at greater risk of a terror attack in light of the Bali bombing?' (*Herald Sun*, 2005f: 19). Of the 472 people who called in to answer this question, 59.7 per cent believed that Australia was at greater risk. Through the power of images and what I argue to be spectacular yet mundane reporting, 59.7 per cent of *Herald Sun* readers believed that the attacks in Bali made Australia more at risk. It is possible to suggest that terrorism in Bali does not make us more at risk, but it may have made us more aware of already existing risks and vulnerabilities. In short, terrorism in Bali may be distant, but it *feels* close. In *The Age* on 5 October, a letter from Ray Sanderson argued that the 'reality' is that terrorism had never occurred against Australians in Australia (*The Age*, 2005b: 16). John Novak wrote in *The Age* that Australia is clearly not safe from terrorism. He believed it is perhaps not probable, but that it is random and could happen without warning, at any time. Alan Freedman, also writing in *The Age*, believed that in Melbourne people find themselves in a world war that 'started on September 11' (*The Age*, 2005b: 16).

In *The Australian*, witnessing is a feature of the letters to the editor section (*The Australian*, 2005a: 15). Barry Jiggins argued that 'We in the West will compulsorily bare (sic) witness to your macabre swan song on the evening news if that's what it takes to enjoy our decadence and freedoms in peace'. In compulsorily bearing witness Barry Jiggins admitted to being unable to look away when terrorism is on his television. Barry Jiggins then decided to share his views by writing to the 'letters to the editor' section of *The Australian*. In this way, Barry Jiggins has helped create the spectacle of terrorism that he witnesses. Rex Condon in *The Australian* offered a critique of the media reporting of the Bali bombing. He asked why so much coverage was devoted to the reporting of Australian interests when the attacks mainly damaged the people and tourism infrastructure of Bali. Rex Condon argued that where the transferring home of an Australian victim received front page attention, the treatment of injured locals was mostly ignored. Judi Cox concluded in *The Australian*: 'Just when you think you've seen all the gruesome images, photos appear of the severed heads of the three Bali suicide bombers. Let's hope parents of young children are turning off the TV news and hiding newspapers' (*The Australian*, 2005a: 15).

A letter from Paul Wilson in the *Sydney Morning Herald* asked what allows the media to show such graphic images of violence and injury on television (*The Sydney Morning Herald*, 2005: 14).

> *Amateur video footage of what seems to be a suicide bomber exploding in a crowded restaurant has been playing at all hours on all the major TV networks. Has anyone seen one warning preceding its use? Do we now need to see a person exploding to have some concept of a suicide bomber and the associated carnage?*

Paul Wilson (*The Sydney Morning Herald*, 2005: 14) argued that the nature of witnessing can be seen to have changed when his five-year-old witnessed 'Bali terrorism 2005' on a news bulletin during a children's programme. Wilda Fong wrote in *The Sydney Morning Herald* that while she understands that 'a picture speaks a thousand words' she questions the purpose of bloodied images of victims from the Bali bombings: 'Where are the ethics and compassion from people of the media?' (*The Sydney Morning Herald*, 2005: 14). Allan Gibson drew comparisons between terrorism news and television fiction. He argued that as we watched the images of Australian Federal Police working with their Indonesian counterparts in the aftermath of the attacks, witnesses should have kept in mind that 'Unlike the scenarios of popular TV programmes, this *crime scene investigation* is reality'[1] (my emphasis) (*The Sydney Morning Herald*, 2005: 14). These letters to the editor in the *Herald Sun*, *The Age*, *The Australian* and *The Sydney Morning Herald* contained sophisticated comment and opinion about images and what it means to be a witness. Terrifying and powerful images clearly had an impact on the letter-writers explored here. Yet these letter-writers are not passive observers of the terrorist threat and its rejuvenation, reconstitution, and reanimation: they are active participants in the everyday, routine, mundane and banal terrorism commentary.

Ann Jenkin asked in *The Australian* why the Australian public was doing the hard work for the terrorists by feeling excessive fears and anxieties and overreacting to the attacks in Bali. She believed it is what terrorists want and 'Thanks to our media, they are being incredibly successful' (*The Australian*, 2005b: 13). In the *Herald Sun*, Phillip Spencer argued that the Howard government was guilty of waging a 'Muslims under the bed fear campaign' analogous to the former Australian Prime Minister Bob Menzies' 1950s and 1960s 'reds under the bed scare campaign' (*Herald Sun*, 2005g: 21). He went on to suggest that the treatment of Muslims in Australia had taken us 'back to the middle of last century'. He argued that an open dialogue, tolerance and understanding could ensure that Australia remained a safe place to live and work (*Herald Sun*, 2005g: 21). A letter in *The Age* from Peter Kartsounis argued against profiling in airports that targets Muslim Australians. He believed that Australia could easily become a place that paints Muslims as the 'legitimate subjects of fear and suspicion in a post-9/11 world' (*The Age*,

---

1 *Crime Scene Investigation*, or *CSI*, is a brand of crime-drama series on US television network CBS.

2005c: 12). Terrorism for Peter Kartsounis was real, but the negative consequences did not have to be.

Terror News – The Bali Bombings

In this analysis of Australia's major newspapers following 1 October 2005 I have suggested that contemporary acts of terrorism – such as 9/11, 7/7 and 3/11 – were rejuvenated, reconstituted, and reanimated in journalistic spaces devoted to reporting the Bali bombings. I presented information from news articles, opinion editorials (op-eds), and letters to the editor from major Australian newspapers in the week following the attack – 2 October through to 8 October 2005 – to demonstrate this rejuvenation. I argued that during times of terror, terrorism becomes a routine and everyday part of life in the city. I suggest that this reporting, particularly in the Murdoch-owned tabloid *Herald Sun*, is directed towards selling 'terrorism' as a brand and a commodity. This terror-reporting forms part of the backdrop to living and working in the city. Bali is a popular holiday destination for affluent Australian workers who, due to favourable conditions for currency exchange and the low cost of consumer products in Indonesia, flock to the island during end of season sporting trips, school holidays and annual leave. While Bali is not part of the Australian homeland, the trend of reporting, opinion and letter writing in the week following the second Bali bombing suggests that for many Australians it feels like part of Australia. Bali is an Australian 'traumascape' (Tumarkin, 2005) – a site of national mourning and 'Aussie' identity. As such, these attacks resonate with working people in Australian cities. Australian workers – and I argue the world's workers – know that they are the targets of terrorism. They are also targets when holidaying in Bali.

Given the response of Australians evident in journalistic space in major Australian newspapers one can imagine that the response would be spectacular if terrorists were to carry out a successful attack in an Australian city. Some have suggested that terrorism *almost* happened – were such a thing possible – in November 2005 when accused terrorists were arrested in Sydney and Melbourne, with authorities suggesting without the burden of evidence that these men were on the verge of committing a terrorist atrocity. I will focus on the spectacular, overreacting and sensational media coverage of these attacks. This terror-reporting placed working people squarely in the crosshairs of home-grown terrorism. In this way it is strikingly different to the response to the attacks on Bali. Terrorism in Indonesia remains distant, no matter how close it felt. While these anti-terror arrests certainly do not equate to a literal act of violence, the hysterical response of many journalists and some sections of the public and law enforcement communities points to something diabolical about terrorism and the threat it poses. These arrests for supposed terroristic intent were treated by some to represent a clear and present danger to people living and working in Melbourne and Sydney. The anti-terror arrests were another crucial moment in terrorism reporting and journalistic spaces again filled with references to 9/11, 3/11 and 7/7 and their rejuvenation in mundane and banal ways.

Too Close For Comfort: Anti-Terror Raids in Australian Cities

Witnesses awoke on 9 November 2005 to images and alarming newspaper reports that declared home-grown terrorism had arrived in Sydney and Melbourne. The raids were conducted at dawn on 8 November, too late in the morning to appear in that day's editions of Australia's major newspapers. Dunn and Anderson (2005: 2) reported in the *Herald Sun* that hidden cells had been planning 'catastrophic' chemical or explosive attacks, and that their plans had been 'smashed' during dawn raids by federal police and security agencies. The Melbourne Magistrates Court was told by prosecuting attorneys at committal hearings for the terror suspects that one of the accused was willing to be a martyr in a suicide mission (Dunn and Anderson, 2005: 2). Another terror suspect who was arrested later on the day of the raids was shot while being apprehended. Dunn and Anderson (2005: 2) argued that it may prove to be 'a day that forever changed Australia'. The authors described the day in this way: 'In the nation's biggest joint counter-terrorism operation, more than 400 federal and state police, along with ASIO agents, swooped on 22 properties in two states, arresting nine men in Melbourne and eight in Sydney, and seizing chemicals and computers'.

The anti-terror raids were framed in the media as essential and necessary actions to thwart an imminent attack on people living and working in Melbourne – little critical thought was exhibited amongst the journalists privileged enough to be tipped-off before the raids occurred. Yet, more than anything, the raids were unmistakably media events – spectacular events – that were used to sell newspapers and ensure a large audience for the nightly news. Whether terrorism posed any greater material or corporeal threat to Melbourne was profoundly irrelevant. The rationale for the arrests was that: 'We were concerned the attack was imminent', Victorian Police Chief Commissioner Christine Nixon said. Premier Steve Bracks said he believed police had disrupted 'probably the most serious preparation for a terrorist attack that we have seen in Australia' (Dunn and Anderson, 2005: 2). In *The Australian*, Stewart and Leys (2005: 1) offered similarly narrow coverage of the raids. They described the anti-terror raids in this way:

> In the largest and most important anti-terrorism operation in the nation's history, hundreds of state and federal police officers in NSW and Victoria raided homes in the dead of night, believing a terrorist attack was imminent. The raids – the culmination of an 18-month investigation – uncovered stockpiles of chemicals similar to those used in the London bombings in July.

The New South Wales Police Chief Commissioner, Ken Maroney, stated that the Australian public could be 'satisfied that we have disrupted what I would regard as the final stages of a large-scale terrorist attack ... here in Australia' (Stewart and Leys, 2005: 1). Stewart and Leys (2005: 1) reported that during the committal hearing in the Melbourne Magistrates Court for the arrested terror suspects, the prosecutor claimed that the accused believed that a holy war should be carried out against infidels and that killing innocent people in some circumstances would be appropriate. The defence solicitors argued that the charges were 'scandalous political prosecutions that shame this nation' and added that there was no evidence to suggest that the group was planning on carrying out a terrorist act (Stewart and Leys, 2005: 1).

On 9 November, Moran and Drummond (2005: 5) reported in the *Financial Review* that the would-be terrorists had tried to obtain chemicals that had not been readily available since 9/11. This point was reiterated in a news article by Tippet (2005: 3) that appeared in *The Age* on November 9. Neighbour (2005: 3), in a news article written for *The Australian*, reported that the men arrested were radicalized and trained in the ideology of jihad. Neighbour (2005: 3) argued that training in military style camps for jihad was a rite of passage before 9/11; in the post-9/11 world it amounted to an admission of guilt. Even those who had attended and left these camps prior to 9/11, before it was illegal, have been held to account for their actions in the aftermath. I argue that the frequent references to 9/11 when reporting the arrest of terror suspects in Melbourne and Sydney demonstrated again how contemporary terrorism was used as a referent that was rejuvenated, reconstituted and reanimated through the latest terror scare.

Walters (2005: 5) writing in the same issue of *The Australian*, argued that 'The biggest counter-terrorist operation in Australia's history has shown just how far the security agencies have evolved since September 11, 2001'. Walters (2005: 5) argued that 9/11 served as a wake-up call for intelligence and policing agencies. Writing in *The Age*, Gordon (2005: 4) argued that Australian Prime Minister John Howard was seeing Australia through a difficult time just as he promised in the aftermath of 9/11. I argue that this is a problematic link that Gordon forges between the anti-terror raids and 9/11. His doing so is further evidence of antecedent acts of terrorism mundanely and routinely appearing in journalistic spaces reporting the latest terror scare. An editorial in *The Australian* explained to readers that there was 'no doubting' that terrorism posed a significant threat to Australia (Editor – *The Australian*, 2005: 17). Emotive terminology was used in this editorial to frame terrorism raids in Sydney and Melbourne in such a way as to invoke memories of 9/11, 3/11 and 7/7. The editor of *The Australian* argued that the 'price of life and liberty' was 'eternal vigilance' and that this was 'crystal clear' when thinking about the meaning of the anti-terror raids in Melbourne and Sydney. More problematically the editor proclaimed: 'Australian cities are on the front line in the worldwide war on terror' (Editor – *The Australian*, 2005: 17). While reminding readers that it is for the courts to decide the guilt of the 16 accused, the editor asserted that the arrests – described as 'a frightening affair' – confirmed what 'sensible citizens have known we faced since September 11, 2001' (Editor – *The Australia*, 2005: 17). The editor of *The Australian* added that terrorism will 'probably' occur in an Australian city and that such an event would transform Melburnians and Australians from distant witnesses to near witnesses. It would seem that the editor in *The Australian* believed that the images of 9/11 marked a dawn in a new era of spectacular terrorism:

> *Every Australian who watched the two aircraft fly into New Yorks' (sic) Twin Towers on September 11, 2001, who saw reports of the wholesale slaughter of Madrid commuters in March 2004 and Londoners in July, knows what terrorists delight in doing. Every Australian who remembers the attempt to bomb the Australian embassy in Jakarta in September 2004 will understand the sort of threat we face. And every Australian who remembers the brutal, indiscriminate destruction that killed close to 100 of our countrymen and women in the two Bali bombings will know.*
>
> (Editor – *The Australian*, 2005: 17)

The editor of *The Australian* suggested that, if a terrorist attack was to occur in Australia, terrorists may target ferries in Sydney, trams in Melbourne, shopping malls, and spaces in and around sporting events in cities and towns – vital coordinates of living and working in Australia's two largest and most populated cities. The editor of *The Australian* stressed that the people who hate us live among us and therefore civil liberties needed to be set aside to find these people, and that criticism of government and the police must be restrained. It was, in the opinion of the editor of *The Australian*, the only way to prevent terrorism occurring in an Australian city. Readers were implored not to forget that people 'in cities around the world have been slaughtered in terror attacks' (Editor – *The Australian*, 2005: 17).

An editorial in the *Financial Review* on 9 November strongly supported the arrest of terror suspects: 'If half of what is alleged sticks, no one will now be able to deny that the nightmare of home-grown terrorism has arrived in Australia' (Editor – *Financial Review*, 2005: 62). The editor of the *Financial Review* described people in Australian cities as lucky: despite watching 9/11, 3/11 and 7/7 and two attacks in Bali on television, Australia remained 'terrorism' free. *The Sydney Morning Herald*'s editor wrote that the terror arrests show that terrorism can be 'grown' in Australia (Editor – *The Sydney Morning Herald*, 2005: 16). The editor added that it was equally concerning that the arrests were stage managed with media crews present during the dawn raids that ensured spectacular televisual footage was captured.

An op-ed by Andrew Bolt in the *Herald Sun* on 9 November described the arrests as a 'wake-up call' that terrorism posed a *real* threat to Australian cities (Bolt, 2005b: 23). Bolt invoked imagery of Madrid and London and declared that people in Australia could be 'blown up' by Islamic extremists, and described scenes of Muslim rioting and violence in Europe that he argued could soon be seen in Australia. This is because, Bolt (2005b: 23) argued, many Muslim immigrants to Australia have been conditioned by an 'archaic and even fossilized culture' (Bolt, 2005b: 23).

Australian newspapers on 10 November contained more news articles, opinion editorials, and letters to the editor that discussed the anti-terror raids. In *The Australian*, Stewart (2005: 1) reported that there have been close links discovered between Islamic prayer rooms and the terror cells that have been exposed by the anti-terror raids. Stewart (2005: 1) argued that some with links to this prayer room believed that 9/11 was a conspiracy of the West and that Osama bin Laden was a good man. In another article in *The Australian*, Gosch and Makin (2005: 5) argued that some people who lived near the houses that were raided during the anti-terror raids were traumatized and had developed sleeping difficulties. In *The Age*, Nicholson and Grattan (2005: 4) argued that Muslim leaders were pleading with the government to clamp down on potential 'rednecks' and vigilantes who may seek reprisal and attack people perceived to be Muslim.

The headline on the front page of the *Herald Sun* read: 'Terror Alarm On Map' (Hunt et al. 2005: 1). According to Hunt et al. (2005: 1): 'A Melbourne office tower housing many hundreds of public servants was among the possible targets of an alleged terror plot foiled by raids this week'. The police and security agencies that conducted the anti-terror raids uncovered a potential plan to target a tall building in Melbourne. The coverage in the *Herald Sun* continued on page four with a powerful image of two Muslim women – the wives of accused terrorists detained in the raids – dressed in traditional Islamic clothing (Hargest, 2005: 5). The eyes of only one of the women could be seen: they are otherwise completely covered by clothing. The picture was large, prominent, and in colour. Below the picture is an article where political and religious leaders appealed for calm: after the anti-terror raids were reported in the media over 200 tip-offs on the identity of potential terrorists were received by the national security hotline (Frenkel, 2005: 5). Australia's

Prime Minister, John Howard, is quoted in Frenkel's (2005: 5) article arguing that only radical elements within Muslim communities were responsible for the threat of terrorism in Australia. He called for calm and warned members of the public against attempting vigilante-style reprisals against Muslims. A Muslim leader urged the government to be ready to prevent 'rednecks' from attacking Muslims and creating 'disharmony' (Frenkel, 2005: 5). On page seven of the *Herald Sun* there was an article about one of the terror suspects, Omar Baladjam, who had once appeared on one of Australia's most popular television soap operas, *Home and Away* (Saleh et al., 2005: 7).

Neil Mitchell wrote an op-ed in the *Herald Sun* on 10 November. His topic was the unruly behaviour exhibited by supporters of the arrested terror suspects out the front of a Melbourne court (Mitchell, 2005b: 23). He argued: 'Hatred erupted on the streets of Melbourne this week, and God help us if what we saw in the eyes of several angry men was a glimpse of the future' (Mitchell, 2005b: 23). Mitchell (2005b: 23) was also critical of the New South Wales Police who had tipped off the media hours before the raids commenced. Australians were able to watch the footage on the morning and evening television news. Mitchell (2005b: 23) argued that terrorism represented not only the threat of violence. He argued that it represented a threat to the preservation of democratic values: 'We must accept that people are frightened and nervous. That is reasonable. They have, after all, been told they were targets in a holy war. But also under threat is the way we work in a crisis. It is the process of democracy and justice that is under pressure here' (Mitchell, 2005b: 23). In the *Herald Sun* an op-ed by Malcolm Thomas (2005: 23), president of the Islamic Council of Victoria, argued: '…in these days of fear and terrorism, it is getting harder to discern legal facts from political spin'. He questioned the need for the more restrictive anti-terrorism legislation when the present arrests were carried out under existing laws. Thomas (2005) also expressed concern over the possibility of retribution attacks being carried out against Muslims in the community following the anti-terror raids. To people who held animosity towards Muslims during this apparent terrorist threat, Thomas (2005: 23) offered the following warning: 'Those in the broader community who claim all Muslims are terrorists are themselves full of hate, and the perpetuation of the same is in itself a form of terrorism'.

Two Liberal Party parliamentarians – Greg Hunt and Jason Wood – also discussed the anti-terror raids in the *Herald Sun*. They argued that the anti-terror raids in Sydney and Melbourne were proof of a direct threat that had existed since 9/11. Hunt and Wood (2005: 22) argued that 'The *fact* an *alleged* plot *may have* involved' chemical agents is a terrifying scenario (my emphasis). I highlight this use of language as an example of what I argue is a bizarre and politically charged turn of phrase. I suggest that the op-ed by Hunt and Wood (2005: 22) represented a tabloid style of writing that is designed to be sensational and spectacular. Hugh White prepared op-eds on 10 November for both *The Age* and *The Sydney Morning Herald*. White (2005a: 15) in *The Age* established early in his op-ed that 9/11 was the referent for the anti-terror raids: 'In the four long years since September 11, 2001, we in Australia, like people all over the world, have been trying to get the problem of terrorism into perspective'. Much like the reporting of the Bali bombing, reporting of the anti-terror raids rejuvenated, reconstituted, and reanimated 9/11 in journalistic spaces. According to White (2005a: 15), terrorism at the time of the raids had become a permanent spectre that many struggled to understand and the anti-terror raids made the challenge of understanding terrorists in our midst more difficult to fathom. White (2005a: 15) argued that terrorism had become increasingly familiar since 9/11 to witnesses in Australia. Therefore, the anti-terror raids, while shocking, should perhaps not be surprising. The Australian Security Intelligence Organization's director had previously warned that a terrorist attack in Australia was inevitable and that this inevitable attack would just as likely be carried out by an Australian as by a foreigner. The anti-terror raids were therefore a 'grim confirmation' of what was already known and not a startling new threat (White, 2005a: 15). I suggest that White's argument frames the anti-terror raids as a mundane and routine occurrence. It was, in White's opinion, nothing new. White (2005a: 15) believed that ongoing threats of terrorism did not represent a fundamental threat to democratic governance or our way of life. The op-ed in *The Age* was essentially the same op-ed that he prepared for *The Sydney Morning Herald* (White, 2005b: 11).

Letter Writing in an Age of (Anti)Terror

These 'attacks' were anti-terror in the most literal sense. There was simply no terroristic violence – only a spectacular, media-generated terror where the only violence was the dawn barrage perpetrated by the police against Australian Muslims who may or may not be guilty. The courts were supposed to decide, but it was the audience of witnesses and victims living and working in Australia's cities that confirmed that terror would be the result.

In the *Herald Sun*, of November 9, D.J. Fraser argued that people of Middle Eastern origin are being targeted as potential terrorists in the Australian community. Stuart Davies in the *Herald Sun* believed that the terror raids had demonstrated that Australian Prime Minister John Howard's strength was in going 'against popular opinion' when it is the right thing to do (*Herald Sun*, 2005h: 18). Stuart Davies argued that the anti-terror raids represented such an occasion. In contrast, Red Bingham in the *Herald Sun* argued that witnesses should not allow their perceptions to be persuaded by 'professional panic merchants' (*Herald Sun*, 2005h: 18). In *The Age* a letter from Troy Cox congratulated the policing and intelligence agencies for their 'successful counter-terrorism raids' (*The Age*, 2005d: 18). Diana Fitzgerald believed that the raids were a political and media stunt designed to gain support for government policy, improve television ratings and sell newspapers. I suggest that the commodification of terrorism was what Diana Fitzgerald was witnessing and reflecting upon. The terror raids that were witnessed first-hand by members of the media – who had been tipped off in advance – meant that others were able to witness the anti-terror raids by watching television and reading newspapers. The result is a better quality commodity of terrorism: the media were not reporting secondhand information as they were present even as the dawn raids were occurring.

It is evident that the letters to the editor in Australia's major newspapers represented polarized opinions on what the anti-terror raids meant. Some believed that the anti-terror raids were media stunts designed to affirm the need for strict anti-terror laws, while others believed that the anti-terror raids had proved that the laws were necessary and that terrorism truly posed a serious threat to Australian cities. This polarization was most effectively displayed in the letters to the editor section of *The Australian*. Ellis Hopper pleaded in *The Australian*: 'protect me and my family's human right not to be blown up' while Lachlan Gardner argued that 'The fundamental freedoms that have made our country the greatest place in the world to live are under attack, not by terrorists but by politicians' (*The Australian*, 2005c: 17).

Letters to the editor in Australia's major newspapers on 10 November offered intense commentary on the anti-terror raids. In the *Herald Sun*, Paul Jeffrey argued that during terror scares: 'All Australians, regardless of religion, race or creed, should realise that only an extremely small portion of the population supports terrorism' (*Herald Sun*, 2005i: 20). Paul Jeffrey explained that not all Catholics should be considered to have a propensity towards terrorism because of the IRA, and nor should Muslims be considered to have a propensity towards terrorism because members of al-Qaeda are Muslims. Glenn Darcy in the *Herald Sun* told the emotive tale of his 10-year-old boy who was scared to go to school for fear of being 'blown up'. He is reminded of how living in Australia is now synonymous with fear and suspicion. Two other letters praised Australian Prime Minister John Howard for the anti-terror raids and condemned 'Greens, Democrats, bleeding hearts, do-gooders, Left-leaning government haters' who opposed strict anti-terror legislation (Herald Sun, 2005i: 20). In *The Age*, Michael Larkin argued that the media representation of the anti-terror raids had reinforced negative stereotypes about Muslims. In *The Age* Ben Coleman saw no problem with targeting Muslims with anti-terror laws (*The Age*, 2005e: 14). He argued that recent acts of terrorism have been perpetrated by Muslims so targeting Muslims is perhaps appropriate. Les Hawken discussed, in the same paper, an attack on a cameraman outside a Melbourne court by supporters of the accused terrorists. He believed it created a damaging image of Muslims in Australia.

A group of letters in *The Age* questioned why the media were informed of the place, date and time of the anti-terror raids before they occurred. I suggest that it should be of little surprise that a media spectacle, a simulated event of the highest order, would be choreographed and synchronized in this way. I argue that something of the same order occurred on 9/11 as the world's television networks took only a few moments to point cameras at the burning Towers in Manhattan and amateur film-makers were already filming when the first plane struck. In a post 9/11, digitally enhanced environment amateur film-makers are always ready, always tipped off: a terrorist attack can occur at any place at any time. As Weimann and Winn (1994) have argued, the camera is like a weapon that anyone can pick up and use.

The guilt or innocence of those who were arrested is not the most pressing concern. Guilt or innocence and truth or falsity I would argue have little meaning in an exploration of a carefully constructed spectacle that unfolds live on television screens in real time. Guilt or innocence and truth or falsity become inconsequential to the power of the images of the accused that shock and terrify. As I suggested in Chapter 1, when it comes to hyperreality, seeing is believing. To be found not guilty in Australian courts would not absolve the terror suspects from their complicity in terrorism as spectacle – their image guilt. I suggest that this complicity extends to witnesses of terrorism and to these letter writers who construct the spectacle they are subject to: the spectacle of terrorism that I have argued is far from spectacular. Much the same, I suggest, happened on 9/11, 3/11 and 7/7: al-Qaeda were accused and convicted by images even though no court proceedings have been brought against this organization. When the terrorist event is filmed there is no such thing as an innocent terrorist. I argue that this is why the media were invited to the terror raids.

John Colville argued in a letter to *The Age* (2005e: 14) that a concern far greater than the terrorist threat was:

> ...the behaviour of the Federal Government, because it highlights just how much the threat of terrorism has become an irresistible weapon in the arsenal of conservative politicians. I thought the whole idea of shrouding arrest-without-charge in secrecy was to avoid the bad guys tipping off their mates. But how can this be a legitimate argument when John Howard and Phillip Ruddock [Australia's Attorney General] are allowed to do so on national television?

And Greg Barron in a letter to *The Age* (2005e: 14) added to this debate:

> So, it appears that some members of the media were tipped off about the raids that occurred on Tuesday. It will be interesting to see what action the authorities take against those who leaked this information. If the threat was as real as we are being told, then did this leak not have the potential to scupper raids and allow the alleged terrorist plot to succeed? Is this not aiding and abetting terrorism? Will anyone be held accountable? Or was the media circus beneficial?

Dave Davis argued in his letter to *The Age* that the arrests were a media event masquerading as a counter-terrorism operation. He questioned why the anti-terror raids did not have to be conducted in secrecy but the court cases, for the most part, did. It must be puzzling for some that while witnesses were allowed to watch the terror raids on news programmes throughout Australia they were not initially permitted to know what the accused were charged with or what exactly they were allegedly planning.

Just as there were those who questioned the constructed spectacle surrounding the anti-terror raids there were others who wrote letters to the editors of Australia's major newspapers who argued that the anti-terror raids could only be seen as effective policing that thwarted a potentially devastating terrorist act. As Andrew Gibb exclaimed in his letter to *The Age*: 'What the hell is wrong with you people?' (*The Age*, 2005e: 14). He argued that there 'appears' to be 'no doubt' that terrorism posed an immediate threat to Australian cities. James Forsyth added that: 'It flied (sic) in the face of common sense to deny the evidence of intention to terrorise that has been uncovered' (*The Age*, 2005e: 14). John Dorman, again in *The Age,* argued that he had *seen* proof that 'an imminent disaster' had been averted. And Alan Inchley in his letter to *The Age* called for an apology to be made to John Howard who was criticized when he said that Australia needed new anti-terror laws: his argument was that we now had proof that they were needed and that the threat of terrorism was *real*.

Ian Semmel observed in *The Australian* that footage of the anti-terror raids was accompanied by images of the London bombings (*The Australian*, 2005d: 13). Adriana Maxwell commented in her letter to *The Australian* that the arrested men were already being discussed as guilty terrorists: being arrested on television was for Adriana Maxwell a clear sign of their guilt. I suggest that since the goal of terrorists is to create fear in an audience then these terror suspects are surely guilty as charged: the hyperreality of terrorism cannot be disproved by appealing to some kind of truth when images are laid bare for witnesses to see – once again, seeing is believing. It is as Max Wilkinson wrote to *The Age*: 'ASIO has a secret raid at 2.30am and they took their television cameras'. Andrew Raivars added in his letter to *The Age*: 'It's so difficult these days to tell a foiled terrorism plot from a successful government one' (*The Age*, 2005f: 14). I would like the final say in this analysis to be made by Michael Burb in his letter to *The Age*. This letter in its simple yet profound entirety reads: 'New York, Tel Aviv, Bali, Madrid, London, Sydney, Melbourne' (*The Age*, 2005f: 14).

A City Whose Terrible Future Has Just Arrived?

South Park is a crudely drawn cartoon series created by Matt Stone and Trey Parker that is well known for its political satire and cutting-edge social commentary on terrorism, war, celebrities and religion. In one episode of *South Park* groups of anti- and pro-war protesters confront each other on the streets and sing anti- and pro-war songs. One of the pro-war activists in *South Park*, a regular character named Skeeter, plays his guitar and sings this song to the crowd with a country and western twang:

> *Did you forget 'dem towers in New York?*
> *Did you forget how it made you feel*
> *To see them towers come down?*
> *Were you like me? Did you think it weren't real?*
> (Skeeter, Episode 7.04, 'I'm a Little Bit Country', air date April 9, 2003)

Australian journalists writing for some of the nation's major newspapers certainly did not forget and I have attempted to show how, during times of terror, other acts of terrorism are routinely and mundanely rejuvenated in the guise of the latest terror scare. I argue that it will be possible for all terror scares to reanimate 9/11, 3/11 and 7/7. The journalistic spaces that I have just explored are similarly explored by other distant witnesses: for many it is a daily routine. I spoke to some of these witnesses and victims – they are working people in Melbourne during a time of terror. I tell their stories in Chapters 5 and 6. A key characteristic of the attacks that I have discussed in this chapter is that they were not attacks that had occured in an Australia. These moments of terror are surely nothing like 9/11, 3/11 and 7/7. Nothing exploded and no-one in Australia died. Terrorism can be avoided by not holidaying in Bali and through the spectacular efforts of Australia's law enforcement agencies. There can perhaps be no tribute and no defiance. While it has become part of the vulnerable and precarious life-worlds of distant witnesses in Melbourne I suggest that the incorporation of terrorism into everyday life and work in the city – even a city like Melbourne that is untouched by terrorism – is testament to the power of terrorism to generate victims and witnesses even large distances from where terrorism occurs. The explosions may have been in New York, Washington DC, Bali, Madrid, London and Bali again, but they are felt in every city, by every worker, in every organization, by every victim all over the world.

Terrorism is produced and reproduced in journalistic spaces in different configurations of time and space as an event, a scene and a spectacle. It is the 'incessant hum' (Pickering, 2005: 52) of terrorism reporting that reanimates 9/11 and positions it as a referent for understanding the latest terror scare. This reporting is mundane, routine, everyday and banal and I argue that this is most evident during intense coverage of terrorism events. The events I chose for closer examination were the 1 October 2005 Bali bombings and the 8 November 2005 anti-terrorism raids in Sydney and Melbourne. These incidences of terrorism as spectacle were far from spectacular. They were obscene, parodic and theatrical: more and more words were used to produce less and less meaning. These news articles, opinion editorials, and letters to the editor are now artefacts in the *black museum of journalism*. It is a museum where the simulations are life-like and real, yet on closer inspection are empty and devoid of meaning. They are mundane, routine and banal, obscene and superficial.

This newspaper spectacle – the mundane hum of terrorism reporting – displays terrorism through its referential image-events: 9/11, 3/11 and 7/7. It offers contemporary terrorism as a commodity that can be consumed by witnesses and victims across multiple configurations of time and space. Working in the city animates these configurations with real world deadlines, commutes, business meetings and everyday life. I explore this co-existence in Chapters 5 and 6. I intend to suggest that working people in cities watch television and read newspaper reports of the latest terror scare as they did on 9/11, 3/11 and 7/7. These witnesses and victims experience fear and dread as a consequence. I suggested in Chapter 1 that terrorism is also routinely reanimated in Hollywood films from *The Matrix* and *Night at the Museum* to *World Trade Centre*. Terrorism continues to be witnessed again and again and working people in cities can be forgiven for thinking that they are living in a perpetual state of *déjà vu*.

Baudrillard's (1988: 30–31) analysis of an exhibit in the Beaubourg is illustrative here. The exhibit depicted naked, life-like sculptures in everyday and banal positions. Intrigued, witnesses examined the exhibit at increasingly close proximities, certain that there must be something more to the mundane scene they witnessed. The closer to the exhibit that one gets, the more one is forced to face the fact that there simply is nothing more to see. Baudrillard (1988: 30) argued that such everydayness has a stupefying effect on audiences. The need to respond, understand and to speak even with nothing to say can be overwhelming. Letters to the editor in these moments of terrorism as spectacle are testament to the need to speak. As with the exhibit at Beaubourg, on close inspection and with expectations that more will be revealed up close, the media image, and the banal and everyday reporting of the latest terror scare, reveals that there is nothing more to reveal. It is plain, mundane, bare, repetitive, and monotonous. I suggest that if subsequent terror scares did not reanimate 9/11, 3/11 and 7/7 they would have scarcely any meaning at all. In the black museum of journalism, contemporary terrorism appears in a variety of guises: artefacts that represent events across time and space.

The Everydayness of Terror News

Kellner (2005) argues that media spectacles have emerged in new and 'novel' locations and spaces. Some of these are found on the internet, although the print media and daily newspapers in particular offer a similarly effective channel for producing witnesses. Terrorism, like pornography, possesses this witness-producing capability, and the images, imagery and reanimation of terrorism in newspaper reporting moulds well with the fascination with televisual images of 9/11, 3/11 and 7/7. As Nunn (2006) argues, images of these attacks have made terrorism the 'boogeyman of the 21st Century' where living in fear is replaced by seeking the next terrorist, identifying the next targeted location and theorizing how terrorism will next occur: 'there is only one way to assuage our fears of sudden, brutal terrorist attacks: convince us that we will always uncover the conspiracies before the explosion, always know who the perpetrators are before they act, always stay one step ahead of them, always arrest them before the carnage' (Nunn, 2006). Moreover, witnessing images of contemporary terrorism has injected the mundane hum of terrorism reporting with sinister and cataclysmic undertones where each reported act of terrorism is given invigorated meaning by reference to 9/11, 3/11 and 7/7.

As the navigation of journalistic spaces and letters to the editor sections provide the public with opportunities to interact with the spectacle of terrorism, newspapers become the platform for interaction and exchange between audiences, reporters, experts and opinion writers, readers and letter-writers. This exchange in journalistic space makes witnesses subject to the spectacle of terrorism that they help create. In Debord's (1983: §44) view the discourse of the spectacle amounts to a 'permanent opium war' – a numbing, banal and meaningless exchange of images, opinions and 'information'. This permanent war is, I argue, characteristic of the mundane hum of banal terrorism reporting – the artefacts of this hum are to be found in the black museum of journalism.

The Black Museum of Journalism

The word museum has often enjoyed positive connotations. With the phrase 'the black museum of journalism' (Virilio, 2002: 23) I intend to suggest that this should not always be the case. In the black museum of journalism, terrorism is a signpost in an emerging understanding of journalistic spaces in which more information flows faster to more people with less and less meaning. It has been a central argument of this book that it was a goal of the 9/11, 3/11 and 7/7 terrorists to affect a population of witnesses beyond the initial victims, and journalism's black museum bears witness and memory to the space provided for terrorism to wield significant powers to terrify audiences in distant cities. Terrorism was reported as it was occurring through round-the-clock, real-time television reporting. McNair (2006: 7) has argued that the use of such real-time feeds has been one of the most important developments in the immediacy of news reporting as it has allowed witnesses to navigate new spaces of spectacular journalism as they arise. This has had the effect of dissolving 'the physical and temporal distances that had separated people in one country from those in another' (McNair, 2006: 7).

I argue that the city is used as a stage for the black museum of journalism. City dwelling witnesses and victims view this museum routinely and sometimes participate in the interactive production of artefacts. I suggest that this is the stage for the theatre of terrorism, a theatre that represents both the spectacular image and routine, mundane, and everyday life. The spectacle, according to Baudrillard (1987a: 21), 'is never obscene'. Rather 'Obscenity begins where there is no more spectacle, no more stage, no more theatre, no more illusion, when every-thing becomes immediately transparent, visible, exposed in the raw and inexorable light of information and communication' (Baudrillard, 1987a: 21–22). This obscenity, I argue, can be seen in the mundane hum of terrorism reporting in Australia's major newspapers following the Bali bombings and the anti-terror raids. Journalistic spaces come to embody the 'forced' and 'exaggerated' (Baudrillard, 1987a: 21) reporting of terrorist events. Reporting of the latest terror scare can have a stupefying effect that entices witnesses to a closer examination as it did for witnesses in Baudrillard's story of the exhibit in the Beaubourg. This close-up view of terrorism images and imagery is *too* close.

Today's terrorism can be seen in the all-too-close – 'more-visible-than-visible' (Baudrillard, 1987a: 22) – newspaper media. When newspaper reports are at their most superficial, and when information is laid bare free from any need to interpret or understand because it is so objectively apparent, this is when the spectacle is at its most mundane. This is the black museum of journalism. A night in this museum uncovers a world that was never hidden, where 9/11 is reanimated in the latest terror scare so that it 'keeps exploding in people's minds' (Virilio, 2002: 22) and newspapers are sold in greater quantities. The black museum of journalism can in this way be seen to be feeding the commodification and branding of terrorism.

Conclusion

Understanding the black museum of journalism is crucial for understanding the consequences of terrorism for working people and businesses. In this chapter I have presented information that situates city-dwelling witnesses and victims of terrorism within a landscape of sensational and spectacular media images and discourses. I have analyzed information drawn from major Australian newspapers at crucial moments following terrorism events: the 1 October Bali bombings and the 8 November anti-terror raids, both occurring in 2005. This analysis had three purposes: to demonstrate the workings of simulations and hyperreality; to frame and contextualize the stories of the distant witnesses that I explore in Chapters 5 and 6; and to demonstrate that the reporting of spectacular incidences of terrorism is far from spectacular, rather, it is mundane, routine and banal. In moving towards these goals I have attempted to show how other acts of contemporary terrorism are rejuvenated, reconstituted and reanimated in journalistic spaces in which terrorism is reported. This is the black museum of journalism. This black museum makes the city a stage beneath which witnesses and victims can be in the audience of the theatre of terrorism.

The world of images, the world that was originally intended to describe something *real*, is now better than the real: it is hyperreal. It is not, however, a detraction, degeneration, or disintegration of the real. Quite the contrary: it is far better. Reality can be seen as a kind of bonus added to the reported event. In this way I argue that hyperreality is the event and the reporters, opinion writers, letter-writers and readers create the world that they simulate. As Baudrillard (1994: 1–2) argued:

> *Today abstraction is no longer that of the map, the double, the mirror, or the concept. Simulation is no longer that of a territory, a referential being, or a substance. It is the generation by models of a real without origin or reality: a hyperreal. The territory no longer precedes the map, nor does it survive it. It is nevertheless the map that precedes the territory –* precession of simulacra *– that engenders the territory, and if one must return to the fable, today it is the territory whose shreds slowly rot across the extent of the map … Something has disappeared: the sovereign difference, between one and the other, that constitutes the charm of abstraction.* (emphasis in original)

In a sense, following Baudrillard, the media reporting precedes terrorism for the witness and the victim. Terrorism is often first encountered in media spaces. I argue that this is inescapable. I am not suggesting that somehow the journalistic spaces were filled with terror reporting before the terrorist event occurred. But I am suggesting that in many instances journalists will be there witnessing terrorist events as they unfold and will pass their firsthand information on to audiences. Witnesses did not need this service on 9/11 as it was occurring live on television. But because witnesses did have real-time terrorism on 9/11 I suggest that it is now craved. It is craved because it improves the reality of the image – it makes the image feel more real if witnesses can watch events as they are occurring.

Here, the mundane hum of terrorism reporting represents deep anxiety for precarious and vulnerable people living and working in the city. One could go to Ground Zero in New York and see the hole in the ground where the Twin Towers once stood as confirmation that 9/11 was real but one can never return to that date or to the event – it exists now only as images and imagery. Attempts to reanimate the reality of 9/11, 3/11 and 7/7 are evident in newspaper reporting in Australia's major newspapers during the latest terror scare. Compared to the spectacular terrorism on these dates, these events are mundane. Yet they now hang in the galleries of the black museum of journalism. If they seem to come to life, as the museum artefacts did in the movie *Night at the Museum*, it is only to confirm their hyperreality and to remind us that the image is not real. *But of course! And now that I think about it I never thought it was!* Terror reporting in the critical moments following the 1 October 2005 Bali bombings and the 8 November 2005 anti-terror raids reanimated 9/11, 3/11 and 7/7 and invoked their images to explain these less spectacular terror scares. People living and working in cities read newspaper reanimations of terrorism in these moments. These reanimations encourage witnesses to recollect images of terrorism. I argue that this can be seen through stories told by working people situated in Melbourne. It is to these stories that we now turn.

CHAPTER 5

Working in a Time of Terror

Introduction: Witnesses and Victims in the Theatre of Terrorism

I intend to argue in this chapter that the city is a theatre where terrorism is performed for people who live and work in a city. These people experience their life-worlds as vulnerable and precarious as they witness terrorism in images and simulations in multiple configurations of time and space. The stories of seven witnesses in the city of Melbourne are presented in this chapter. These witnesses face the daily, mundane, everyday, routine and banal reanimation of terrorism in reports of the latest terror scare – what I have argued to be the black museum of journalism. The meanings and consequences of terrorism in the lives of seven working people in organizations in Melbourne are explored here. I argue that as these witnesses and victims are confronted by spectacular terrorism they become consumed by suspicion, fear, and dread. In doing so, the important relationship between witnesses and victims, simulations and images of violence, distance and the city and the organization as a site for counter-terrorism is illustrated. It is a relationship that keeps changing and the city and the corporation becomes an unstable yet emergent laboratory for terrorism and business research. I argue that reflexivity in reporting this research becomes significant as the meaning of the interview changes across time and space. Even after the interviews are completed these meanings continue to change as what it means to be a worker in a city changes. I argue that this change is twofold. First, the interview itself changes. The dialogue returns to me as a cleaned transcript with a meaning evident in the cold thereafter that was elusive in the heat of the interview. Second, the world changes as the interview lies dormant on tapes and as a transcript. As time passes the interview is reflexively reinterpreted as terrorism, the world, the city and me, as the researcher – and a witness and victim of terrorism – continues to change. As 9/11, 3/11 and 7/7 continue to explode in the minds of people living and working in cities, other terror scares come and go. The dialogues that I explore in this chapter represent particular configurations of time, space and meaning – meanings that are situated and change with the passage of time. In this way I suggest that the interviews are much like terrorism itself. The meaning can be interpreted and reinterpreted, played and re-played and understood across multiple configurations of time and space.

The purpose of this chapter is to explore the stories of seven witnesses who work in inner-city Melbourne. Six of these stories were collected between 21 February and 3 April in 2005 and a seventh was collected on 13 December in 2005. These stories represent perceptions of terrorism in these particular configurations of time and space. I argue that the dialogue generated through in-depth interviews produced important insights into what terrorism means to working people who are witnesses and victims of contemporary terrorism. In this chapter I introduce the informants and myself to contextualize the stories they provide – stories that highlight what it means to be a worker, a witness and a victim in a time of terror. I then explore the stories of Patrick, Paul and Courtney – all three of whom worked for the same retail organization in the inner city – and Marcus and Timothy, who worked elsewhere in inner Melbourne. For these witnesses, terrorism was closely related to images. Not just images on television, however. I suggest in this section that these witnesses had an acute awareness of the importance of images and imagery and their responses highlight the significance of not only images of terrorism on television and in newspapers, but also images of the Self and Others. Following this I begin a reflexive re-appraisal of the stories of Patrick, Paul, Courtney, Marcus and Timothy. On re-examination I am aware of certain biases and presuppositions that I had held when I first explored their stories. By re-exploring the interviews in a different time and space I shed new light on the consequences of terrorism for working people and businesses. This re-examination incorporates new stories – Evelyn and Owen's stories. Images continued to play a crucial role in the reflexive analysis and I become more aware of the significance of 9/11 in understanding terrorism. This re-examination also reveals how these post-9/11 workers had incorporated 9/11 and the threat of terrorism into their everyday routines and rituals. They knew that terrorism could strike at any moment – they believed that the best thing to do was not to think about it and to get on with their lives. I conclude this chapter by suggesting that spectacular terrorist attacks like 9/11, 3/11 and 7/7 in many ways never end: they continue to explode in the minds of witnesses and victims of terrorism throughout the world, reanimated in and by the latest terror scare. The importance of images is not limited to the television screen, however, as images of Self and Others also invoke the spectacle of terrorism.

Workers, Witnesses and Victims

The stories of seven workers are presented in this chapter. Each worker is a witness and a victim of terrorism. They all have a story to tell. It is a story about the consequences and meanings of terrorism and what it means to be a worker in the city in a time of terror. They work in various industries and sectors in various positions within their organizations. They bring to their work a variety of culturally and socially specific attitudes and beliefs. Allow me to introduce them.

PATRICK

I identified the retail organization where Patrick worked as a location to recruit respondents for my research because of its potentially vulnerable emplacement in the city. The store was a 'flagship store' housed in a prominent shopping strip in the heart of Melbourne's central business district (CBD). I approached the organization's management by completing an online form in November, 2004. A representative of the organization contacted me and, after some discussion, permitted me to recruit respondents in this store. I posted a sign on a notice board in a communal staff area of the store explaining my research and what participation would entail. The sign invited those who were interested in participating to contact me. This was how I came to interview Patrick, Paul and Courtney all of whom work in the inner-city Melbourne store of this retail organization. Patrick was the first person that I interviewed on 21 February 2005. He was a manager in the Melbourne-city store of a major clothing retail chain. He indicated that he was in the 25–36 age group. He seemed more youthful than this in both dress and physical appearance. He explained that it was a requirement of his job to look this way. Patrick told me that he was probably successful in his interview for his management position because he was modern, trendy and very outgoing. He certainly struck me as being extroverted and he seemed to have a positive attitude. He appeared relaxed; he cracked jokes, and was evidently comfortable with being an informant in this research. He was short and stocky and his hair was spiked and fashionable. During our introductory discussion he told me a number of things about himself. He completed high school but did not go to university although he had been accepted to study. He was of Asian descent: his family had emigrated from the Philippines in the early 1980s and were devout Christians, although Patrick did not practice anymore. He was gradually building a career in the retail industry and planned to work in the highest levels of management at this firm. Watching 9/11, the Bali Bombings and 3/11 had affected Patrick in a number of ways that he considered to be 'profound'. He believed that the world had changed forever, that his life and the life of his family and friends would never be the same, and that 9/11 in particular was the most monumental event he would ever witness. He watched television frequently and news programmes in particular – it was a more dangerous world for Patrick and he believed that he needed to keep on top of the latest events.

PAUL

Paul was the second person I interviewed from the retail store. I interviewed Paul on the same day that I interviewed Patrick – 21 February 2005. He was a retail employee in the same retail clothing store that Patrick managed. He was aged between 26 and 35 – again, Paul looked more youthful than his age suggested. Paul was outgoing, very confident, extroverted and trendy. He had a stylish haircut and a thick 'five o'clock shadow'. He told me that it was the image that the company wanted to create. He was positive about his work and life but, unlike Patrick, his career aspirations did not involve working in retail. Paul held a Bachelor of Science from a major Australian university and was in his first year of a degree in secondary teaching. He had committed a lot to his studies and he wanted to teach science to high-school students. He told me that he was Catholic and had attended Catholic primary and secondary schools. Paul hoped to eventually teach at a major Catholic college. He had a thick Australian accent and he spoke clearly and articulately. His family were of Irish descent and had lived in Australia for several generations. Paul was a casual employee who worked at the store around 11 hours per week. He had been offered a full-time management position that he declined. The impact of witnessing contemporary terrorism was significant in Paul's life. He believed that terrorism had been a monumental event that affected his personal and working life in many ways. As he witnessed 9/11 he called loved ones not to see if they were safe but to share the enormity of the experience. He had a sense that he was watching something that would perhaps define a generation and made several comparisons to the Vietnam War. He said that terrorism had meant almost nothing to him prior to 9/11. After 9/11 he frequently thought about terrorism. 9/11 made Paul think about terrorism in a new way and he began to pay more attention to the news. After 9/11 he had a better understanding of what it meant for the IRA to be called terrorists. He also remembered hearing about an act of terrorism occurring at an Olympic Games in the 1970s. It is perhaps no coincidence that at the time of the interview *Munich* (2005) – a feature film depicting these events, and starring Australian actor Eric Bana – had recently been released.

COURTNEY

Courtney also worked in the same retail organization. She was in the 18–25 age group. Courtney was confident, stylish and outgoing. She was wearing makeup, her hair was extravagantly styled and she was wearing many clothing items available for sale in the store. She had an olive complexion, with dark hair and dark eyes. She was the third person I interviewed on 21 February 2005. She held a Bachelor of Arts from a small, regional Australian university that she planned to return to for a second degree in secondary teaching. She was intelligent and energetic but did not enjoy her work as much as she perceived her colleagues did. Courtney was a casual employee and worked in the store around 18 hours per week. She had many goals – some she had realized, many she had not. However, she was not someone who dwelled on these concerns. She also felt that religion had a greater impact in the world than it should. Courtney believed violence, conflict, war and politics could all be traced back to religion. It was religion that she held primarily responsible for the violence and images she witnessed on 9/11, during the Bali Bombings and on 3/11 in Madrid. As traumatic as 9/11 was for Courtney, her family believed that the world was becoming less violent. Courtney was born in a Southern-European country that had experienced terrorism in the past and she believed that terrorism was not an effective method for getting what you wanted. She did not believe that terrorism would continue to have a major impact, but she believed that contemporary terrorism represented something else – something seemingly more than just terrorism.

TIMOTHY

I identified the organization in which Timothy worked as another potentially vulnerable location in inner-city Melbourne in November 2004. Timothy spent most of his work days in tall and prominent buildings throughout Melbourne's CBD as a law clerk for a private contracting firm. I explored the occupancy of many of Melbourne's tall and prominent buildings from the signs fixed in the ground level of most buildings. I would then search the internet for contact details for the organizations I had identified. After speaking to a manager at the organization where Timothy worked I was permitted to advertise for respondents in much the same way I advertised on the notice board in the communal staff area of the retail firm. Timothy contacted me with a special interest in terrorism and world affairs. I interviewed him on 15 March 2005, several weeks after I interviewed the group from the retail organization in inner-city Melbourne. He described himself as left wing in his political beliefs and actively engaged with popular dissident media and popular culture including Noam Chomsky books and Michael Moore movies. He was a young man in appearance and was in the 25–36 age group. He had tanned skin, short black hair, and was short and stocky. He looked different to the retail workers – more business-like in a striped shirt under a woolen pullover complementing brown, checked slacks. Timothy told me he had an active sporting and social life and was very concerned about politics and the general state of the world. He was not wearing branded clothing and had no gel in his hair, but he sported all the confidence of the workers I spoke to at the retail organization. Yet as he spoke he maintained a permanent frown. He said that while he was Australian-born, his mother was born in Britain. He had recently travelled to Europe on a British passport. He worked around 32 hours per week in the job that he performed for two different contracting firms. He completed high school but never considered attending university until he was in his early twenties. He applied once, unsuccessfully, and decided not to try again. He believed terrorism appeared in many guises of which 9/11 is only one example. He spoke of attacks on Muslim people and mosques after 9/11 and of the wars in Afghanistan and Iraq. He explained that to include these things as terrorism did not downgrade 9/11, but it did put 9/11 in perspective. In one sense he believed 9/11 had no impact on his day-to-day life, but he also thought about 9/11 often.

MARCUS

Marcus was another respondent who worked in tall and prominent buildings in Melbourne's CBD. I had recruited Marcus in much the same way that I had recruited Timothy with one notable exception – in the case of Marcus, I had identified organizations housed in a particular building in Melbourne that had been the subject of 'terror scares'. I interviewed Marcus on 3 April 2005. Marcus had previously worked as a professional consultant in a tall and prominent building in inner-city Melbourne. In the time between securing his participation and conducting the interview he had left this job and pursued a career as a small businessman in the retail-clothing industry. Marcus was average in size and build. He had flair and style and wore a pinstriped suit and very fashionable and expensive-looking frames on his glasses. He studied business at a major Australian university and he was in the 26–35 age-group. He did not play much sport but he did enjoy watching cricket and football. He was confident, but not particularly relaxed. He spoke freely and articulately with what some may describe as a 'private-school' accent. Marcus watched the nightly news, read newspapers and articles on the internet, and he considered himself a knowledgeable person in 'a practical way'. I was unsure what this meant at first but as I interviewed Marcus I understood that he was referring to 'business-smarts' – learning the tricks and unspoken rules of the corporate world. Marcus believed conflict was everywhere and that it was an inevitable part of life. He told me at the outset that he believed the United States did the right thing in ousting Saddam Hussein because he was a dictator. Iraq and terrorism were closely linked in Marcus' view. He did not understand how anyone would want to inflict the damage that was caused on 9/11. Marcus described himself as a Christian and he said that followers of any religion that would allow terrorism were deeply misguided. He said that while Christianity was once a violent religion it had changed to become more peaceful and Islam should follow the same path. He believed that events like 9/11 were an inevitable part of the world and his life.

EVELYN

I identified the industry in which Evelyn worked as being potentially vulnerable to terrorism. Evelyn worked in the sporting industry and was periodically employed for major sporting events. Academics writing in the terrorism studies literature had long explored sport as an attractive symbolic target for terrorists. Having lived and worked in Melbourne for most of my life – and being an avid sports fan – I was familiar with the major sporting events that Melbourne regularly hosted. I searched the internet for the contact details of organizations that operated in this industry and sought permission to advertise for respondents in the usual way. I found Evelyn to be a particularly interesting informant. As I introduced myself, she jumped in with: 'You know, I am not going to repeat to you what I hear on the TV'. Evelyn considered herself to be an intense thinker who always attempted to understand the underlying meaning rather than just the surface meaning. I interviewed Evelyn on 16 March 2005 and she was in the 26–35 age group. Evelyn worked casually in the sporting industry and was called in during its biannual peak periods. She explained that this was common in her industry and she followed seasonal work when it was available. Evelyn sparked my interest due to her involvement in a major sporting event in Melbourne where she had worked in the security department. Her job required her to be friendly and outgoing but she said that she was not particularly outgoing or extroverted. Evelyn was very down to earth and seemed to me to be intelligent. From the beginning of the interview she had stated her wish to be honest and reflexive about her opinions and her perceptions of public opinion. Evelyn believed the two were at odds. She had completed a science degree at a regional Australian university and had since returned to study philosophy and psychology. Her goal was to do a PhD and practice as a psychologist. Evelyn said that she did not know much about terrorism but she did know about 9/11. She watched 9/11 as it was occurring and it was the only act of terrorism she had paid attention to. For this reason Evelyn thought that it might be better described as something else. She thought that religion and politics were most responsible for events like 9/11. Michael Moore was a key source of information about terrorism for Evelyn: however, she said that Moore contributed to the perpetuation of the divide that existed between people.

OWEN

I recruited Owen through an advertisement that I posted on the company notice board of the public transport organization where he worked as a senior manager. Owen was the second-in-charge at this organization. He joined the organization from a major airline company and he brought with him a wealth of experience in managing major public transport organizations. I interviewed Owen on December 13, 2005 in the company's Melbourne offices. The interview was conducted two days after the infamous Cronulla Riots in Sydney where people of Middle Eastern-appearance were chased and attacked by an estimated 5000 so-called white Anglo-Australians. Owen had been less active in counter-terrorism security than his colleague Louis (an informant featured in Chapter 6) and had no direct responsibility for ensuring the safety and security of his business, but Owen still had a keen awareness of what terrorism means, its potential consequences and how business leaders and managers should respond. Owen was in the 46–55 age-group and considered himself to be both a successful business and family man. He wore a stylish suit and looked well-groomed. He spoke clearly and calmly. Owen believed that terrorism was best characterized as 'anarchy' and a desire to displace social order and harmony. For most of our discussion Owen argued that terrorism was a minor nuisance that never really affected his personal life in any direct way. Yet, as a management employee – in a non-security capacity – in a potentially vulnerable public transport company, Owen believed that terrorism could have alarming and far-reaching consequences. Owen believed that these consequences, however, should not become all-consuming and that we should not allow fears and anxieties to become paralyzing. Instead, Owen argued that everyone needed to be comfortable with the fact that events like 9/11, 3/11 and 7/7 were unavoidable and had most likely changed the business world forever.

I-WITNESS TERRORISM

I am a key player in this research. Not only am I an academic and a researcher in the corporatized university system, I am a worker in a major city. In this way I am a witness and victim of spectacular terrorism. This is my story. When I was young I was never allowed to see any of the great movies of my generation. The 1980s were a showpiece for movie violence and like all girls and boys under ten years old I wanted to be a part of it. To my dismay I did not get to witness *Predator* (1987) and *Predator 2* (1990), *Robocop* (1987), *A Nightmare on Elm Street* (1984), *Friday the 13th: The Final Chapter* (1984), *Rocky IV* (1985) and *Rambo III* (1988) to name a few. Many of my friends would discuss these movies in the schoolyard and, of course, act out various violent scenes. This was as close as I got to *seeing* these movies until many years later. It was not until I was studying terrorism and in particular my studies of the *Irish Republican Army* (IRA) that I began to wonder why this was so. My family are Catholic – some adhere strictly to its teachings, others not. My grandparents were especially devout. I attended a Catholic primary school and a Christian Brothers Catholic secondary college. Perhaps by limiting my exposure to Hollywood violence the adults in my life were attempting to protect me from shocking possibilities of violence. Restricting what I saw on television and in movies seemed to be a reasonable thing to do (I didn't play with toy guns until I was older either). However, I was allowed to watch *The Omen* series and *Star Wars* which was then a trilogy. *The Omen*, while a satanic thriller, remains a religious movie and perhaps my family felt it added to my education in matters of religious doctrine and good and evil. The reasoning for allowing me to watch *Star Wars* is less clear, but perhaps it is related to my family's Irish heritage. As I was growing up the IRA were never openly considered terrorists in my household. They used violence, which was regrettable, but the reasons why they fought were considered sound. I was told that the British had oppressed the Irish for hundreds of years and that my family had been the victims of discrimination, mostly for being Catholic, throughout their lives in Australia. I realized later that *Star Wars* was a movie about a legitimate insurgency. It is about the necessary use of violence to achieve a just end. I was being taught as a very young child that some violence is good and some is bad.

On the night of 11 September 2001 I was in my bedroom watching *The West Wing* – a drama about a fictitious President of the United States and the trials and tribulations of his senior staff. A commercial break towards the end of the program reported an apparent accident where a passenger aircraft had crashed into one of the Twin Towers. I am almost ashamed to admit that I gave the incident little thought when it was reported this way. As *The West Wing* concluded the television network cut to live coverage of the 'accident' and announced that it was now believed to be a deliberate act. I watched in shock and a voyeuristic awe as many did on that night and the following morning[1] as a second

---

[1] This is dependent on your vantage point to 9/11. Mine was Geelong, Victoria but it could have been anywhere in the world. The witness was anyone with a television.

plane appeared to the left on the television screen and sliced through the other Tower. In my sleepless night that followed, I saw the Twin Towers in New York collapse, I saw the Pentagon on fire, and I saw the wreckage of a crashed plane in Shanksville, Pennsylvania. I changed the channel frequently to make sure that this was really happening – I saw the same scenes on every station. I watched the Towers fall again and again.

As I arrived at the university where I was a final-year undergraduate it seemed that there was nothing else in the world that was important. The attacks were discussed in every class and over every coffee. It seemed that many people felt as I did: that we had witnessed something incredible. I wondered what would happen next, what the effects would be, and whether it would happen again in the United States or cities elsewhere. It seemed that the city was the focus and it seemed that the fear around campus was a good indication that fear existed in other places too. Years later as I recruited informants for this research it became clear that many people were concerned that terrorism would affect their city, their building, and their families. I interviewed 55 people in total from varying walks of life. Some were managers and business leaders; others were entry-level employees and casual and part-time workers, or contractors. Some were professionals, others were unskilled and untrained. They represented many age groups and socio-economic classes. They were Christian, Muslim, Jewish, Atheist, Agnostic and Buddhist. Some were born in Australia, some were born overseas. Most were men. They all had something in common – they all lived and worked in a city distant to 9/11 and other terrorist attacks and they all witnessed the attacks on television.

During the interviews that I conducted during 2005 I became a participant in dialogues with other witnesses to terrorism. These witnesses had many stories – some told with passion and emotion. For some, our discussions never quite got to terrorism as a political, religious or ideologically motivated act. These informants preferred to talk about their children as little terrors, their pets being terrorized by the neighbours' teenager, the terror they experienced when watching horror movies, and the terror inflicted by gangster rappers, homeboys and Eminem's music and its role in the degradation of society. There had been both simple and sophisticated responses, some separating personal perception from community perception, others describing changing perceptions over time, and others providing detail into how the media has impacted on their perceptions of safety and their lives both at work and at home. In seeking out witnesses and participating in these stories I was trying to capture a segment of the world, not a generalizable mass – a small piece of the real. I wanted to understand people in the contemporary city, people in the 'desert of the real'.

Images of Islam

Patrick entered the small room at the back of the busy store. He was the '2-IC', or the second in charge, and had been a floor manager with the organization for several years across a number of regional and suburban shopping malls. The organization had 'roaming' regional managers who oversaw the performance of store managers (Patrick, 21 February 2005). The chain of command was strictly followed by the regional manager who in turn answered to a centralized management structure at the organization's Sydney head office.

I asked him what he believed terrorism was. He struggled initially to respond and asked for clarification. He eventually began to speak, although somewhat awkwardly.

Terrorism I think is, in my opinion, I believe it's (pause). It's people (pause). It's like (pause). I can't really define it. I can give examples of it. I can't say, I can give you examples. Terrorism to me is like people, for example, like September 11, bombing the Twin Towers. Terrorism is suicide bombing. Terrorism is kidnapping people and executing them. All that kind of stuff.
(Patrick, 21 February 2005)

Patrick's difficulty in responding was perhaps not surprising. Certainly the academic, political and diplomatic communities have also struggled to define and articulate what terrorism is. It should not be surprising that witnesses in distant cities find the question difficult. Patrick was able to articulate a response by referring to examples of acts of terrorism and who he believed to be terrorists. As our discussion continued, it became more focused on who carried out acts of terrorism.

Terrorism and terrorists, especially when I worked at [Melbourne city shopping strip], I found it very difficult. When I think about terrorists and the terrorist threats I think about the certain race, I think about what's happening in Iraq, I think about people of that kind of race. As soon as I see one [a Muslim] I think shit, you know. Especially if they are walking around [Melbourne city shopping strip], I think to myself it is such a big complex and there are a lot of those people around there; it really wouldn't surprise me if something happened to that place. Like every time you hear a fire drill, an alarm, or you hear something happening, for example, like … fire drills, the sirens, anything to do with that. You maybe think shit, something has happened and they [Muslims] are the first people you think about (emphasis added).
(Patrick, 21 February 2005)

There was a perceived link for Patrick between terrorism and Muslim people who he believed were the most likely to be terrorists. It was a view echoed by others in this organization – their stories appear in the coming pages. Literature that examines how people perceive terrorism would seem to support this. According to Freyd (2002), anger directed at people perceived to be Muslim was demonstrated on many occasions following 9/11. This included the heckling of a Lebanese man who had run the arts centre at the World Trade Center as he was searching for survivors (Freyd, 2002: 5). A Wyoming mother and her children were chased from a 'Wal-Mart' because they appeared Muslim. A mosque in Texas was firebombed. An Egyptian worker won a payout for discrimination after being fired from a restaurant because his manager believed that having someone who appeared Muslim as a staff member would be bad for business (Freyd, 2002: 5; Sixel, 2003). I asked Patrick if he believed he treated people differently after he witnessed an act of terrorism like 9/11, the Bali attacks or 3/11:

I certainly treated people differently. As soon as an Arabian, a Musso, as soon as a Muslim walked in, what I classified as a Mussi, I would genuinely try to stay away from them only because I didn't want to come into contact or have to deal with people like that. It sounds a bit racist but, just the mentality after September 11 and what you see on TV does make me have this kind of, I've given them a stereotype basically.
(Patrick, 21 February 2005)

I suggest that admission of stereotyped or discriminatory attitudes represented a sophisticated and reflexive awareness of his views and biases, yet perhaps paradoxically the substance of the stereotype could be considered simple and xenophobic. Patrick also believed that he was less impacted than his colleagues by this. He believed that he was not alone in his views and that his views were comparatively moderate.

We [the 2-IC manager and his staff] would have in depth conversations about what happened on September 11. We would talk about what's happening over in the Middle East and they would have the same reactions ... I thought I kept a medium kind of take on the whole situation. These guys were just completely [saying] 'I hate them'. If I see them, probably nine times out of ten a Muslim walked into the store and we wouldn't serve them just based on the Fact that they were Muslim and they looked like they were up to something. But that's how people were (emphasis added).

(Patrick, 21 February 2005)

Patrick was talking about an image of Islam where he associated headdress, particular garments, facial hair, skin colour, accents and language differences with being Muslim. Paul, a young, fashionable and confident employee at this store, shared similar views. He explained that he had often treated people differently when he perceived that they fit an image of Islam.

Paul: It's like, also another bad thing to say, a horrible thing to say, but you look at Aboriginals and I know for me, I class them as a certain type of people. Yet I know when I look at people who may look of an Islamic or Muslim faith and that sort of stuff, I class them as a type of people now.

Howie: It's funny that they probably only have to look like they are Muslim.

Paul: Exactly, and it may be that they are as Aussie as you or I but at the same time if they look a certain way, I judge them straight away. I don't consciously think about it. I don't remember any specific thing I have ever thought to myself but in my conscience I know it's there. Just thinking about it now. It comes to mind now. I know I must think it whenever I see them ... my take on terror would be someone who fits a certain stereotype.

(Paul, 21 February 2005)

The role of stereotyping through images of Islam is important when understanding the impact of terrorism on working people and business in cities. Such attitudes are fed through subtle and unsubtle reporting in the media (Manning, 2006). According to Manning (2006: 3), Australia is a country where Islamophobia has 'run riot' and where people appearing to be Muslim, who fit an image of Islam, are subject to prejudice and discrimination. For Paul, it was contemporary terrorist attacks that had generated these feelings.

Paul: [I held] a different view of the people that walked in after September 11. It's not something that I deliberately took upon myself to view people as. But it's just little messages that come through the media that it [terrorism] is possible.

Howie: And this in the heart of Melbourne?

Paul: Exactly. And the Western suburbs of Melbourne too. And it is an area with a lot of Muslim and Eastern European people and you can't help it. I'm sorry. You can help it but at the same time you instantly (pause). You don't look at people and think that they are going to commit a terrorist act but you class them as a certain type of people which is totally wrong to do. It really is.

(Paul, 21 February 2005)

These attitudes could perhaps be expected to be more pronounced in an organization that operates in a popular shopping district in Melbourne. It is a place where culturally diverse people interact almost constantly. Patrick described the area outside of his store as a 'multicultural sea'. When religious motivations are central to media discourses about terrorism, people living and working in the city focusing attention on all people who fit the stereotypical perceptual requirements of a 'Muslim' may be an expected outcome. Courtney, a stylish and sophisticated looking woman who had a modern haircut and liberally applied make-up articulated her perceptions of images of Islam:

Muslims are people who want to follow a different culture. The way they dress, the way they speak, their beliefs, making the women cover everything. They are usually dark, they dress funny. You know, funny to what is normal. No, I mean not the way Australians do. They come here and they think they still have to do the things they did back home.

(Courtney, 21 February 2005)

In an interview conducted on 3 April 2005 with Marcus who worked for a consultancy firm, views such as Courtney's reappeared. In particular, Marcus believed the *hijab* was a particularly ostentatious form of symbolism contributing to his perceptions of images of Islam: 'Like in India and Afghanistan where the women wear the things over their faces. When they come over here they believe they still have to wear them. It's part of their culture. It's what they want. When they come over here they still do it' (Marcus, 3 April 2005).

It is likely that images of Islam play an important role in how witnesses in distant cities formulate opinions about terrorism. Poynting and Noble (2004) have documented many cases where Muslim women and men have been targeted for discrimination and abuse. This occurred particularly during the first Gulf War in the early 1990s and following 9/11. Among the discrimination and abuse, Muslim women reported having their hijabs pulled from their heads.

You Could Just Tell

The dialogue with Patrick, Paul, and Courtney uncovered beliefs that were associated with a critical incident where the possibility of terrorism in Melbourne was thrust to the forefront of their minds. I asked Paul how terrorism affected his life when he was at work. He had no hesitation in offering the following story:

Paul: Funny you should mention that. A funny example is the other day on, I think I must have worked Wednesday. There was a fire alarm go off and everyone shit themselves and started walking out. And everyone was going, well what does that mean, what's going on. And everyone came up and said 'I think it is a fire alarm, it's just a test'. And others were like 'nah, nah, that's not a fire alarm. And now (pause)

Howie: And did you hear the word terrorism used once or twice?

Paul: Well, I didn't really, but you could just tell people were panicked like something was going on. It was like, you know, the time of the year and all, you know. It's the time of year, you know if anyone was going to try and make an impact. And that was the funny thing, you could just tell. Whenever there is a problem or some stuff like that people instantly think the worst... But as far as working in malls and stuff I don't really, it hasn't really entered my mind too much.

(Paul, 21 February 2005)

Paul in one sense played down the impact of terrorism yet his response revealed important insight into how he perceived terrorism. It was after I intervened in the response that I discovered that even though there was no suggestion that the alarm may have had something to do with terrorism, on some level 'you could just tell' (Paul, 21 February 2005).

I asked Paul whether these beliefs had caused emotional and psychological stress and anxiety even though he argued that he did not regularly think about terrorism:

I think it is more so just the fear that it could create. That we [terrorists] can inflict casualties anywhere, whenever we want. And you know, it could mean that geez! [They] create fear that, you know, what if I go here, what if they decide to do it there, what if I go here, you know. Will they do it there? I think it is more so the fear that it can create. It causes people to be worried about where they are going.

(Paul, 21 February 2005)

While Paul did not discuss stress in responding to my question, he once again provided an important insight into terrorism and the impact that it had on his work and life. As he shied away from describing his concerns about terrorism as stress, he seemingly equated stress with fear. But is 'fear' really an accurate description when a Melburnian talks about terrorism? In the philosophical traditions of Kierkegaard and Heidegger, fear is always fear of something. Kierkegaard (1957) argued that where there is no object, or subject, for fear to rationally be attached to, dread – not fear – is the outcome. In this way, dread can be seen as a fear of nothing. As Melbourne has never been the site for a significant act of terrorism, one could argue that 'fear' of terrorism in Melbourne is problematic. I intend to suggest that dread is equally problematic because terrorism has occurred in Melbourne as an image-event in contemporary times particularly on 9/11, in Bali, on 3/11 and 7/7. Indeed, it could be argued that terrorism occurs wherever it is witnessed.

Terrorism has occurred in many places throughout history but rarely in Australia. The most notable in Australia was the bombing at the *Hilton Hotel* in Sydney in 1978 (Hocking, 2004: 83). A bomb placed in a rubbish bin near the hotel's entrance on George Street was detonated killing two council workers and a police officer. The bomb coincided with the Commonwealth Heads of Government Regional Meeting (CHOGRM) that was commencing that day. The *Hilton* housed several delegates. These attacks were quickly characterized by Australia's security community and by politicians as the first act of terrorism in Australia (Hocking, 2004: 101). Other incidents of terrorism in Australia included acts perpetrated by people belonging to communities who were originally from the former Yugoslavia, the targeting of the Indian High Commission, the targeting of a Jewish social club in Sydney, and attacks against judges of the Family Court (Hocking, 1993). A report on terrorism and the threat to Australia, the *Protective Security Review*, prepared by Justice Hope and released in 1979 argued that international terrorism potentially posed a threat to Australia 'in response to foreign issues' (Hocking, 2004: 111). Perhaps the most obvious terrorism in Australia's history is the one that it so often conspicuously absent. For many, the displacement of Australia's indigenous populations during European settlement clearly meets the definitional requirements of terrorism.

These acts do not feature in dialogues generated through interviews with working people at any stage. I asked Patrick and Paul to list five incidences of terrorism in the order that they recalled them. In this post-9/11 but pre-7/7 time and space, invariably 9/11 was the event most recalled. The second most recalled was the first Bali bombings on 12 October 2002. Outside of these incidences there was often confusion. Paul recalled something about an attack at the Olympic Games in the 1970s. Patrick remembered that there had been attacks in England and Ireland carried out by the IRA and he was aware of many other groups that were violently anti-government although he did not know the name of any of these groups. It was 9/11 that was for these workers the central event through which perceptions of terrorism were formed:

I think September 11 definitely brought it to the forefront but other than that, it [terrorism] didn't mean anything to us because, it was almost just because it wasn't used as often [before 9/11]. They spoke about it as much, but it didn't mean as much to us. That's what it did for a lot a people. It's brought it right to the forefront as a problem yet it's been a problem for a hundred years.

(Paul, 21 February 2005)

I argue that 9/11 has infused new meaning to the word 'terrorism'. In much the same way that the Matt Stone and Trey Parker movie *Team America: World Police* (2004) defined terrorism through 9/11: (*It will be 9/11 times 1000. What, 911000? Exactly!*), working people in Melbourne in early 2005 understood terrorism in reference to 9/11.

Stress, Anxiety and Fear

In answering my specific questions relating to stress caused by terrorism, feelings of fear and dread were often discussed and in all instances 9/11 was considered the source for these. Timothy worked as a clerk in a legal firm that provided services to law firms throughout Melbourne's central business district and suburbs. As such, Timothy worked in and around many of Melbourne's tall and prominent buildings. His beliefs and attitudes towards terrorism were formed through this potentially risky work environment in Melbourne. 'It was just that after September 11, and then Madrid, that people who had to work, and had to get there with public transport, trains and stuff, suddenly felt different about things. You couldn't be sure anymore that, you know, something wouldn't happen. Because now we know they can' (Timothy, 15 March 2005).

Patrick also believed that stress, fear and anxiety remained associated with terrorism and people he identified as potential terrorists:

Bourke Street [in inner city Melbourne] was basically covered [with people] like every second… it's such a multicultural [city]. It's not until you actually work in the city that you notice how big Melbourne is multiculturally. It's huge and then you walk around and you'd see these people and it really is very difficult to go to work there knowing that it is the place where something could happen as it did in New York.

(Patrick, 21 February 2005)

Evelyn, a sporting industry employee whom I interviewed on 16 March 2005, believed that many people in Melbourne were fearful of terrorism even though she was not:

My parents have brought it up in conversation with me. I was thinking about going to New York for a year. My parents have brought that up as a fear they have. It shows that a lot of people do have these fears, but it is not something that I would see as realistic.

(Evelyn, 16 March 2005)

Some management and organizational studies literature examines the impact of terrorism on perceptions of stress, fear and anxiety. Much of this literature discusses organizations in large American cities in the aftermath of 9/11, the November 2001 anthrax letter attacks, and the 1995 Oklahoma City bombing (Alexander and Alexander, 2002; Alexander, 2004; and see Barnett, 2002; Perry and Lindell, 2003; Pfefferbaum et al. 2000, Liverant et al. 2004). These authors argue that people in cities that are close to where terrorism occurs will continue to experience negative consequences in the months and years that follow an attack. Among these negative consequences is fear and anxiety including the serious medical condition Post Traumatic Stress Disorder (PTSD). More generally, people often experience stress in work and life that is caused or worsened by an act of terrorism. This can lead to maladaptive coping strategies such as misplaced discrimination, drug and alcohol abuse, and unwillingness to participate in socially acceptable ways (Alexander, 2004).

These issues were the subject of a conference on terrorism and business in 1979 that examined mostly communist terrorism and the threat it posed to business and organizations. Terrorism as a cause of stress and anxiety in an organizational setting was a driving theme (Alexander and Kilmarx, 1979: xiii). The proceedings were published and the authors' arguments can be seen as significant and prophetic. Ochberg (1979: 113) argued that increasing incidences of terrorism worldwide had 'underscored the psychological, as well as physical, needs of victims – and *potential victims* – of terrorism' (emphasis added). Ochberg (1979) argued that the unique threat posed by terrorism resulted in irregular coping strategies. Chief among these coping strategies was engaging in discriminatory and racist behaviour against communities to which perpetrators of terrorism are perceived to belong. An exploration of two critical incidents in Australian history lends credence to Ochberg's argument. On 12 March 1868 at Clontarf in New South Wales, an Irishman attempted to assassinate Prince Alfred on his tour of Australia (Dunn, 1998). Following the attempt to kill the popular prince, anti-Catholic and anti-

Irish sentiment spread rapidly throughout Australia's major cities. Rumours quickly circulated that the perpetrator was a Fenian – a radical Irish revolutionary – and Catholics and Irish were attacked as enemies of the nation. Public 'indignation meetings' that discussed ways to prevent Irish terrorism were held in many parts of the country (Dunn, 1998). It was a problem that was being tackled in England and had been reported in the Australian media.

Following these attacks, Ultra-British and Ultra-Protestant groups became more active and attracted many new members in Australia. Many Irish Catholics and Northern Irish Protestants were attacked in the street by vigilante gangs during this period. Over a century later, in the aftermath of 9/11, the Bali bombings, 3/11 and 7/7, anglo-Australians rioted in Cronulla in Sydney's south in protest to the presence of violent gangs in the region who the rioters believed were of Lebanese descent. The mob quickly turned violent and began targeting and violently confronting people perceived to be foreign. Bangladeshi students were chased. Dark-skinned men were kicked and punched. Seemingly average Australians were featured in news reports justifying the violence and discussing the merits of revenge for violence perpetrated by so-called Lebanese gangs. A federal politician, Bruce Baird, justified the attacks as revenge for 9/11 and the Bali bombings. Home-grown neo-fascist groups seized on the opportunity and heightened xenophobia to recruit and spread propaganda (Australian Associated Press, 2005).

Freyd (2002: 5) argues that in the wake of terrorist attacks 'Hatred May Mask Fear'. She believes that racist and discriminatory responses to terrorism are common and most likely stress related. In this view, the response to fearing terrorism is based on the 'fight or flight' behavioural principle. When flight is not an option – as it sometimes is not when facing the threat of terrorism in routine and daily life – 'identifying and hating an enemy' can be a coping strategy (Freyd, 2002: 5). Freyd (2002: 5) argues:

> *Surely we know that all Arabs or all Muslims are no more responsible for the horrific tragedy than are all Irish or all Christians responsible for terrorism in Northern Ireland. Surely we do not want to repeat acts reminiscent of our own history of severely mistreating innocent Japanese Americans during World War II. Surely we do not want to engage in the same sort of racism and hatred of innocent people that we find so abhorrent in other lands.*

Thinking about the stories of the working people that I have interviewed and Freyd's argument I am reminded of a scene in the film and political satire *Starship Troopers* (1999). In this film, the human race is waging a war against giant alien bugs in distant space. On Earth, the population is urged to support the war effort. In one scene, women and children jump around the sidewalks of suburbs and cities squashing garden-variety bugs, all the while laughing hysterically and cheering. The suggestion here is that by squashing Earth bugs, citizens can help in the war effort. The movie's catch-cry is: 'war is hell, bugs are worse!' This unlikely scenario is a metaphor for some reactions to terrorism. Witnesses who feel hopeless and powerless in confronting terrorism routinely in their daily lives may feel empowered by discriminating against people perceived to be Muslim. It could be argued that Patrick adapts a coping strategy that manifests in some discriminatory attitudes. Paul, whilst more reflexively aware of his prejudices, also holds discriminatory attitudes and beliefs.

The Media Spectacle

While terrorism for Australians remains a phenomenon that occurs overseas, for many Melburnians it is real in the impacts it has on witnesses and victims. As I have argued, physical distance is problematized by simulations and images of violence that are transmitted through media spaces on television, in newspapers and on the internet. For Paul, the media makes the prospect of terror *real*, and following 9/11 this has created a new awareness of the potential for terrorism to affect the daily lives of witnesses in routine ways:

> *That's the thing though now; you hear a loud bang or see something suspicious you instantly think 'terrorist bombs building'. More so because they [people in New York] have had it [the terrorist threat] drilled into them. The thing too is there are also people who don't have it drilled into them who simply watch TV or read the paper and think things as well and they haven't even had it drilled into them.*
>
> (Paul, 21 February 2005)

On numerous occasions respondents discussed the role of the media in forming perceptions and opinions on terrorism. Patrick spoke of how he interpreted messages from the media that allowed him to build a stereotype and an image of Islam into fear. He acknowledged a central role for media images of violence in allowing terrorism to be witnessed by a greater audience of witnesses than the violence alone. When discussing potential terrorist targets in Australia, he was careful to build publicity considerations into his discussion:

> *I thought it [terrorism] would strike the major cities like Sydney or Melbourne. I would say I would think if they were to do something in Sydney maybe like a big sporting venue. For example the Commonwealth Games are coming up now. They are going to get a big television coverage. If that was going to happen. Sydney I thought something was going to happen at the Sydney Olympics.*
>
> (Patrick, 21 February 2005)

For Paul it was televisual images of terrorism that had the most significant influence. He received information from the commercial television networks because they were easily accessible, not because they provided high quality or nuanced information:

> *Network news; Channel 9. Channel 9, Channel 10, the commercial television stations and commercial newspapers as well. Not so much independent publishings and broadcasts as such. Only, because it is not something that I seek out, it is what is readily available to me. And the most readily available is where I gain most of my information from so, it is not the most reliable source but at the same time it's all we have to go by really.*
>
> (Paul, 21 February 2005)

Manning (2006) argues that racism and prejudice is encoded within media discourses reporting issues dealing with Arab and Muslim Australians. This reporting, Manning (2006) argues, systematically portrays Islam, Muslims and people of Middle Eastern appearance as shady Others polluting traditional and pure 'Aussie' values and practices.

This trend is similarly documented by Pickering (2005) in her study of media portrayals of refugees arriving in Australia by boat. Through powerful linguistic technologies and techniques, Australia's major newspaper media providers depicted refugees as inherently immoral and illegal actors benefiting from incomplete and ineffective Australian and international laws.

I asked Paul whether his perceptions of Muslims were influenced by reports in the media. He did not directly answer this question. Instead, Paul offered an explanation of how he may have developed potentially skewed opinions from the media on all issues regarding terrorism:

You are in the majority [watching commercial news] but it doesn't make you right. But at the same time it's not that I don't want to know or I'd rather be ignorant to what is going on, it's just that I don't have the time to invest into finding out more, finding out more about what is actually being spoken about. Like most people they get a brief understanding of major issues and stuff, not necessarily gathering the full view of everything. But that's my most obvious outlet to learn what is going on.

(Paul, 21 February 2005)

Melburnians witness images and violence in distant locations through the media. Through these interviews in early 2005 – post-9/11 but pre-7/7 – a picture began to form of how terrorism is real in its impacts. Media reports of terrorism have generated particular perceptions among these workers that have led to discrimination against people perceived to be Muslim. It can be argued that these perceptions increased fear, dread and stress both at work and in daily life. Yet, as Timothy argued:

I don't just watch commercial Australian television. In the elevators at work they play FOX News. Also I watch docos. Michael Moore. Much of what I know come from these sources. Also newspapers, the Herald Sun. And books. I have read a few Noam Chomsky books. I think it was called Pirates and (pause) and Empire. Pirates and Empire. I know they are all crap though. Mike Moore is left wing. The Media is right wing. What is left?

(Timothy, 15 March 2005)

What is left? Timothy acknowledged the problems and shortcomings that he perceived in the media and felt left with no other alternative. Turning off the television is apparently an unacceptable option.

Moving Through Time and Space

This study of the consequences of terrorism for working people and businesses explores how witnesses and victims in cities have perceived contemporary terrorism across multiple configurations of time and space. Through interviewing people who work in Melbourne I was able to interpret and re-interpret, analyze and re-analyze and understand and re-understand during the interviews and long after the interviews ended. The dialogues were collected between February and April 2005 and transcribed, analyzed, and written-up in the months and years that followed. These dialogues transcend their historical emplacement in time and space in much the same way terrorism has and continues to. In May 2006 I revisited and reanimated these encounters with workers in Melbourne. I reanimated our discussions and re-examined and reinterpreted the data in a different configuration of time and space. Naturally the interviews had a different meaning on re-examination and my new interpretations uncovered other meanings not immediately evident.

I attempt here to revisit the interview dialogues by reflexively re-analyzing the interviews themselves. By May 2006 the world of images and terrorism had changed. In July 2005 bombings in London, known as the 7/7 attacks, caused incredible death and destruction in another symbolic city. Bali was again attacked on 1 October 2005 with several Australians killed and injured, and in November of the same year anti-terror raids were conducted in Melbourne and Sydney resulting in a number of arrests and the uncovering of an alleged plot to launch a terrorist attack in Australia. These frequent peaks in terrorism reporting made me aware of some deficiencies in my original approach. Instead of Melbourne being populated by unfortunately duped masses – people fooled by mass mediated interpretations of terrorism – I have come to see these people existing in a world of work and life, images and violence, precariousness and vulnerability, and fear and dread. Images of terrorism are viewed in distant locations because they exist, not because of ignorance or delusion. These are representations and constructions of reality, not a state-fashioned control mechanism.

Some insights from informants that seemed insignificant in my first analysis were strikingly important to me in May 2006. I suggest that two key themes emerged in my reflexive re-examination. The first was the significance and the importance of '9/11' as a symbolic event. It was clear that the word 'terrorism' was almost incidental to the impact of 9/11 on working people in Melbourne. Overriding importance was placed on that one day when workers were targeted in the corporate nerve-centre of the globe – I suggest it is the importance of being 9/11, an idea I will discuss in the following pages. This was the 'mother' all of events as Baudrillard (2002: 3–4) suggested and it has had a significant impact through its reach as an image viewed in many diverse and distant cities. The second was cultural change within the city. Melbourne was sometimes referred to as a multicultural and diverse city inhabited by tolerant, relaxed and comfortable city-dwellers. These mythical cultural cornerstones were exposed in the face of reactions to terrorism that resulted in intolerance, discrimination, fear, and dread. I will discuss these two points in the sections that follow.

The Importance of Being 9/11

As I re-examined the transcripts of dialogues that I had participated in and cleaned in the process of transcribing I am aware of the meanings, lying within, that were initially hidden in the first analysis. I became aware that there had been little discussion of 'terrorism', yet many discussions centred around '9/11'. Informants scarcely mentioned 'terrorism' at all. I argue that few events have had the impact of 9/11. The spectacle of 9/11 was advantaged by the instantaneous, round-the-clock media coverage even as the events were occurring. Patrick, when asked what terrorism was in his opinion, responded:

> *Terrorism to me is like people, for example September 11, bombing the Twin Towers. Terrorism is suicide bombing*
>
> (Patrick, 21 February 2005)

And this from Paul responding to my question that asked him to list some examples of incidents of terrorism *other* than 9/11:

> *I think September 11 definitely brought it to the forefront but other than that, it [terrorism] didn't mean anything to us because, it is almost just because it [the term] wasn't used as often [before 9/11]. They spoke about it as much, but it didn't mean as much to us.*
>
> (Paul, 21 February 2005)

And this from Timothy:

> *I don't know shit about terrorism. I know September 11. When I was watching the news, people immediately ringing up like radio stations, mosques and leaving abusive messages and threatening messages on the answering machines of the Muslim people. That's terrorism. If someone did that to me, rang me up and threatened me, obviously I'm going to feel scared. Being scared to me is terrorism. If you threaten someone and they feel intimidated or they feel unsafe, that's terrorism.*
>
> (Timothy, 15 March 2005)

Terrorism for Timothy was in some respects something different to 9/11. It was not simply about a politically violent act that is labelled 'terrorism' but also an emotional and psychological response. While 9/11 produced terrifying and powerful images, other terrorism does not. In a pre-7/7 world, 9/11 was seemingly the stand alone signpost, despite the significance of the Bali and Madrid attacks. Terrorism was associated with fear, dread or intimidation, and violence and threatened violence. 9/11 seemed paradoxically both more and less knowable and more and less fathomable for these witnesses. It was an amazing event that would have been appropriate as fiction – a phantasmagoric occurrence perhaps never to be repeated but, as I have argued, already seen in pop culture and its stories. Perhaps because of this it was almost instinctively captured by cameras and viewed by witnesses and victims in both near and distant cities. It is in this sense more knowable and more reachable as personal experience for working people. It was televisually *real*.

Tall buildings were often discussed as risky sites in contemporary cities. Watching towers fall to the ground in New York had created a lasting image witnessed in other cities. My informants subsequently expressed feelings of anxiety associated with working in tall buildings. For some it was simply a comment here and there that working in tall buildings after 9/11 would create fear and stress and that they would be more likely to take their sick days and annual leave as soon as it accrued. Others down-played tall buildings as risky sites and believed that after 9/11 life in buildings 'continue[d] as usual' (Marcus, 3 April 2005). Some expressed significant concerns. Marcus explained his personal concerns when working in a tall building:

> *I used to work in the Rialto [a very tall and prominent building in Melbourne]. I was already a bit worried after September 11. One day our boss, or the building management, or something, got a call. It was the federal police saying that there is a concern about the Rialto for tomorrow and that you should tell your workers that they can work from home tomorrow. I was shit scared. We had just seen it happen [in New York].*
>
> (Marcus, 3 April 2005)

The spectacle of 9/11 had attached to Marcus' psyche. While terrorism remained a concept difficult for some people to explain, the same difficulties did not extend to explaining 9/11. It was 9/11, or more precisely the images it generated and supported, that could be more easily understood and explained than the amorphous term 'terrorism'. For informants, the meaning of 'terrorism' was often difficult to locate. But 9/11 was laid bare by images and its meaning was obvious – the meaning of 9/11 belonged to everybody. Witnesses reacted by developing techniques for evading the next 9/11 – avoiding tall buildings, avoiding Muslims, avoiding major cities. Melbourne had all of the props, the scenery and the characteristics for a theatre of terrorism. An act of terrorism in Melbourne, if choreographed as 9/11 (or 3/11 or 7/7 for that matter), would also create powerful and terrifying images that would combine with violence to create something greater than the violence or images alone.

Images of the Self and Society

In conducting this reflexive re-examination of the stories of working people in Melbourne, I wondered whether 9/11 had really changed the world forever. After all, it was the catalyst for a variety of events including the Global War on Terror, significant changes in legislation in many countries, and a world of people anxious of where the next major attack would be. I argue that it had become for these workers – these witnesses and victims – ordinary and mundane to live in a city and a world threatened by terrorism. Informants had said that they thought about terrorism a lot, and that it was an extraordinary threat, but few have made any significant changes to their routines and behaviour. I suggest that 9/11 had not altered routines but had become part of existing routines – it was just one more concern in precarious and vulnerable city living. I suggest that the everydayness and routineness of terrorism is partly the result of the unreality of images of terrorism that communicate violence without the heat, shrapnel, death and destruction – just as in *Night at the Museum*. Now that I think about it, I never thought it was real – at least not in the same way. If the workers that I interviewed had watched passenger aircraft crash into some of Melbourne's iconic buildings, or suicide bombings on Melbourne's rail network, surely I would not be arguing that spectacular terrorism in Melbourne is routine and everyday. It would seem that there is a link between the power of images and witnessing at a distance. I argue that if you are close to an act of terrorism – in a geographical sense – it is violence. At a distance it is terrorism. It reminds me of the actions of the government of Myanmar in November 2005. Analysts believed that due to fears of an invasion from the United States, the Myanmar government began relocating to deep jungle in another part of the country (Mydans, 2005). The unlikely prospect of an American invasion is immaterial to the effects that the threat had on this Burmese city. There was no violence, but there was certainly terror. The government of Myanmar had seen it before of course – their government noted that the United States had invaded other small countries such as Panama, Grenada, Somalia, Kosovo, Afghanistan, and Iraq. *They had seen it all before.*

The city of Mumbai was targeted on 11 July 2006. Nearly 200 people were killed when seven simultaneous bombs were detonated targeting the rail network. This attack received far less attention in the Australian media than the comparatively smaller attacks in London on 7 July 2005, and the second Bali bombing on 1 October 2005. Regardless, the bombings in Mumbai demonstrated to city dwelling witnesses that the reach of terrorists is long. I have suggested earlier in this book that witnesses and victims in Melbourne have allowed the threat of terrorism to change their work and daily lives. I argued that this was an 'own goal' of sorts – it was the terrorist's intention that we respond in such a way. Complicit in this predicament were security experts who were paraded in the media discussing a variety of issues about being safe and avoiding terrorism, 'shoot to kill' and bag search provisions in new legislation, and the need to be alert but not alarmed. In a time of uncertainty working people in Melbourne viewed countrywomen and -men arrested for crimes of terrorism on television news and in newspapers. Rarely, I suggest, have Australians been so security conscious. Even a near-war with Indonesia in 1999 barely raised a concern in the public and politicians did not find it necessary to prepare the nation for such an event (Birmingham, 2005). Yet, we are led to believe that terrorists lurk in every corner of our cities (Mickelburough, 2005: 9). This 'own goal' does not exist because of the duped masses. They are far from duped as they witness really real terrorism on their evening news and in journalistic spaces at critical moments. Reanimated in these moments are spectacular events like 9/11, 3/11 and 7/7. In this way, terrorism can be seen as a real and tangible source of fear. The workers, witnesses and victims are not duped. I suggest they are the true terrorism experts as they know the impact of terrorism better than most – they are the targets and as such they know how terrorism feels. This can be seen to have helped foster security aware cultures in cities. Issues of safety, security and counter-terrorism are routine and banal aspects of discourse for city dwellers. This is life in a distant city for a victimized population – Welcome to Fear TV! Even without terrorism in Melbourne, *witnesses have seen it all before*.

Both the terrorism studies literature and the workers I interviewed have argued that there is a relationship between the problems caused by the threat of terrorism and the culture and harmony of the city. Studies examining the impact of terrorism on work and cities, while making little direct reference to culture, frequently allude to culture and changing culture in the city following acts of terrorism (see Alexander and Alexander, 2002; Alexander, 2004; Alexander and Kilmarx, 1979; Mankin and Perry, 2004). As Alexander and Alexander (2002: 45) argue, 'The aftermath of the World Trade Center and Pentagon attacks and the danger of a slumping economy led some corporations to reduce costs, fire employees, cancel acquisitions, delay transactions, and postpone investments'. Terrorism became a justification for layoffs and cost cutting to improve productivity. While the economic hardships predicted by Alexander and Alexander (2002) did not eventuate and the United States' and the world's economy recovered quickly from a minor slump, it was nonetheless treated as evidence of the need for fostering strict security awareness. For witnesses in Melbourne, terrorism was a cultural issue. Informants believed that terrorism arose from cultural difference, and impinges upon any culture it disrupts. With the far reach of the spectacle of terrorism through the image, this cultural impinging was not limited to cities close to terrorist violence. Paul believed that:

> *Terrorism is ... someone who wants to affect the way that we live as a culture and live as a society ... someone who necessarily disagrees with* my *cultural views and wants to do their best to disrupt that (my emphasis).*
>
> (Paul, 21 February 2005)

I challenged Paul by saying that this understanding of terrorism could include not only terrorists but also his family and friends who disagreed with Paul's lifestyle choices and intervened in his life in an unwelcome way. I asked Paul if he would like to review his response. Encoded in Paul's response was not only his understanding of images of Islam but his understanding of images of the Self:

Paul: A different nationality, other than Australian. A different religion.

Howie: A different religion?

Paul: I mean to Christianity, of course. Usually Islamic. Has a hatred of all Western society. It's part of their culture. It's what they want. When they come over here, they still do it [hate our culture]. It's just a different point of view.

Howie: So, it's a big cultural issue.

Paul: That's the way I definitely see it.

(Paul, 21 February 2005)

A report to the Human Rights and Equal Opportunity Commission in April 2004 by Poynting and Noble (2004) found that Arab and Muslim Australians live with significant racism in their daily lives. Of the 186 respondents from Arab and Muslim communities in Melbourne and Sydney, two-thirds had personally experienced an increase in racism since 9/11 and only one-fifth of the respondents reported no increase in racism. Moreover, 93 per cent of respondents believed that their community was now more targeted by racism, violence and abuse and 64 per cent believe that this was best represented as 'a lot more' (Poynting and Noble, 2004: 6).

White (in Birmingham, 2005: 37–38) argues that 'primal fears' have taken control in the lives of many people in Australia. In White's view, Australian witnesses of 9/11 are fearful of terrorism for four key reasons. First, the reaction of witnesses to 9/11 'has been strongly, and strangely, personalized – that is, people have had a strong sense of being personally at risk from terrorists ...' (White in Birmingham, 2005: 37). I argue that this response can be seen in Paul's discussion of Muslims. Second, there is often exaggeration in experiencing the threat of 9/11-style terrorism because 9/11 was infused by comments from political and expert spokespeople, and by the media that exaggerates the threat that terrorism poses. Third, the response to 9/11 was militarized: the integration of military discourse into accounts of 9/11 worked to frame the reaction of audiences. Fourth, 9/11 was barricaded inside a debate about good and evil and terrorism subsequently became a moral issue. Audiences were encouraged to adopt a universal moral position in a collective war against terror: 'Be alert, not alarmed' was the motif for the anti-terrorism as public relations campaigning in Australia. Personalization is an outcome of images of the Self developed in confronting terrorism. Fear perhaps not surprisingly is an emotion evident in Paul:

Howie: If a terrorist act were to occur in Australia, where do you think it would happen? When is probably relevant as well.

Paul: I think it is more so just the fear that it could create. That they can inflict casualties anywhere whenever we want. And you know, it could mean that geez [pause] they create fear that, you know? What if I go here, what if they decide to do it there? What if I go here, you know? Will they do it there? I think it is more so the fear that it can create. It causes people to be worried about where they are going. A place with a high profile as well like symbolically high profile. Westgate Bridge, Sydney opera house, Rialto towers.

(Paul, 21 February 2005)

These fears should be situated in the context of perceptions held by other Australian witnesses. In a survey in the *Sydney Morning Herald* in 2004, 68 per cent of respondents believed that terrorism was inevitable in Australia (Michaelsen, 2005). The views of the Assistant Commissioner of police in Victoria, Simon Overland, were featured in the *Herald Sun* in the week following the second Bali bombing on 1 October 2005: 'we will have an attack here' (Mickelburough, 2005: 9). Evelyn explained where she believed such an attack may occur:

If there was any attack on any major event in Australia, any sporting, particularly sporting events in Australia because we are in love with them. If anything was attacked like that, that would be used as a catalyst for even greater control over our country [by the government] and we would go exactly the same way as America is going. There's two kinds of ideas that would make something a target. Either the value that it holds to the country or the amount it is seen by the country. The media coverage that it gets. Anything that draws a crowd, or anything that is looked upon as an asset of Australia would be the perfect target for a terrorism attack.

(Evelyn, March 16, 2005)

Evelyn believed that attacking a symbolic location would generate the most fear. These symbolic targets are the most attractive to terrorists. As Jenkins (1987: 583) once wrote; terrorists 'want a lot of people watching not a lot of people dead'. Evelyn described a number of scenarios where terrorism would be an effective means for spreading fear including the Melbourne Cricket Ground on the Australian Football League's Grand Final Day:

A lot of people would die if the MCG was targeted on Grand Final day. I think they go for a combination of symbolism and numbers killed. Yep, that might be an equation they would work on. But I don't think number of dead would be their main goal, unless they were pathological people behind the attack: unless they really wanted to kill people. I think more it's what could they do to make Australia feel vulnerable. I think that would be more the key and I think in that way attacking the symbol of Australia would be the way to go.

(Evelyn, 16 March 2005)

Encoded within this discussion of the symbolism of terrorism was an important role for images and spectacles. Publicity, audiences, spreading fear and witnessing were all important factors in Evelyn's account. The suggestion here by Evelyn is that terrorists in many instances only intend to harm people incidentally. The goal is to have a lot of people watching. For Melbourne, a sporting event would be a particularly powerful theatre. Melburnians enjoy sport: I can think of no better way to shock this city than to make their sporting events appear vulnerable to terrorism. A number of commentators have attempted to understand the potential targeting of sporting events. Among these is Toohey and Taylor (2004) who argue:

> *A lot of terrorism is seen as theatre, and it depends on what message that the terrorists want to convey in terms of symbolic intent, with a lot of the targets that have been hit recently, have represented a certain aspect of Western culture that the terrorists want to signal that they disagree with, so in Bali it was the nightclubs, in Morocco the nightclubs, a lot of the other targets were economic. So it depends on the message they want to be sending.*

Toohey and Taylor (2004) believe that events such as the Olympic Games, the Commonwealth Games, and the Melbourne Cup pose special security challenges. Much of the post-9/11 discourse on terrorism and counter-terrorism focuses on Islamic terrorism, but threats will come from a variety of sources. Toohey and Taylor (2004) note that ETA targeted a major stadium during a sporting event, and that it was an anti-abortionist who targeted the Atlanta Olympics. According to Wright-Neville (in Eastley, 2006) terrorists will often avoid targeting major sporting events as the greater security that these events attract make them more difficult targets for terrorists to attack.

As Patrick argued, attacking a sporting event would create images that would generate fear in anyone who witnessed the attacks whether they attended the event or witnessed the reports on television or in journalistic spaces. Terrorism creates images as it did on 9/11 and 7/7 and terrorists rely on this to spread fear and dread. As Toohey and Taylor (2004) argue the attractiveness of sporting events to terrorists relates to the television coverage that sport attracts and the spectacle that sport generates: 'because terrorism isn't necessarily directed at the victims'.

Incorporating Terrorism Into the Everyday Routines of Work

My re-examination of the meanings and consequences of terrorism for the working people that I interviewed for this book also revealed how terrorism had become an everyday and routine part of what Virilio (2002: 82) calls *business being business*. In particular, Owen's story – a story that I collected many months after the other stories featured in this chapter – articulated what it means to be a precarious and vulnerable worker in a time of terror. At first, Owen downplayed the consequences of terrorism in his working life:

> *No one considers it [the threat of terrorism]. I don't believe that any of us really worry about it too much. We walk down the streets. We are not looking at anybody. I don't think it concerns too many people. I think we show that by attending major sporting events. We attend big gatherings. And I think we are a pretty cosmopolitan population here [in Melbourne] and, generally speaking, I think we live pretty harmoniously. Not to say that it [disharmony] doesn't happen.*
>
> (Owen, 13 December 2005)

As I inquired deeper into how Owen perceived terrorism, however, he began to reveal how he was affected by terrorism in his working life. He believed that in a time of terror, in a world that he sometimes thought of as post-9/11, it was difficult to not think about the meanings and consequences of terrorism:

> *... as far as the airports are concerned and the railway stations are concerned, if anybody wants to look at that, there is lots and lots of places around the place that are vulnerable to terrorism. There is a fire this morning in England that is the biggest fire, or biggest explosion, since the war. And everybody assumes, everybody knows, that when you go on the West Gate Bridge on the left hand side, crikeys! If you can get in there and put a bomb there, you could make some damage. I guess you can do that, no matter where you are talking about, no matter what you do. If somebody wants to make damage, they will do it.*
> (Owen, 13 December 2005)

Locations that Owen viewed as risky were also difficult to avoid – people travel to the city on public transport, people fly around the country at their leisure, and the West Gate Bridge in Melbourne carries millions of commuters during the peak hour rush. Owen admitted to sometimes having some fears and anxieties when he 'stop[ped] long enough to think about it'. But he argued the key was to not stop and think about it for too long. Terrorism, in his view, can most likely not be stopped. Owen seemed to be suggesting that living and working with the almost constant threat of terrorism was a routine and everyday part of working in the city.

On re-examining the stories of the other informants that I interviewed I became aware that they were also often talking about incorporating terrorism into their everyday working lives. As Evelyn explained of working in a time of terror:

> *I was more interested in the day to day of what I was doing. I dare say after three weeks of working there it [terrorism] did not cross my mind once and it was not brought up by management – nothing was indicated. We were working in the security department and no, nothing ever came up so it clearly wasn't a focus of theirs. But [pause]. I don't know. So many errors could have slipped through in their security process. It would have been very easy for an attack. I do remember thinking the security is not great and I slipped a few people through that I probably shouldn't have. And I know other people were doing it, but it wasn't, there was nothing mentioned by management. They weren't really that strict.*
> (Evelyn, 16 March 2005)

I find this to be a fascinating response. Evelyn's response is illustrative of how terrorism has slipped into the everydayness of working in the city and how she had felt anxiety because she had witnessed many 'errors' and moments when 'security is not great'. On the one hand, Evelyn claimed that she did not think about terrorism at work, yet on the other hand Evelyn noticed that management were perhaps not taking security very seriously and that her workplace was perhaps not well protected against terrorism. It was nothing that would send Evelyn into a panic but it was important enough that she decided to mention it to an academic researcher studying terrorism and work in a post-9/11 world. Evelyn believed that thoughts such as the ones she had about her organization's security were a product of the post-9/11 world. She felt it was unlikely that she would have been worried about terrorism in this way before 9/11.

Views such as these were also evident in the stories of other respondents. Patrick, for example, believed that the threat of terrorism, as insignificant as he claimed it was, also caused him stress and anxiety when he was at work:

You talk about stress levels, it does play on your mind … it's probably not enough for me to take a sick day off work or anything. It certainly elevated the fact that something could happen … When it came down to the crunch, the bottom line was … if I was in the store and a terrorist attacked, what would I do? What would I do if something happened? That was my major concern, that kind of thing. Coming to work, you don't go to work thinking I would die in a terrorist attack today, but you do think if there is a bomb thing today what am I going to do? How am I going to get home? It was always if I was in Melbourne, that was my biggest concern. If something happened what was I going to do. But it never affected the fact that I have got to come up [to the city] to work. That I am going to be scared going to work because of the terrorist threat. It was always what if it happened.
(Patrick, 21 February 2005)

It was this 'what if' factor that explains the impact that terrorism has on the everyday and routine working lives of city-dwelling workers. While the terrorist threat would not make Patrick stay at home, he had spent some time thinking about what he would do if terrorists launched an attack whilst he was at work. Being trapped in the city during a major disaster would be a significant problem for the city based workers who travel large distances to and from work in cars on major arterial routes and on public transport. There were floods that affected several areas around Melbourne several years ago and I was unlucky enough to be at Southern Cross station in Melbourne when the announcement was made that no trains will be departing – I was a one hour train ride from home and suddenly confronted with no way of getting there. This was not a major disaster and there was no panic but I was, along with many other commuters, stuck in the city. Following 9/11, 3/11 and 7/7 the cities of New York, Madrid and London were quite literally shut down. Indeed, the violence of terrorism was only the beginning of the consequences of terrorism. It was these consequences – in addition to the violence of terrorism – that caused fear, stress and anxiety for Patrick.

Owen believed that it was not only workers who needed to incorporate terrorism into the everyday routines of work. He believed that managers in organizations could also make terrorism and the threat it posed an everyday and ritualized function of business and part of good corporate citizenship:

what we are trying to do in this company is put in place good management [in responding to terrorism]. And it should be there all of the time anyway. The simple part of watching people get on board a bus, not leaving luggage on board that doesn't belong to anyone. They're all good business practices that should be and have always been done, even before 9/11. You just need to be careful – that's all. Everybody says, look its very simple, don't get too carried away with it. You're taking people for a ride on a bus from A to B. That's it. People have their own luggage they are all going to get on board. If you see someone acting stupidly … you say, 'hey, that doesn't seem to be right'. That is not what we are all about. So we're a very simple product.
(Owen, 13 December 2005)

Through these 'good business practices' Owen believed that terrorism should form part of the everyday concerns of business. He believed this partly because 'No one will stop a suicide bomber. That's the ultimate. If someone wants to give their life to do something or to say something, it doesn't matter what we do' (Owen, 13 December 2005). Business leaders and managers should not obsess about the possibility of terrorism targeting their organizations just like all people should not obsess about leaving their houses for fear of the danger posed by criminals, wild animals, lightning strikes and a host of other threats – something bad may happen if you leave your house, but not leaving your house would have far-reaching consequences. Fear of terrorism threatens to turn the contemporary organization into a pathological patient that sees danger lurking in every shadow in every corner of the city. But by incorporating terrorism into the routine and everyday *business of being business* there can be hope of responding to terrorism in ways that do not leave workers paralyzed by fear and do not require millions of dollars be spent to turn organizations into fortresses.

I asked Owen if he believed that there would be significant consequences for an organization where counter-terrorism security becomes an obsession:

[It is] Terribly important [to maintain a customer, not security, focused culture]. Keep it simple, keep mindful of what we are doing, don't let terror drag on you because … the only real terror we could possibly have is a suicide bomber. You're not going to stop that person. That's the exception. But we can't worry about it. We just take proper, genuine, normal work care and study situations. You just go about business as normally as possible … We have always been security oriented. But now it is framed in a different paradigm. We are just telling people well there are some pressures. What should we do? Do we have to do something better? No! But, however, if you see a piece of luggage sitting on the tarmac anywhere on the drive instead of doing nothing – what you may have done before [9/11] – the proper course of action is to tell the police. A suitcase sitting on its own. Invariably it is probably a guy going to get his car or something, but you've done the right thing. At least you have taken action. *If somebody comes on board the bus and leaves a suitcase and nicks off and disappears well what you need to do is get everybody off the bus. And I think we would want to know why he was doing that anyway.* So, small changes. No big deal *(my emphasis).*

(Owen, 13 December 2005)

The phrase '*So, small changes. No big deal*' represents a crucial goal for business counter-terrorism. This phrase represents how business leaders and managers might incorporate the threat of terrorism into the everyday practice of doing business in ways that do not undermine customer service, employee well-being, and bottom-line productivity. If your core business is not counter-terrorism security then *small changes* may be all that is necessary.

Conclusion

Global television audiences are witnesses and victims of terrorism and will continue to be victimized as terrorism is reanimated over and over again through every subsequent terror scare. The idea that the witnesses that I interviewed were duped masses is now revealed in its absurdity. The witnesses are far from duped. They are the true terrorism experts. They are the ones who experience terrorism and the ones who can defy terrorists by trying to ignore the fears, dreads and anxieties that terrorism has caused. Witnesses continue to live despite seeing proof that terrorism is real through the images generated by terrorism and through spectacular terrorism's reanimation.

The mind has no time to repress the terrifying and powerful images that were generated on 9/11, 3/11 and 7/7. I argue that these images are weaved into the fabric of city life and that workers are condemned to witness these images again and again. Any possibility of repressing or forgetting is, I suggest, circumvented in advance – terrorism has been seen again and again, and it will continue to be seen. Since 'terrorists are seeking a larger audience than those that they actually inflict damage upon' (Toohey and Taylor, 2004) the city provides a theatre for this global audience of witnesses. Attacking the contemporary city ensures witnesses both near and far.

Contemporary terrorists – especially those responsible for the attacks on 9/11, 3/11 and 7/7 – have demonstrated a penchant for targeting working people and businesses. The stories of the workers that I explored in this chapter demonstrate that working people are aware of this possibility and have attempted to incorporate terrorism into their everyday working lives. I suggest that workers throughout the world are witnesses and victims of terrorism and that these stories are unlikely to be isolated occurrences. Yet these stories will change across time and space. Workers in different cities will have differing experiences, and workers in the same city at different times will have similarly different experiences. The consequences of this can have demoralizing affects on employee well-being, organizational cohesion as well as human security, safety and harmony. So what can *managers and business leaders* do? In the next chapter, I explore some of their stories.

CHAPTER 6

Simulated Security: A Business Response to Terrorism

Introduction: Managers in Times of Terror

In this chapter I explore more stories of working people, witnesses and victims of terrorism in a major city. These stories are different from the stories of mostly non-management employees and witnesses explored in the previous chapter in two key ways. First, most of the stories in the previous chapter – except for Owen's story – were collected before the occurrence of crucial moments of terrorism in 2005. These crucial moments – the July 7 London bombings (7/7), the October 1 Bali bombings, and the Melbourne and Sydney anti-terror raids – had a significant influence on the stories explored in this chapter. Second, the witnesses that are the subject of this chapter were managers and business leaders responsible for the security of organizations, employees, public spaces and other people who live and work in the city.

I have argued in this book that images play a central role in understanding the impact of terrorism on working people and witnesses in cities. Included in this understanding of images are images of culture and religion, images of violence and images of the Self. Would it be surprising then if those who are charged with protecting Melbourne from terrorism chose to use images as a weapon in combating terrorism? As Georgio Agamben (2001) argued after 9/11, people in many places face 'extreme and most dangerous developments in the thought of security'. I argue that security was once almost exclusively the domain of the state but now operates from decentralized stages in the city where organizations are asked to close the gaps to help in countering terrorism in Australia's cities. My data and analysis suggest that reluctance on the part of managers and business leaders combined with their belief that terrorism poses only a minimal threat to the city means that it is often only images of safety – simulated security – that are produced in countering terrorism. For one of the managers I interviewed, securing organizations, city spaces and other witnesses from terrorism boils down to one key question: *What would I say to the Coroner's Court or the Royal Commission if I had to testify following an act of terrorism?* As these workers, business leaders and managers confront images of terrorism, their perceptions of terrorism are complicated by their need to secure the city against the next terror scare.

In this chapter I explore three stories. These stories were provided by managers and business leaders of organizations in inner city Melbourne from three different industry sectors – Allen, a partner in a prestigious law-firm housed in a tall and prominent building; Sean, the security manager at a major events venue; and Louis, the general manager of a Melbourne-based public transport organization. Each story is framed by their responsibility to secure the safety of organizations, workers, spaces and people.

Managers, Witnesses, Victims

The stories of three managers and business leaders are presented in this chapter. They are workers, witnesses and victims in a time of terror. However, their stories are different to the stories of the workers presented in Chapter 5. These managers and business leaders are responsible for the safety and security of organizational and city spaces, workers, customers and clients that inhabit this space. They wear the burden not only of living and working in the vulnerable and precarious city in a time of terror, but they are on the frontline in the urban battlefields in the so-called 'War on Terror'. They are compelled by legal and moral convictions to be corporate counter-terrorists. Much like their workers, they too are true terrorism experts.

ALLEN

I recruited Allen from an organization housed in a tall and prominent building in Melbourne's central business district (CBD). I had identified Allen's organization as an occupant of such a building and called the switchboard at this organization seeking permission to recruit informants for my research. I was permitted to post advertisements and my contact details on a company notice board. Allen contacted me and agreed to be interviewed. Allen was an image of success. He was a lawyer and partner in a profitable legal firm. He had family, friends and wealth. He was the eldest of my key informants, falling into the 46–55 age-group. He had slick, jet-black hair and an expensive looking suit with matching shoes. He was cheery and at ease during our conversation: not surprising, perhaps, for a lawyer. I would say he exhibited class and confidence. I interviewed Allen on 12 July 2005. He spoke regularly about his family and the affection he felt for his wife and children. He was eagerly looking forward to a trip they were planning to *Disneyland*. Allen spoke with a refined yet unmistakably Australian accent. He also questioned me as much as I questioned him. He was eager to know about my studies, what I hoped to achieve from life and where I thought I would be in five years. Allen seemed interested in my perspective on terrorism and related issues and I offered to talk to him about these issues after I understood what he thought terrorism meant. We were sitting in a large boardroom with a spectacular view of Port Phillip Bay on the shores of which Melbourne is located. It was a cool yet beautiful sunny day and the sun shone through the office windows and his assistant brought lattes and café style cookies into the boardroom. It dawned on me that Allen was in a position of significant power and I wondered about the impact of this on our interview and the information I collected. I made a vow to myself to engage Allen as I would have any other less-intimidating informant. He believed that terrorism had a minimal impact on the world despite the initial shock that he and his family experienced when witnessing 9/11. However, he believed, paradoxically, that 9/11 had changed the world forever. Allen was not concerned about his trip to *Disneyland*, but admitted, after I mentioned the possibility of terrorism affecting his trip, that it was perhaps something that he could have considered when planning the trip. He was adamant, however, that it was perfectly safe to travel after 9/11, perhaps more safe than before 9/11, because airport security was more stringent than ever.

SEAN

Sean worked in a potentially vulnerable location at a major sporting events venue. When this venue holds major events massive security operations are undertaken. The venue is considered by journalists, academics and security experts to be an attractive target for potential terrorists. I identified this venue for this reason and I searched the internet for an appropriate contact from whom I could seek permission to advertise for respondents. I found the contact details for Sean, a manager working in security at this venue. He denied my request to recruit his employees but offered to participate himself. I interviewed Sean on 4 October 2005. He struck me as a serious and highly-professional person. Sean spoke with a thick Australian accent. He was articulate and a diligent follower of the news media. Sean considered it an important part of his job to keep up-to-date on all issues affecting his city. He was in the 26–35 age-group. Sean was keenly interested in current affairs and had detailed and nuanced opinions on terrorism: I suspected that he had been reading about terrorism in preparation for our interview. He was well informed on many cultural issues. He was tall and strong looking, and an altogether imposing figure. I interviewed Sean in a windowless room deep in the basement offices of the major events venue. Sean was interrupted many times in the 45 minutes we were talking. He told me that he was heavily relied upon by low-level security professionals but that he considered himself more of a line manager than a strategic planner. In the interview it became clear that risk-management strategies were a significant part of Sean's job and he felt that he was aware of many threats and risks that his organization and his city faced. He was Anglo-Australian, and a fan of football and cricket. He had a goatee beard, short-cropped hair and looked rugged and strong. He was appalled by terrorism. He hated it when people used violence to try and change other people's views. It was pathetic, in Sean's opinion, when this happened in any 'walk of life'. In Sean's view, intelligent people talk, the unintelligent fight. For Sean, 9/11 made terrorism an issue of public concern but he spoke frequently about other acts of terrorism – especially the second Bali bombings that had occurred three days before our interview. 9/11, however, was the referent for other terrorism for Sean. He believed that this was because 9/11 was witnessed as it was occurring whilst other acts of terrorism were reported by the media after they occurred.

LOUIS

I identified and recruited Louis in a very different way to my other key informants. It was during a major counter-terrorism and security conference in 2004 at which I attended a session that explored how terrorism was impacting on the public transport sector in Australia. Louis was one of the presenters and he identified himself as the managing director of a privately-owned niche public transport provider in Melbourne. Louis' talk explored many of the issues that I was examining at that particular time – employee stress, anxiety and well-being, occupational health and safety and risk management. During the conference delegate's lunch, I approached Louis and started a conversation. He said that he would be very keen to participate in my research. I contacted Louis shortly afterward and arranged our encounter. I interviewed Louis on 20 November 2005. Louis was particularly active in the counter-terrorism community. He attended conferences and seminars on terrorism and had taken a pre-emptive attitude to the possibility of terrorists targeting his company. He fell into the 36–45 age-group and appeared youthful despite holding the position of managing director in this organization. His company had around 80 employees which was small in relation to other public transport organizations in Melbourne. This organization operated as a niche provider, however, and was not in competition with larger transport providers. Louis was a very professional, well spoken, and well-dressed individual. He was a family man who took his job very seriously. Louis was keen to strike the right work–family balance: something that he found difficult to attain. He described his workforce as 'ocker-ish'. Louis attended a major Australian university and was an accountant by education and trade. While he was politically conservative he felt he was sensitive to a wide range of opinions on many issues. While he was shocked and appalled by what he had witnessed on 9/11, he was sceptical about the possibility of terrorism occurring in Melbourne and affecting his life, family or business. Regardless, as the managing director of a public transport organization he felt obliged to take steps to protect his organization from terrorism. Louis was keen to secure peace of mind for his customers, clients and staff. He did not fear terrorism in his personal and family life, but when he went to work he believed that his job required him to consider terrorism a serious threat.

Allen's Terrorism: From the Ground Looking Up

The stylish and successful Allen asked an assistant to bring us a pair of lattes and some cookies as we sat down in the plush offices of a legal firm housed in a tall and prominent building in Melbourne's central business district. Allen was jovial and relaxed and was eager to talk about terrorism with me. It was 12 July and Melbourne had offered another cool yet sunny mid-winter's day. More significantly it was four days in Australian time since images of the London bombings of 7 July 2005 – the '7/7' attacks as they have come to be known – had been blazoned across televisions and newspapers around the country.

I asked Allen what he believed terrorism to be. He replied:

Terrorism is something out there. It doesn't really affect us here in Melbourne.
(Allen, 12 July 2005)

While it was not the usual response that I had become accustomed to in conducting interviews with working people about terrorism, it was certainly not the first time I had heard this belief expressed in this way. It was interesting to hear that terrorism does not always play a significant role in people's lives and that the threat of terrorism was perhaps overblown. But first I wanted to engage with Allen's assertion to explore its context and the assumptions and beliefs that supported it. If Allen was to dismiss the possibility that terrorism had influenced working people and witnesses in Melbourne he would be the first that I had encountered. I asked Allen: 'What do people you know think? Your friends and family?'

To which he responded with a smirk:

> *I don't think they think about it at all. [deliberate pause] Is this something people think about?*
>
> (Allen, 12 July 2005)

I was not sure what to make of this initially and it sets the trend for the continuing dialogue with me on the back foot in our encounter. The transcripts betray my memories of shifting in my chair and feeling uncertain about continuing the interview. In the moment I broke stride from my planned questions and asked more directly: 'What things changed in this building after September 11?' I regretted it almost immediately. I had intended not to direct Allen's thinking to a specific act of terrorism. I nonetheless got an answer that I had hoped for which provided me with an opportunity for deeper interrogation: 'Well … ' Allen began before pausing:

> *… things were different after September 11.*
>
> (Allen, 12 July 2005)

As I inquired further into Allen's experiences of working in this tall and prominent building, his references to images of terrorism were becoming increasingly apparent. While he had originally resisted, mostly in a playful and sarcastically good-humoured way, he began to describe how 9/11's images reached him and altered his feelings about his building as a vulnerable and precarious place in a city. I asked Allen whether terrorism had impacted on his life and work:

> *Allen: No, not at all.*
>
> *Howie: Really? (I look out the window at a view stretching out over the city and the bay) Because it would seem …*
>
> *Allen: Nope. Never.*
>
> *Howie: Fair enough.*
>
> *Allen: Well, I mean, of course I thought about it. How could I not?*
>
> *Howie: Well, I …*
>
> *Allen: I mean, look at it.*
>
> *Howie: Yeah, no I agree.*
>
> *Allen: It is harder to imagine though when you are in the building. I find it easier to picture when I am on the ground looking up.*
>
> (Allen, 12 July 2005)

Months after this interview I began to understand Allen's perception of the city and its sites and spaces in terms of Baudrillard's critical examinations of 9/11's meaning. Baudrillard (2002: 44–45) argued that 9/11 represented a unique event in the history of cities and the destruction of the Twin Towers represented an ending or 'disappearance' of not only the buildings but the world system of capitalism, work and commerce they represented. I argue that such meaning is located here by Allen. His employment as a lawyer and partner in a prestigious law-firm is symbolic of the same world system: overwhelmingly affluent, hegemonic, and, at times, exploitative. The imagery of this disappearance was reanimated for Allen when he viewed his building from the outside. The destruction of the Towers in New York was the referent for the potential destruction of buildings in cities throughout the world, and people in their shadow are compelled to look up.

Baudrillard (2002: 4–5) argued that everyone has dreamed of this event: it is a fantasy played out regularly in Hollywood disaster movies. The terrorism on 9/11, 3/11 and 7/7 would perhaps be more appropriate in a disaster movie. Washington DC blogger Wonkette (2007) described 9/11 as a 'terror porn fantasy' that satisfied the American desire for 'blowing shit up', especially when the target is a city 'full of minorities and homosexuals'. Wonkette (2007) pointed to disaster novels and movies that saturated American culture before 9/11 including the series of *Die Hard* (1988) movies, *Armageddon* (1998), and *Independence Day* (1996). In short, it was all too easy to imagine. Indeed, witnesses do not imagine, they simply recall the image, projecting themselves back to 9/11, 3/11 and 7/7 or some other terrorist atrocity. Perhaps all that is needed is to close one's eyes and picture the moment when two aircraft crashed into the Towers causing them to collapse, or the newspaper images of the destruction caused by the bombing of London's public transport networks. On 9/11 the buildings collapsed in the most theatrical manner fulfilling the lust experienced while watching the building tension of the foreplay leading ultimately to the climax of the wildest disaster fantasy:

> *The countless disaster movies bear witness to this fantasy, which they clearly attempt to exorcize with images, drowning out the whole thing with special effects. But the universal attraction they exert … shows that acting-out is never very far away, the impulse to reject any system growing all the stronger as it approaches perfection or omnipotence.*
> (Baudrillard, 2002: 7)

Allen, while adamant that the impact of terrorism on his personal and working life was minimal, described in some detail the changing security arrangements in his building following 9/11. The building's management had considered the possibility of being targeted by 9/11-style terrorism and conducted a number of drills to evacuate the building and increase security at entry points. Allen said he was often not in the building when drills had taken place and was told about them later. From his perspective the increased security amounted to little more than more diligent screening, by existing security staff, of employees as they entered the building. Allen believed the building functioned as it had done prior to 9/11. This perspective of minimal change in post-9/11 cities has been a focus for research into urban spaces. White (1999: 23, 33) has argued that New York was 'peculiarly constructed to absorb almost anything that comes along', and New Yorkers had coped through many challenges by 'a sort of perpetual muddling through'. While terrorism in New York and London had an initial economic impact, and fear and dread is expected to linger, Savitch (2003) argued that these and other cities have changed only negligibly.

Contrary to this business-as-usual mentality and way of coping, Eisinger (2004: 115) argued that: 'The terror attacks of September 11, 2001, on New York and Washington,

D.C., were fundamentally challenges to American values, optimism, and global economic dominance, but they must also be seen as assaults on cities as urban places'. Cities are mostly unprotected places where many socially, economically, and culturally diverse people gather to work and go about their daily lives. Many of those who were killed on 9/11 were involved in knowledge-driven industries 'of the new cosmopolitan economy in signature buildings that had to come to represent some of the most powerful symbols of modern urban achievement'. An attack on these symbols represents an attack on the 'very essence of American cities' (Eisinger, 2004: 116).

I suggest that 9/11, rather than representing an attack on the essence of cities, can best be described as an attack on the *image of cities*. The skyline of New York, featured in so many movies, sitcoms and cartoons (think *Permanent Vacation* (1980), *Friends*, and *The Simpsons* respectively), changed alongside less tangible changes in the images Americans held of themselves and their nation. In this way 9/11 can be seen as a threat to the skylines of all cities. After the attacks there were predictions that tall buildings would no longer be built because occupants would be difficult to find, that organizations would move out of such structures to lower pastures, and that there would be an out-migration of labour to regional and suburban areas (Eisinger, 2004: 116; Kantor, 2002). Others argued that business travel would be curtailed and holidays in distant locations would represent an unreasonable travelling risk. In addition, it was suggested that people would stop viewing going to work as necessary and instead embrace technologies for telecommuting where business can be conducted from remote locations (Alexander and Alexander, 2002). A change in one part of life in response to terrorism may have unintended consequences in others – an example of this can be seen in estimates that over 1000 more road deaths resulted in the months following 9/11 from motorists driving large distances in preference to domestic air-travel (Gardner, 2008). Similarly, business leaders and managers that encourage telecommuting will need to be prepared for the social and behavioural consequences of significantly reducing human interactions and isolation. In minimizing social interaction a number of other problems may be encountered, even if people who telecommute are safer from terrorism. These problems may include mental health issues arising from working in an isolated environment, lower work satisfaction and motivation arising from decreased social interaction, and physical health issues arising from less physical travel and exertion (such as the exercise one incidentally undertakes in commuting to work).

Allen spoke about a family trip he was planning to *Disneyland*. I asked Allen whether terrorism was a consideration as he planned the trip. The smile slowly lessened on Allen's face betraying his typical joviality:

No, not at all. I guess now that I think about it perhaps there should be some concern. I don't know though. I am not afraid and neither is my family' (Allen, 12 July 2005). When I had asked him about the London bombings that had occurred only a few days earlier, he had little to say: 'These things happen. It is a strange world. You just have to hope.

(Allen, 12 July 2005)

When I had asked him about the London bombings that had occurred only a few days earlier, he had little to say:

These things happen. It is a strange world. You just have to hope.

(Allen, 12 July 2005)

The tall and prominent building that housed the firm where Allen was a partner was like others that can be found constructing the skylines of cities throughout the world. Each morning and evening business women and men congregate outside and in the foyers of these buildings. City dwellers, workers and visitors often find themselves in or below these structures.

For Allen, images of 9/11 were critical in his perceptions of terrorism and the threat it posed to Melbourne. Allen most dreaded terrorism when he could picture the point of impact of aircraft crashing into New York's Twin Towers. I argue that terrorism has had a lasting impact, in everyday ways, on Allen's daily life. 9/11 is routinely reanimated by Allen when he is at the base of his building looking up. Despite our interview occurring only five days after a major terrorist attack was staged in London, 9/11 remained for Allen, as Baudrillard (2002: 4) had asserted, the 'mother' of all events.

Sean's Terrorism: Other Than the Obvious

I interviewed Sean on 4 October 2005 in the management office of a social, cultural and sporting venue in Melbourne: an empty, windowless and sterile room underneath the venue itself. It was three days after bombs were detonated in beachfront restaurants and cafés in Bali, killing 26 people. Newspapers in Australia devoted considerable journalistic space to these attacks – as demonstrated in Chapter 4 – and what they meant for witnesses in Australia's major cities. This venue hosted many sporting, cultural and social events of national and international significance and the venue's operators regularly managed the security of major events and the crowds that they attract. Sean was a security manager. He appeared large and muscular, and spoke with a thick Australian accent.
I asked Sean what he believed terrorism was:

Personally, I just think a lot of it is political but it is also religion I suppose. I don't sort of try to understand why they do it. I think it is personal as well to victims, more so. As to why they do it? Who knows?

(Sean, 4 October 2005)

I was dissatisfied with this response so I tried a different approach to get more detail. I asked Sean what things he considered to be terrorism:

Apart from the obvious we have had around the world, bombings, things like that. Probably it could be local. Just society in general against a particular people. This would be classed as terrorism, at a low level. Probably a threat against the masses more than individuals themselves though. Or a particular race or country. A threat against the masses really.

(Sean, 4 October 2005)

To my surprise, Sean did not mention the most recent terrorist attacks in Bali. To my direct question that asked what things he considered to be terrorism he replied: 'Apart from the obvious'. I was concerned that I had given him the impression that I wanted a response that was other than the obvious. Among Sean's arguments was his belief that terrorism involved a 'threat' against a group of people. I asked Sean whether a threat is sufficient for terrorism to have a significant impact without an attack occurring:

Sean: I don't think it has to [be an act]. It could be, for example, your suicide bombers. It's not what ... there is no consideration where personal life is concerned for their reason behind doing it. I don't know.

Howie: The reason why I ask is that Australia has had some incidences of terrorism. The Hilton Bombing in Sydney. Attempts against Jewish interests. Attacks between communities from the former Yugoslavia. But people in Melbourne usually think about 9/11, Bali, London, Madrid. We haven't experienced terrorism on that scale on our homeland. It makes me wonder if we can still be significantly affected even though we don't witness terrorism on our streets.

Sean: I've probably got a couple of degrees of separation. The Russell Street bombing which, although it was a long time before September 11th, my father-in-law was an ambulance officer who was at Russell Street. Now that can be classed as terrorism to me although locally. Things like 9/11 happen in Iraq and Pakistan and that all the time. But we don't witness that all the time. So when it does happen here it is huge. Over there it is nearly everyday life. I think that's where Australia is so shocked when something does happen. Although they are starting to get used to it.

(Sean, 4 October 2005)

The Russell Street bombing occurred on 27 March 1986 when a bomb was detonated in a car out the front of the Russell Street police headquarters in Melbourne (Hocking, 2004: 174). It made national headlines and images of destruction, horror and bewilderment were viewed throughout Australia. Rather than 9/11 representing new and unprecedented violence it invoked, for Sean, a reanimation of the Russell Street bombing. Sean believed that the Russell Street bombing can be 'classed as terrorism' and he noted that it occurred some 15 years before 9/11. In this way, Sean's witnessing of 9/11 gave the Russell Street bombings new meaning and significance.

I asked Sean what acts of terrorism he believed had the most impact in Melbourne. I assumed that Sean's response would include 9/11, like it had for almost every other witness that I had interviewed. Sean responded quite differently:

I think probably not so much September 11 although it was a shock to the world in general. The closer to home, your Balis, especially the one recently. The ones more close to home. Being that it does involve Australians. There were Australians involved in September 11 although not to the degree of the first bombings in Bali.

(Sean, October 4, 2005)

I asked Sean whether the same could be said about the London attacks: that it was more relevant to Australians than 9/11; that it was 'closer to home':

Howie: What about London? People often comment to me that even though London is a long way away, we feel very close to Londoners. Many of us have stories of people we knew, people frantically jumped onto the phone to make sure everything was okay in London.

Sean: Yeah. One of the guards here is from London. He is from London himself and he has family over there. I made sure he was okay and didn't have to go there, have some time off and things like that. But he was sort of affected because he had close relatives and immediate family over there.

(Sean, 4 October 2005)

Some commentators have suggested that Melbourne is home to *indirectly affected* witnesses because spectacular terrorism has not occurred there. Indirectly affected witnesses are loosely defined as witnesses in distant cities – the concept of distance, however, is not clearly definable. It most commonly refers to geographical distance, but also temporal and interpersonal distance. Pfefferbaum *et al.* (2000) and Schuster *et al.* (2001) argued that interpersonal distance is created when members of a population have a direct or perceived link with victims of terrorism either through friends or family or other perceived affiliations and empathies. As Schuster *et al.* (2001: 1508) argued: 'The events of September 11 were widely described as attacks on America, and most or all Americans may have identified with the victims or perceived the attacks as directed against themselves'.

Sean argued that while people in some cities around the world have been more accustomed to terrorism, Australians have not been. But he argued that people in Melbourne were becoming more accustomed to terrorism because of the interpersonal closeness between people in Australia and victims of terrorism overseas. Sean suggested that 9/11 played a lesser role than other acts of terrorism in forming perceptions of terrorism in Australia but that it remained part of a powerful backdrop through which other terrorism is understood. For Sean, this closeness between people in Australia and victims of terrorism overseas meant that terrorism did not need to occur in Melbourne for people in the city to be witnesses and subsequently be affected by images of terrorism. Sean's story was infused with his memories of the explosions on Russell Street in Melbourne. Sean was not there, but a close relative was involved in the medical response to the attack. For Sean, Russell Street provided lasting images of terror and violence in Melbourne. I too remember hearing about the explosions, seeing the destruction, and watching television footage of bewildered police officers wandering around the wreckage. Sean was also sensitive to the feelings of a work colleague from London following the London bombings. Interpersonal distance from terrorism, associated with a perceived feeling of closeness, was an important factor for Sean as a security manager and witness to terrorism.

Sean was beginning to see a pattern in the terrorism of contemporary times. While he argued that major acts of terrorism like 9/11 played a less-significant role than other acts of terrorism for witnesses, he had obviously been paying close attention to these major acts:

What seems to be happening to me is that it is happening every 12 months. When you look at it, it is every September and October. Something happens.

(Sean, 4 October 2005)

First there was 9/11. Until now, Sean had played down its importance but it returned as his referent and he incorporated 9/11 as part of the 'obvious' acts of terrorism that have occurred that had consequences for people living and working in Melbourne. Second, there was October 2002 when Bali was targeted for the first time. In September 2004 the Australian embassy in Jakarta was targeted and in October 2005, Bali was targeted for a second time. Was Sean a dedicated chronicler of terrorism events throughout the world?

Perhaps, but there could be another explanation. I think (and I realized this long after I conducted the interview) that Sean probably read the previous day's *Herald Sun* on 3 October 2005.

Pages eight and nine of the October 3 edition of the *Herald Sun* provided a timeline of recent acts of terrorism with the starting date on 9/11. Later in our discussion I asked Sean what media sources he used most when gathering information about terrorism. Sean responded: 'Personally? The *Herald Sun*'.

Sean noted that the London attacks do not fit this pattern. I asked him if that may be because they were not carried out by international terrorists but by British citizens:

Yeah that's true. But I think with the way that London happened with taking out critical infrastructure. The underground in London is massive and it is their [Londoners] main way of commuting to and from the city. Because parking is so expensive, it's hard to get into the city in a car ... that's why it is huge when they stop public transport. And I think here would be, if they ever had to do it here, just my thoughts, things like our water, because our dams are so open. Things like power are our major (pause). Melbourne probably couldn't function that well if your water was polluted or your power stations were taken out. Melburnites would find it hard if you are not ready for it.

(Sean, 4 October 2005)

The targeting of critical infrastructure has been a significant concern for counter-terrorism experts, agencies and governments since before 9/11. It was perhaps not surprising to hear somebody in charge of managing a site containing critical infrastructure to share these concerns.

I think water is huge. Power you can live without, water is an essential service. Even when you speak to people from your local water companies, no matter how long you don't pay your bill they can't cut you off, because it is an essential service. It seems like everyday living, helps people survive. You need that water. If you were going to hit something that is what you would want to hit.

(Sean, 4 October 2005)

Sean had carefully considered what the strategic objectives of terrorists might be. It was perhaps to be expected that a security manager would have considered the possibility of terrorism affecting his workplace and city. Sean was responsible for a site of cultural and social importance and the lives of those who attended major events. A successful terrorist attack against this venue would have disastrous consequences for Sean, myself and other working people and witnesses in Melbourne.

The Appearance of Security

As I attempted to direct our conversation towards how terrorism impacted on workers and witnesses in Melbourne, Sean returned the conversation to the vulnerability to terrorism that he perceived in areas outside of the city.

Howie: But what about in the city? Inner city Melbourne? What might be targeted?

Sean: More outer Melbourne, which in turn affects inner city. Your reservoirs up Dandenong way, your Sylvan dams, they are probably not as big and your Upper Yarra dam and the hydro electrical station up there. One of the major water infrastructures that supply Melbourne with their clean water. I really wouldn't think they would hit sporting venues, because everyone plays sport, and they haven't hit one yet and I don't think they would. Sport's played all over the world, different codes, and everyone gets involved, everyone plays. It is not for one culture or one religion. Take cricket for example. It is played everywhere. It is played by Muslim countries, Christian countries, Catholic countries. So I don't think they would hit a sporting event or a sporting stadium anywhere in the world. It would be political, for example, 9/11 they hit the Pentagon. It might be infrastructure such as in London.

(Sean, 4 October 2005)

I was surprised to hear that a man in charge of security at a major social, cultural and sporting venue did not consider it likely that a sporting event would be targeted. He held the firm belief that terrorists would prefer to target power or water infrastructure – targets that Sean considered to be the 'holy grail' for terrorists. For Sean, sport worked as a kind of universal language and he inaccurately stated that sporting events had previously not been targeted. 9/11 and 7/7 were referents for his understanding of terrorism in this context and his argument that terrorists would rather target a political site or critical infrastructure.

For Sean it was the nature and structure of the city that would determine the target that terrorists would select. In New York it was the financial sector and large iconic buildings. In London, targeting the public transport network had the effect of interrupting the normal functioning of the city. As such, terrorists would seek to target Melbourne where it would most disrupt the city.

I think again with 9/11 to put a massive city on hold and the city that they hit (pause). Not only did they hit the biggest infrastructure in the USA in the stock exchange, it stopped it to a halt. It's like when they hit London they hit the underground 'cause it stopped the city. Which in turn creates other issues in the world economy. It's one of the main players in the whole thing.

(Sean, 4 October 2005)

I seized on this response as an opportunity to question Sean on the Melbourne Commonwealth Games that were to be held in March 2006, some five months after I conducted his interview. This major sporting event received global media attention and passed without a major security concern. I asked Sean whether he believed the Commonwealth Games would be a target for terrorists given that an attack at the Games would be likely to significantly disrupt Melbourne.

I don't believe so. Obviously, things are going to be stepped up by the authorities. Your Vicpol's [Victoria Police], your army, defence forces. But I just think that because there are so many, because it is the Commonwealth Games and not the Olympic games, there is a big difference between the two although a lot of people don't see it. Commonwealth Games is the Commonwealth Games for a reason. I still don't think that they would target something like that. It is always possible though, you never know. It's that all terrorisms are irregular, erratic.

So the response is all reactive. You can only be proactive to a certain extent. Then deal with it as it happens.

(Sean, 4 October 2005)

Sean spoke freely and candidly. He had clearly given some thought to what he might say in preparation for our interview. Sean would be unpopular in some circles for downplaying the possibility of terrorism at the Commonwealth Games. Similarly, his belief that counter-terrorism security is a reactive endeavour could make many attendees at this major venue feel unsafe.

The Trusted Information Sharing Network (TISN) (2005), an Australian national organization of security and counter-terrorism professionals, argues that 'almost daily terrorist events throughout 2005 demonstrate that cities remain a favoured terrorist target'. In attacking cities, terrorists hoped to kill and injure the most number of people possible, to destroy buildings and cause disruption and generate as much devastation and fear as possible. Attacking mass gatherings and major events would seem to achieve this purpose. According to Barnes and Ker (2005) special units were readied for the Commonwealth Games to deal with biological, chemical and radiological terrorist attacks. The authors argued that counter-terrorism was the 'centrepiece' of security at the Games (Barnes and Ker, 2005). The position of the Australian Security Intelligence Organization (ASIO) was that an attack at the Commonwealth Games was 'feasible' (Eastley, 2006). Others argued that the Games may not have been the only Australian target during this period. According to Wright-Neville (in Eastley, 2006),

There's ... a tendency in the past for terrorists to avoid high profile events, because they know that they are much more difficult targets to attack, and they're much more likely to consider trying to take advantage of the fact that attention is focused on Point X and therefore they might strike at Point Y.

Many security and counter-terrorism analysts have suggested that this phenomenon was observed during the 7/7 bombings with the G8 summit being held in Gleneagles while attacks were carried out in London.

For Sean's part, he could offer little as reassurance to people attending major events in Melbourne or who frequently find themselves in crowds:

Infrastructure is the target. The scaffolding that supports the system. They [terrorists] are trying to make a statement. With yourselves [suicide bombing], you can do some damage. We need to rely on our intel. and our government. There is not a lot your average Joe on the street can do much about.

(Sean, 4 October 2005)

It was difficult for Sean to imagine a scenario where security could be guaranteed. This was perhaps especially so when picturing the archetype of contemporary terrorism: the suicide bomber. It was suicide bombers that caused the destruction in New York and Washington D.C. on 9/11, on rail networks in Madrid and London, and twice in Bali. This, added to almost daily reports of suicide terrorism in occupied Iraq, paints a picture of terror for witnesses and victims in distant cities that I argue has had a lasting impact.

A determined suicide bomber is an organic, thinking, reacting, improvising killer. Most likely they cannot be stopped.

Sean nonetheless believed that there were a number of practical steps that managers could take to mitigate the consequences of terrorism. Many of these, Sean argued, should focus on the well-being of the worker. He believed that it was important to be sensitive to his workers' needs during the times of high stress and high anxiety that terrorism can create. He again mentioned how the 7/7 attacks had special significance for one of his employees: 'As I said, one of the guards here is from London. I was really worried about him. It is hard to know what to say at times like that' (Sean, 4 October 2005). Sean believed that managers need to be aware of special cases like this and actively seek out anyone especially traumatized by acts of terrorism. Sean also believed, however, that in the post-9/11 world, especially for people in the security industry, a renewed sense of precariousness and vulnerability were normal and that his workers needed to be ready to work in everyday and routine ways in post-9/11 business security:

Security is such a major industry, especially since September 11 ... Being in the security industry you expect 80 per cent of [the difficulties of working post-9/11]. You expect increase in procedures and things like that. Although all the guys here love working at the [major venue]. I think the only thing they want is more money. Their procedures have increased over the last 2 years dramatically. Myself, being a security manager, I spoke to the guys at one stage, being that [the procedures] had increased so much and of course they are going to expect more compensation for it. They're the last to leave the site during evacuation! (my emphasis).

(Sean, 4 October 2005)

Perhaps the added burden of working in post-9/11 security could be accompanied by higher compensation, although this would be problematic for many businesses. As Sean aptly points out, if an act of terrorism was to target the major venue where he worked, his security team would be the last to leave. This potential compensation management problem that Sean described would seem to be a looming dilemma in the city-dwelling business world, but it is a dilemma that has been around for some time. St. John (1991), in his study of airplane hijacking, argued that low-skilled, low-paid, bored, and dissatisfied security staff at the world's airports represented a major flaw in counter-terrorism security. In contemporary times of terror the focus of international terrorists has extended well beyond the airport and, as such, it may be that this same flaw has also shifted. To improve the appearance of security, low-skilled and low-paid security staff may be appropriate, but I would like to suggest that hiring only this type of security is a risky policy. It remains that highly-paid impeccably uniformed, gun-toting, ruthless looking security will do far more to deter a would-be terrorist. But would workers feel safer in the presence of such security staff? It is likely that the presence of this sort of security – perhaps coupled with bomb and metal detectors – would create more panic, fear and alarm. It seems clear that an appropriate balance must be struck. There may be significant consequences for either over- or under-reacting during times of terror. It would be difficult for me to offer any universal method for addressing this dilemma except to say appropriate security responses should be determined only after first understanding the nuances of each particular organization and the nature of the threat of terror they face. For people in office buildings, for example, it may be that the emotion 'terror' will have more significant consequences given that the probability of a violent act of terrorism occurring on office

Simulated Security: A Business Response to Terrorism 151

buildings is low – attacks on office buildings of the kind witnessed on 9/11 are thought to be unlikely given the stringent nature of airport security post-9/11. A rail operator on the other hand may be justified in implementing a significant security presence during peak times at it may be that employees will appreciate this added security attention.

100 per cent Bag Searches and Security Simulation

Sean suggested that there a number of other practical steps that managers and business leaders can take to prevent terrorism and mitigate its consequences. Many of these practical steps stemmed from what Sean saw as his legal and moral obligation to create a secure environment for employees and patrons who attend major events at this venue. Since complete security was, in Sean's view, not possible, an appearance of security was Sean's goal: this was simulated security through creating an image of safety. Sean and his colleagues worked tirelessly to simulate security in preparing for major events:

> A lot of people are asking did we do anything extra [in preparing for a major event]? We did heaps. Probably more so for peace of mind for the general public. Also to stop anything untoward coming into the ground. We did things like 100 per cent bag searches which usually we would only do for [a major event]. We do it in [a major event] because we have more time to do it. It's very hard to do something like that during football season. You haven't got a lot of time to get people in. At [a major event] you have [many thousands of] people and to get them into the ground it is a matter of 45 minutes to an hour at the most. To do a 100 per cent bag search is mind boggling to say the least. We can never be sure if stuff is getting through.
> (Sean, 4 October 2005)

The importance of 'peace of mind' in understanding terrorism – and the attempts of terrorists to shatter this 'peace of mind' – has long been a topic of theoretical debate. Horgan (2005: 3) argues that terrorism is designed to 'create levels of heightened arousal … disproportionate to the actual or intended future threat posed by the terrorist'. In a similar vein, Friedland and Merari (1985) suggested that terrorists seek to create perceptions of terrorism disproportionate to any actual danger posed and that terrorism has the ability to affect witnesses far beyond the initial destruction and death caused. It is therefore important to consider and manage public perceptions when delivering security for major events. Since terrorists seek to psychologically influence a population through a targeted and symbolic act of violence it would seem appropriate to respond with security measures that create an image of safety and deliver perceptions of a secure venue. In many respects this is symbolic, simulated security. Witnesses to major acts of terrorism need to witness image-security in order to defy the power of terrorism and go about their everyday lives feeling safe, secure, relaxed and comfortable.

In the unsecurable city the metaphor of '100 per cent bag searches' is symbolic of the simulation of security through an image of safety. As a witness to 9/11 and patron of this venue from time to time, predominantly for football and cricket matches, I had assumed that everybody in the ground with a bag had been searched. I had always volunteered my bag when I had seen a bag checking table. However, I know of a friend of my late grandfather's who took pride in missing the bag searches and avoided security guards with a skip that belied his age. I realize now that such absolute security through 100 per cent bag checks was always unlikely (come to think of it, I never thought it was realistic). I shared my story of my grandfather's elusive friend with Sean. This did not surprise him and he explained that 100 per cent bag searches are a goal more than a reality:

> *With 100 per cent bag searches, we try to emphasize it is 100 per cent. We try to check everyone's bag. That's why we have tables external to the ground, we have fencing external to the ground. We have a guard force at those peak times. I mean the [a major event] is probably the wrong day to initiate it as it was probably the first time we had ever done it. The problem is having all of those things permanently. The cricket we have a lot longer, we open earlier, we have enough time to do it, to set it up.*
>
> (Sean, 4 October 2005)

Using concentric barriers to securitize a venue was considered good policy. It required significant manpower and planning and was only feasible for large and special events, such as the Commonwealth Games. And as Sean explained, patron volume was related to the ability of security staff to successfully carry out 100 per cent bag searches. Security in such a scenario was comprehensive but gaps remained. These gaps were filled with simulated security created by an image of safety. Declaring in the media that 100 per cent bag searches would be conducted, and then searching 95 per cent would mostly be good enough in Sean's view as long as there was a visible security presence and patrons walked freely through the venue feeling safe and secure. In this way, the 100 per cent bag search is as metaphorical as the economic concept of full employment: full employment does not mean everyone is employed.

Hire Security Guards Until the Entrance is Blocked

Was there any way of achieving full security at this major venue of cultural and social significance? Sean believed that it would be possible: he could hire security guards until the entrance was totally blocked:

> *Different events cause different issues. There is always a chance that people will miss the bag search when we don't have the 100 per cent bag search. It happens, you can't get everybody, we don't have the man power and you can't put any other facility in place to counter that. Because you have your event staff monitoring the tickets, and that's what they do. And you've got as many guards as you can have* without blocking the entrance. *'Cause we've got to think about leaving and the emergency procedures, so we can't block exits totally. That's why when we do 100 per cent we do it outside the ground so we don't have things coming inside. A lot of things like that come under consideration (emphasis added).*
>
> (Sean, 4 October 2005)

Practicality intervenes in attempts to securitize most sites. Insecurity is characteristic of life in the city and life at this major events venue. It could not be totally secured and total security was not a goal: simulated security through the image of safety provided the necessary *psychic* protection for Melbourne's population. It was a Faustian pact of the city-dwelling society that clings to a belief in security. It is a security, however, based on images of safety. There are many benefits of living in the city that are juxtaposed to possible risks and dangers: the city is home to the affluent and the worker, the criminal and the terrorist. As Žižek (2002a) might say: Welcome to the desert of the real!

This 'image of safety' approach to security was applied especially at the beginning of major events. It was Sean's view that you only get one first impression. As he explained of the security for the Commonwealth Games:

If they see it at the opening ceremony then they will be more comfortable for that two-week period. With the Commonwealth Games, the security is going to be huge anyway. My opinion is if you want to break into a car, you break into a car. If terrorists are going to hit, they are going to hit. As I said before, you can only be proactive to a certain extent. And then it is all reactive as long as your emergency plans or whatever are in place then I don't believe that you will have any major problems. Obviously if you get a situation such as Bali or September 11 you're going to have deaths and injuries but you're going to have to be able to control that a lot better with your emergency procedures. As long as they're in place.

(Sean, 4 October 2005)

Sean argued that perceptions of terrorism in Melbourne and perceptions of the threat to the Commonwealth Games were significantly affected by media coverage of terrorism. Indeed Sean had proved himself to be a diligent follower of news about terrorism in the *Herald Sun*. Sean's description of security leads him from time to time to examples of terrorism that illustrate his point. In the following passage he referred to the 1 October Bali bombings. Our conversation occurred during a week of intense reporting of these attacks:

The footage that they have got this time around is pretty graphic. You actually see the bomb go off. I haven't seen a lot of it. I try not to look too deeply into it. It is what it is but, pictures don't lie. I suppose I'd rather look at a picture of something like that than read about it. The picture is going to tell you more than what the journalist who wasn't even there is saying. They may have been there after the fact and their perception of it is different to someone sitting at a café in Bali. As is the person at home has a different perception also.

(Sean, 4 October 2005)

Neither the journalist nor the distant witness was there and both rely on the media to provide images. The faith that Sean had in images was perhaps startling. Sean felt that 'seeing is believing' and that the televisual construction of the explosions was somehow analogous to 'sitting at a café in Bali' in a way that written journalism was not: the image, for Sean, was closer to reality. The people sitting at home, the distant witnesses, form their perceptions through these images. Images can be both the ultimate reality and a diabolical corruption. I suggest that most commonly, images of terror will be both at the same time.

Sean made a series of startling admissions about securing sites and fellow witnesses in the city. Sean believed that total security was not possible and should not be a goal. Rather, the simulation of security through creating an image of safety was Sean's goal. I argue that it is unsurprising that image creation may be the best way to fight fear and dread created by images of terrorism. Terrorism as spectacle has paved the way for security as spectacle. It allows witnesses to feel safe even if complete safety remains elusive.

Louis' Terrorism: London, Madrid and That Stuff in New York

Louis was the managing director of a privately-owned public transport company that provided services to a niche market in Melbourne and the surrounding suburbs. Our conversation occurred in Melbourne as fine weather returned to the city on 20 November 2005. We met in the boardroom of the company's head office in an historic four-storey building in Melbourne's central business district. I had met Louis at a security conference the previous year and had learnt that he was deeply concerned for the security of his company. He believed that participating in this research provided him with an opportunity to learn something that might enable him to better pursue safety for his workforce, customers and infrastructure.

Many commentators have argued that public transport is an attractive terrorist target (Yates, 2005). Public transport was targeted on 11 March 2004 in Madrid and on 7 July 2005 in London: on both occasions to devastating effect. Managers in transport organizations are in many ways on the front line of countering terrorism in cities where they operate. But, according to Yates (2005), the response of Australian security and intelligence agencies has been reactionary to emerging threats. As such, considerable attention during the second half of 2005 – in the aftermath of the London bombings – focused on mass-transport security and the possibility of it being targeted. Not only is public transport infrastructure considered vulnerable but also the 'mass gatherings ... general malls and shopping centres, and other, so called, 'soft targets' that are connected to urban transport systems' (Yates, 2005).

Before the attacks in New York, Madrid and London, terrorists had frequently targeted public transport. From 1991 to 1999, the IRA had reportedly attempted attacks on transport infrastructure requiring the British transport authorities to manage over 6000 threats and inspect over 9000 suspicious objects. Suicide bombers in Israel have targeted buses and al-Qaeda linked groups have planned attacks against the Singapore metro (Fleckner and Stevens, 2005: 6). What Holt (2006: 6) calls mass-surface transportation, or MST, was the target for 195 terrorist attacks worldwide between 1997 and the end of 2000. According to figures from the *Brookings Institution* in Washington D.C. (in Holt, 2006: 6), between 1991 and 2001, 42 per cent of all terrorist attacks around the world were directed against MST. Holt (2006: 6) argues that the attractiveness of targeting MST is based on four factors. The first factor relates to the vulnerability of crowds that gather to use MST, often in narrow or confined public spaces such as underground train stations. Attacks against such spaces are likely to cause many casualties. Second, MST was designed for efficient and effective transport of large numbers of people. Any security arrangement for public transport must not operate at the expense of economic imperatives such as customer service. Excessive delays in travel would often be considered unacceptable by managers and customers. Third, as passengers using MST are enclosed in confined spaces as they travel, any explosion that occurs is amplified causing more damage than an explosion would in non-enclosed areas. Finally, an attack on MST can significantly disrupt many related sites such as rail tunnels that also house communication and power infrastructure. Economic production in large cities would be significantly interrupted by a shut-down of transportation networks, and companies operating with Just-In-Time inventory procedures would come to almost a complete halt in production (Alexander, 2002; Alexander and Alexander, 2004).

Given these concerns, Louis had undertaken a variety of measures to protect his company against terrorism. I expected that the attacks against public transport would be of most concern to Louis, particularly the attacks in London that had occurred four months earlier. I asked Louis what he believed terrorism was.

Louis: I understand terrorism to be the actions of people to terrorize, to put fear into the minds of the public. People who have no specific responsibility for some political stand or otherwise. The actual actions and objectives of terrorism are things done to terrorize, typically things done to injure or kill or otherwise seriously disrupt the lives of ordinary people.

Howie: I sense that a psychological impact is important in your perceptions of what terrorism is.

Louis: That's what I feel it is. If there was a way for a terrorist to kill a whole bunch of people in a way that wasn't going to make the news and make other people concerned, they wouldn't do it. They want to attack people in a way that's going to attract the media, that's going to be a concern to other people who haven't been directly affected.

(Louis, 20 November 2005)

In the opening exchange of our dialogue Louis and I arrived at a familiar stance in understanding how distant witnesses and victims understand terrorism. Terrorism is a milieu of violence, media images, and an audience. I asked Louis to list five incidents of terrorism in order of significance to his working and daily life. He responded with the two London attacks (one that killed more than 50 people, the other two weeks later that failed when bombs malfunctioned and there were no casualties), Madrid, September 11 or as Louis described it, 'stuff in New York', and finally, since he was pressed to answer, he finally answered 'Bali'. He did not specify which Bali attack.

As it did for Sean, 9/11 formed a backdrop for Louis to talk about terrorism. Sean's 9/11 was part of the 'obvious' occurrences of terrorism. It did not need to be mentioned for its presence to be felt. Similarly for Louis, it warranted a mention that affirms its importance, obviousness and everydayness: 9/11 is that 'stuff in New York'. Not surprisingly Louis felt deeply affected by the Madrid bombings, the London bombings, and the attempted bombings in London two weeks later. Indeed, it was his job that this be his foremost concern. I argue that for many people it was the last of these events that would be most easily forgotten. Nobody died, nobody was maimed or injured, yet the transport network was still significantly interrupted. This attack was attempted on 21 July 2005 against the rail and bus commuter networks in London. Five bombs were planned to be detonated and the terrorists predicted that their bombs would cause massive damage and death. However, only the detonators of four of the bombs exploded causing minimal damage and only one minor injury. The fifth was dumped by the would-be bomber without attempting to detonate it. The rail and bus networks in London were completely shut down regardless. For Londoners terrorism was quickly becoming part of the everyday routine of life in the city. Their distant witnessing had suddenly become up-close witnessing: too close one could argue. Britain's then Prime Minister Tony Blair said after these bombings: 'Sept. (sic) 11 for me was a wake-up call. Do you know what I think the problem is? A lot of the world woke up for a short time and then turned over and went back to sleep again' (in Melvin, 2005). The day after these failed attacks an innocent young Brazilian, Jean Charles de Menezes, was shot in the head multiple times on a train in London by police officers who believed he was a suicide bomber poised to carry out an attack. Like a bad plot line in a B-grade movie, de Menezes was guilty of nothing but being a foreigner in a fearful city.

Louis primarily thought about the two London attacks and the Madrid attack when considering the possibility of terrorism affecting Melbourne. As he explained:

I guess from my perspective the bombings are probably the closest related to my day-to-day concerns as a public transport operator.

(Louis, 20 November 2005)

His choice of the word 'close' when referring to the London attacks is particularly noteworthy. Louis was not referring to a geographical closeness but a psychic and collegiate closeness. He *felt* close to these attacks: if this terrorism had occurred in Melbourne, it would profoundly and directly impact Louis' life. The London bombings figured heavily as the interview progressed and with every opportunity that presented Louis worked it in as an example. For example, in response to my question about whom he considered terrorists, Louis responded:

The London bombing again is one that comes to the top of the mind. They can be ordinary people who can, in the case of the London bombings, belong to the society. They don't need to be imported people. Sometimes they are. Sometimes it will be people come in from across borders. I understand in Lebanon, gee my Middle Eastern geography is not so good, was it in Lebanon where Iraqi's came in to carry out acts? Syria? ... But in the case of the London Bombings it was local Muslims from the UK who were well educated, employed members of the society there.

(Louis, 20 November 2005)

For other informants examples such as these were framed in their awareness of 9/11. I saw a different emphasis from Louis, and to some extent I saw something similar in Sean. What was apparent in these instances was a shift towards more personalized concerns. I asked Louis how he would describe the terrorist threat to Melbourne:

I think there is a real threat of terrorism in Melbourne in that Australia has been cited as being on the list of US allies but we are still participants in the coalition in Iraq and that our government is strongly supportive of the US actions in Iraq. We have got a significant Muslim population including some more radical elements. So I think there is the opportunity there and a reason for potentially choosing Melbourne as a target. Geographically we are actually a long way away. There are some bits of the world that are maybe more exciting for terrorists to attack. And I suppose also if I was looking at Australia just like a tourist, I would probably choose Sydney rather than Melbourne as a terrorist target.

(Louis, 20 November 2005)

I listened as Louis started by affirming the threat to Melbourne and then as he suggested that the city was not highly ranked as a target from the terrorists' perspective. Also encoded in his account is the widely and frequently articulated underlying belief that contemporary terrorism has something to do with Muslim populations. Terrorism perpetrated by Muslims has certainly received the bulk of the world's media attention and figured prominently in my conversations with respondents in this research.

Believing that terrorism was more likely in Sydney than it was in Melbourne was not, in Louis' opinion, an acceptable position to adopt given the responsibility he had to the company, its workers, customers and the general public. As the managing director of a public-transport organization with responsibility for the security of sites and fellow witnesses, Louis needed to engage in a variety of activities that lessened the possibility and impact of terrorism. I asked Louis whether he knew how people who worked in his organization felt about terrorism and whether the proactive position he adopted towards counter-terrorism had had an impact on others in the organization.

> *My impression is that they perceive that there is an increase in threat in the current environment just because there is probably an increase in terrorism throughout the world. But my belief is that I have seen from the way they operate, that they don't feel that it is something that they (pause), that makes them change the way they live and work. Either the way they approach their work or the willingness for coming to work in a transport operation.*
>
> (Louis, 20 November 2005)

Certainly there seemed to be consensus in some circles that there had been more terrorism in the world in contemporary times. This contemporary terrorism has been witnessed throughout the world, sometimes as distant events on television and in newspapers. While distant witnessing of 9/11 and terrorism has not caused a paralysis of the will and a befuddlement of the mind as Fromkin (1975: 684–85) once suggested, I argue that it is an additional burden to an already stressful, precarious and vulnerable city lifestyle.

Taking Action and Creating Images

Louis and the staff in his organization had undertaken a variety of activities and measures to protect sites under his control where terrorists could feasibly strike. Louis described at length his 'management security-level plan' that incorporated risk-management methods into a counter-terrorism protection and mitigation strategy. An evaluation of terrorism-related risks was undertaken by security managers and the possible impacts of terrorism that could significantly disrupt the organization were identified. At the management security-level, detailed plans were formulated for terrorism prevention, recovery and response. At the operational level, an awareness program was developed and scheduled for implementation in the weeks following our interview. This programme involved communicating the management level plan and identifying and establishing better staff awareness of terrorism threats. Louis pointed out that the awareness program did not involve 'sitting people down in classrooms', but rather a comprehensive sharing of the risk-analysis planning undertaken at the management level and the encouragement of a full and frank dialogue on the status of the terrorist threat to Melbourne and what it meant for the organization: 'Which means we understand that Australia is on a medium-level security alert and we don't believe that there is a significant risk of attack against [company name]' (Louis, 20 November 2005).

Staff would then undergo training in identifying potential threats to the organization during operating times. Staff would be trained to look out for suspicious packages and passenger behaviour, foster security awareness and develop techniques for responding to an incident or a threat. This would involve liaising with authorities, informing management and emergency services, and looking after themselves, passengers, customers and members of the public.

However, these extensive measures were not, according to Louis, primarily about physically securing the organization, its people and its infrastructure. Rather these measures were designed to create an image of safety, security and terrorism awareness to satisfy employees, government regulators, customers and the public.

> *I think it is important from both sides. That management demonstrate that we are interested, concerned and are doing something. But also that management demonstrate that we don't believe it is a big risk. That we are doing something, not because we are particularly concerned but we are doing something because we think it is the prudent thing to make sure we are at an appropriate level of alertness. But similarly if we are to be effective staff need to be aware of what they need to do, they need to participate, they need to be alert and have that interest in participation.*
>
> (Louis, 20 November 2005)

In short, counter-terrorism business security should always be implemented with the help, advice and support of the precariousness and vulnerable workers – it should never be imposed from above. In this way, counter-terrorism techniques may prove to be a method to build organizational cohesion and unity. Moreover, cynicism about the threat of terrorism must make way for being seen to be 'doing something' to protect the organization and the city from terrorism. Louis believed it was important for staff to see that the organization was taking the threat seriously and was willing to do something about it. Louis, seemingly sensing the perceptions of many Melburnians that terrorism was a significant threat, had responded in kind with a programme to mitigate and respond to a threat that he did not believe would materialize. Much as it was for Sean, terrorism represented a source of extra work for Louis, rather than physical danger.

There were significant changes to the operations of this organization associated with these measures to counter the threat of terrorism. In particular, organizational culture had to change to be more security-focused.

> *I think it [terrorism] has always got to be well down the list as a secondary part of the culture where the culture of the organization has to be customer service and it largely is. A customer service focused culture. I'm pretty confident, and I would be very disappointed if I found out differently, that we will be able to include a security awareness as part of the culture without staff's relationship to customers, passengers actually changing to become more distant or suspicious or anything like that.*
>
> (Louis, 20 November 2005)

Customer service would likely always come first in this public transport organization. Not only because of competitive pressures, but also because terrorism was not calculated to be a likely event. Despite being acutely aware of the terrorist's destruction in Madrid and London, and despite the significant planning that Louis believed he had undertaken that demonstrated his company's ability to be terrorism-aware, Louis believed that terrorists would likely strike elsewhere.

Louis had mentioned Muslim terrorists as part of his understanding of who terrorists are. I asked him what role race and religion played in his counter-terrorism plans and amongst his workforce.

> *It is something I'm concerned about. So that people who look different, the guy who looks like he is coming from the Middle East, and he has a backpack or he is carrying some luggage or a parcel or whatever, it is important that we don't as a matter of course act in a suspicious or unwelcoming way to those people. But my feeling is that our staff are so used to dealing with a big range of different people that they will continue to be welcoming to everybody who comes along. And I suppose in a way it is a reflection of, yeah we need to be as alert as we can about all of this terrorism stuff but if a terrorist comes along, unless they are actually acting terribly suspiciously they're going to be able to turn up and get onto our service and do whatever they want and I think that is the nature of public transport. It is an open service and we won't be able to do any sort of luggage or bag or body checks for mass transit services and be able to carry the same number of passengers. It just won't work. Even in London and New York everybody can walk onto the public transport systems with all the baggage they want.*
>
> (Louis, 20 November 2005)

Louis' arguments mirrored much of what Sean had already explained. A terrorist, particularly a suicide bomber, would most likely succeed if determined enough to carry out an attack. For industries of the kind that Sean and Louis managed, this apparent vulnerability poses particular problems for management and workers. It is perhaps noteworthy that Louis mentioned these inherent insecurities of public transport in response to questions about the role of race and religion in his counter-terrorism plans. Louis seemed to be suggesting that any form of racial and religious profiling would not be particularly effective for identifying possible terrorists – the fact is that many people of many different races and religions gain access to public transport on a daily basis. Overreacting at the sight of someone who might fit a simplistic stereotype of a terrorist can have significant consequences – the tragic and unnecessary death of Jean Charles de Menezes at the hands of some heavy-handed policing is testimony to this.

Public transport organizations have been targeted many times. Organizations have responded by spending money on counter-terrorism and security. Governments have encouraged the public to be vigilant and to report anything suspicious. Yet Louis believed that little could realistically be done to stop terrorism occurring. Louis' concerns stem less from his inability to fully secure his organization, to close all of the gaps, than from the added burden that creating simulated security – an image of safety – entails:

> *For me, I've got concerns on two levels. One is the real concern about doing something to address a threat for the obvious reasons that you don't want a threat to eventuate. The other one is from a liability perspective, which I don't like to be the reason to do something, but in a way it is almost* more *real. That I know that as someone in charge of a company's operations, there are a certain amount of things that you need to do to cover yourself and in a lot of ways that is driving me more than concern of a threat actually eventuating (emphasis in original).*
>
> (Louis, 20 November 2005)

Louis abided by a simple rule, and it is the golden rule, for security simulators in cities eager to create an image of safety: 'What would I say to the Coroner's Court or the Royal Commission to defend the company's and my actions?' (Louis, 20 November 2005).

In protecting his organization from terrorism, Louis adopted methods for simulating security by creating an image of safety. Rather than trying to provide complete, no-gaps security – a goal that Louis believed was not really attainable – he created security to a point where he could answer questions in front of a court, a coroner's inquest or a royal commission. I argue that Louis perceived a moral imperative, but it was an imperative that extended only to appearances, images, and simulations. The company had to seem as though it was doing all that it could to prevent terrorism and mitigate its impacts and, in a way, Louis was achieving this. It reminds me of a line from the Bret Easton Ellis (1991) novel, *American Psycho*: 'inside doesn't matter'. It is unsurprising that images of terrorism are perhaps best countered by more images: images that paint a picture of security and safety.

Louis believed that he had worked hard towards his goals for counter-terrorism security – he believed that he could show a Coroner's Court or a Royal Commission in great detail the actions taken by himself and his workers in responding to terrorism. I asked Louis to explain the practical steps that he had taken to protect – and be seen to protect – his workers and his company:

We've got two things we have done. One is a management-level security plan, risk analysis, where we have looked at the terrorism related security risks and looked at where we think those are likely to affect our business and what we should do about them. We have planned from a management perspective what our response would [be] ... what our preventative and our reactive measures are for terrorism instances.

(Louis, 20 November 2005)

Louis stressed the importance of strategic and management-level planning for setting the conditions for the organizational response to terrorism. This involved formulating plans for responding to worst-case scenarios and for responding to the day-to-day impacts of the threat of terrorism. Louis believed that these day-to-day impacts could be understood – albeit imperfectly – through the risk management mechanisms that he had adopted for his company. These mechanisms had been developed in association with local and national regulatory authorities and he had been keen to follow their advice which was considered in some security circles to be 'best practice'.

Louis also believed that the strategic and management-level planning was only part of the story. He argued that any counter-terrorism planning must primarily be focused on the management of precarious and vulnerable workers:

At the staff level we have prepared [counter-terrorism procedures] documentation and next week we roll out the training which is really an awareness programme – we are not sitting people down in class rooms. [The awareness programme] covers a few things. One is sharing with workers our risk analysis ... The other thing is the preventative things we are doing. Teaching people about the 'hot principle' for left items. Looking for suspicious people in just the normal day-to-day and typical actions that workers would be engaged in anyway – making sure in their normal process of end of trip checking of vehicles that they are aware of security as well as looking for rubbish and lost items as well. And then in terms of reactive things we have a very

brief procedure for them in the event of a terrorist or other major incident that could happen to us which is basically to notify the appropriate authorities, notify management, looking after themselves, customers and the general public, and cooperating with authorities.
(Louis, 20 November 2005)

The training programme that Louis developed for his company was designed to empower workers and to alleviate their fears by returning control of counter-terrorism to them. By training workers in 'terrorism awareness' managers and business leaders can foster a more securitized culture, provide workers with a sense of control over the amorphous and dreaded threat of terrorism, and alleviate their fears and anxieties. Perhaps more importantly terrorism awareness training can fulfill the need to be seen to be doing something. It can be used as evidence to defend the actions of managers and business leaders should an unpredictable and unpreventable act of terrorism occur. What is more, this training may provide the foresight and awareness to prevent terrorism from occurring or – at the very least – provide the necessary conditions in which an effective counter-terrorism response can be launched:

without overdoing it in terms of making something too complex I want to have a structure there that says I have done a risk assessment, I have looked at appropriate preventative measures … I've done an appropriate awareness program to make staff and management understand what they need to do and to understand perception of the risks. And I have put things in place so that if an event happens that we will react as appropriately as we can.
(Louis, 20 November 2005)

We can learn much from Louis' story about what businesses must do – and be seen to do – when responding to terrorism. I argue that Louis' counter-terrorism efforts were designed to confront terrorism as both an act of violence and as an emotion. Louis worked to communicate with his workers what he believed to be the state of the terrorism threat, he formulated plans for dealing with a threat that was unlikely to eventuate, and he worked to put the fears and anxieties of his workers in a context that stressed training and knowledge as weapons against the low-probability 'risk' that terrorism posed. Louis did these things lest he be required to testify at a Coroner's Court or a Royal Commission to explain his and his company's actions in preventing and mitigating the impact of terrorism on his business. In this way I argue that Louis and his colleagues relied on a sense of simulated security. He was aware that total security would be difficult and expensive to achieve – Louis did not think that airport-style security involving bomb detectors, metal detectors and closed-circuit television was possible without detracting from the customer service culture in his organization and causing more fear and anxiety for workers and customers. But by rolling out terrorism awareness training he believed that his company would be seen to be doing something to prevent the potential damage that an act of terrorism would be likely to cause.

Conclusion: The Security-Appearance Paradox

I will conclude this chapter by suggesting that there is an inherent paradox between security and appearance. Securitizing spaces and people is not about creating powerful, impenetrable, no-gaps security. Rather, it is about simulating security by creating an image of safety. I suggest that spaces and people only need to appear secure to maintain effective protection from terrorism. As such, those witnesses who are charged with protecting sites and fellow witnesses – workers, places and people – should not solely be trying to prevent the physical violence of terrorism; they should also be trying to prevent the emotion 'terror'. This is not to say that there should not be real security: real security can prevent ordinary crime and violence. But this security should not hope to stop an emotion. Preventing terrorism with security can be seen as a metaphor, much like the metaphor of the 'War on Drugs': police are not shooting syringes, pills and bottles on a battlefield. Security will not protect the witness against the emotion 'terror'. But it can put their minds at ease. Creating images of safety achieves this goal: it may be the only true counter-terrorism tactic.

In this sense, securing organizations, workers, spaces and people is primarily a task of image creation. If these practices of security simulation were prevalent in other organizations in Melbourne and other near and distant cities you may expect that it would be theatrically exposed from time to time. For example, in Dubai a two-year-old was detained after his name was registered on a terror-alert database. He was removed from his flight but later cleared of all wrongdoing (Associated Free Press, 2006). In New Zealand a dildo in a box arrived in customs only to be mistaken for a bomb. Security mechanisms were enacted and the 'Sex bomb' was placed in a bombproof safe. *The Daily Telegraph*'s Wellington correspondent (2007) explained: 'The incident has prompted a Customs investigation into why emergency services were not immediately contacted, leaving a potential bomb in a safe overnight'. On this occasion it was a sex aid, but the actions taken by Customs officials had demonstrated to witnesses that if it had been a real bomb, a potentially devastating explosion may have resulted. There was no real threat, but those in charge of security had failed in providing an image of safety and air travellers in New Zealand may be more anxious as a result. The paradox of security and appearance continues as long as nothing explodes. For as the distance between violence and witnesses disappear, understandings of terrorism change. The distant, dreaded threat can quickly become up close and violent. To be aware of this possibility is terrorism.

Witnesses who are responsible for organizations, workers, spaces and people in the city are compelled to close the gaps in security lest they find themselves before a coroner's inquest or a Royal Commission. Their response – to create an image of safety by simulating security – may do little to prevent violence, but it may prevent and mitigate terrorism. Images of safety foster faith and trust in the city's institutions and allow witnesses to engage in insecure and risky activities with peace of mind. This counter-terrorism prophylactic holds all of the content of the simulations described by Žižek (2002a): it is coffee without caffeine, beer without alcohol, war without casualties. Here the simulation re-emerges as security without security: an insecure security. What better weapon can one think of to counter powerful and terrifying images of terrorism? Perhaps business leaders and managers should devote much of their energies for counter-terrorism towards counter-imaging.

CHAPTER 7 Terror-work

An image, I believe, affects us directly, below the level of representation: at the level of intuition, of perception. At that level, the image is always an absolute surprise. At least it should be.
(Baudrillard, 2005: 91)

I'm used to it! Y'know, like cafeteria food or the constant threat of terrorism.
(JD, 'My Choosiest Choice of All', Episode 3.19, *Scrubs*).

You're only as good as your fans.
('Play Mistral For Me', *TISM*)

what science may never be able to explain is our ineffable fear of the alien among us; a fear which often drives us not to search for understanding, but to deceive, inveigle, and obfuscate. To obscure the truth not only from others, but from ourselves.
(Scully, 'Teliko', Episode 4, Series 4, *The X-Files*)

Introduction: The Spectator

In this book I have attempted to demonstrate how the spectacular terrorist attacks on 9/11, 3/11 and 7/7 have had many profound affects and consequences for working people and businesses in contemporary cities. I have argued at times throughout this book that contemporary terrorism has been spectacular and monumental while also, perhaps paradoxically, mundane, routine, everyday and banal. Much like JD's comment from the popular television programme *Scrubs*, the threat of terrorism is something that everyone has had to adjust to. I have suggested that terrorism is popularly understood as a contranymous concept that ranges between acts of physical violence and the emotion *terror*. Terrorists choreographed the 9/11, 3/11 and 7/7 attacks so that there would be a lot of people watching, not just a lot of people dead. These events were certainly successful in achieving this end. Moreover, through these events, terrorists have exhibited their unique penchant for targeting working people. I doubt that this represents a divine hatred of the need to work or even toward capitalist economies. Rather, I suggest that targeting working people and businesses can be viewed as strikes against what it means to be human in so-called 'Western', 'industrialized' and 'developed' cities. The everyday and routine mortgaged, car-loaned, entertainment-driven contemporary consumer would likely not survive for long without steady employment. Perhaps for the same reasons even the casualized and part-time workforces may be expected to have a particularly acute fear of terrorism.

In this concluding chapter, I argue that there exists a powerful and terrifying link between terrorism, workers and businesses. In some respects, this represents a leap.

Terrorism can perhaps in one sense be seen to form part of the amorphous external business environment. But it is my argument in this concluding chapter that terrorism is – in a post-9/11, -3/11 and -7/7 world – an integral part of 'business ... being business' (Virilio, 2002: 100).

I do not want the leap to stand alone, however. The outcome of this leap, I suggest, can also be seen as a logical outcome of the argument and evidence I have presented to this point. In many respects this book has come full circle. I wanted to demonstrate that images hold meanings that exist in multiple configurations of time and space. Images are – by their very nature – vague and ambiguous, yet persuasive and seductive. Pictures and images can attract witnesses and audiences and generate victims in a time of terror. Because working people are the targets of choice for contemporary terrorists they – and the businesses that employ them – are positioned as especially precarious and vulnerable. Sometimes, if the image is special, it can be a spectacle that attracts something more than an audience. The spectacular image, I suggest, attracts spectators: cheering, screeching, yelling and shouting spectators – as the quote from Australian alternative band *TISM* suggests, terrorism perhaps only has meaning through its fan base. Terrorism is only as powerful as the audiences of witnesses and victims allow. The terrorism debates that have occurred during critical moments when terrorism filled journalistic spaces have the unmistakable feel of a supportership and a fan base – who do you support in protecting the world from terrorism? Are you with us or with the terrorists? – to borrow an aphorism from George W. Bush. While distance and the city remain critical points of convergence for understanding the impact of images of terrorism on witnesses across time and space, I suggest that they can be superseded. This is partly because distance is problematized by the image. When the image evolves, distance devolves. Terror-work – representing the everyday, mundane, routine and banal world of work and business threatened by terrorism – has little role for distance, but it still relies on locations and sites. Here the city is a site of convenience, and the spectacle of terrorism can be consumed wherever images can be witnessed.

I set out in this book to show how contemporary terrorism has consequences for working people and businesses in contemporary cities. I also wanted to show how terrorism transcends the time and space in which it first occurred – the flashpoint – in order for it to be reanimated as an image over and over again. In this way, the Twin Towers continue to fall and trains and buses continue to explode in the minds of the world's workers. These attacks set in motion powerful forces that continue to play a significant role in war, politics and society. I wanted to show that terrorists wanted people watching, not just corpses. I hope to demonstrate here that terrorism does not occur where there is death and destruction – this is violence – but where people witness terrorism as a simulation, an image and a spectacle. In short, terrorism exists where terror is felt.

Terrorism as Political Violence and Emotional Response

For some of the best analysis of the meaning of terrorism, one can go to the modern origins of terrorism studies and the work of Paul Wilkinson (1974). I suggest that Wilkinson's (1974: 9) lessons have almost been forgotten, but they are worth revisiting in this concluding chapter.

What do we mean when we speak of terror? In its most important and general sense the term signifies a psychic state of great fear and dread. Our modern words terror, terrorize, terrible, terrorism, and deterrent, are derived from the Latin verbs terrere, to tremble or to cause to tremble, and deterrere, to frighten from. The word terror also came to mean the action or quality of causing dread and, alternatively, a person, object or force, inspiring dread.

(Wilkinson, 1974: 9)

This conception of terrorism should resonate with working people and business – *terrorism* can involve inspiring terror and deterring terror. Terrorism and the responses to terrorism are linked in complex and powerful ways. Humankind has always tolerated fear and dread and the many forms that fear and dread take. Wilkinson (1974: 9) argued that 'Mankind's only final defence against the King of Terrors has been his (sic) beliefs in a form of life after death, his small cries of faith in the face of disaster'. In contemporary times of terror, an unwavering faith in life after death has been associated more with the problem of terrorism than as a form of 'defence'. It is more likely that the best security from terrorism can be found in the institutions that sustain city living and working. Or at least, I suggest, this is what many believe.

In spite of the many diverse consequences of feelings of fear and dread, for people experiencing these emotional states there can be many constants. Gardner's (2008: 27) exploration of the biological and evolutionary meaning of fear can highlight the importance of fear for safety and survival but also how fear and dread are rarely the products of a process of rational understanding or the examination of evidence.

The rather uncomfortable feeling most of us have when we're around snakes is evidence of how this ancient experience continues to influence us today. Throughout the long prehistory of our species and those that preceded it, snakes were a mortal threat ... So natural selection did its work and the rule – beware snakes – was ultimately hard-wired into every human brain. It's universal.

(Gardner, 2008: 28)

This holds, according to Gardner (2008), for all cultures and societies on the planet, even for those who never encounter snakes. Moreover, he argues that this holds for primates in laboratories. In short, humans fear snakes whether this fear originates from learned experience or otherwise. Naturally, not everybody is afraid of snakes. Some people have been socialized into close association with snakes.

In responding to *terrorism*, business leaders and managers must not lose sight of its complex meaning. As Wilkinson (1974: 11–12) highlighted: 'It is ... important to bear in mind that terror is in the heart and mind of the victim, it is a *subjective* experience. Individual reactions to terroristic experience will vary according to their individual psychology and situation'. Yet some situations will have many things in common with other situations. Contemporary terrorists have shown a particular penchant for targeting working people and working people throughout the world share a uniquely devised vulnerability. Working people and businesses have been used for spectacular terroristic effect and terrorism works best as a tactic when 'its psychological effects are out of proportion to its purely physical result' (Wilkinson, 1974: 13). In this way, terrorism might be viewed as the snake in the grass of the working world. Terrorism is feared almost instinctively – this may prove to be an important survival mechanism. That is unless fearing and dreading terrorism becomes more damaging than terrorist violence itself.

Terrorism and Multiculturalism

Bryan Turner (2006: 126) argues that despite extraordinary medical, scientific and technological advancement human life has not been made considerably less-vulnerable or precarious. Similarly, I argue that despite many billions of dollars being spent on so-called counterterrorism and anti-terrorism efforts (Stiglitz and Bilmes, 2008; Wilson, 2007), working people and businesses are not considerably safer or more secure. This should not be misconstrued as an argument supporting the possibility of complete and total security – I argue, following Turner (2006), that vulnerability is a universally experienced human-condition. According to Turner (2006: 127) 'We suffer because we are vulnerable, and we need, above all else, institutions that will give us some degree of security'. This is why working people know their insecure workplaces are vulnerable to terrorism. This is why witnesses and victims feel empathy for the victims of terrorism – those people killed live on television on 9/11, and those people dragged out of the burning public transport networks on 3/11 and 7/7 in plain view of the world's cameras. This is why city-dwellers who see terrorism in New York, Madrid and London know that Berlin, Buenos Aires, Melbourne and Glasgow are also vulnerable and probably targets of terrorism (indeed these cities have all experienced terrorism in one form or another).

Businesses in cities throughout the world rely heavily on their multicultural workforces. During times of terror, the so-called multicultural harmony of the city is revealed in its frailty. For Žižek (2002a: 11), multiculturalism refers to little more than 'the Other deprived of their Otherness'. In this way multiculturalism can be seen as a site of oppression where some people praise the 'idealized Other who dances fascinating dances' or produces international cuisine and services yet refers disparagingly towards those who don't work, learn to speak the domestic language, or socialize outside narrow cultural groups. This distinction is important but problematic. For Turner (2006: 129–31) there is a quirk in the contemporary English language. This quirk begins at the origin of the word(s) 'stranger/guest'. Its Latin origins are *hostis* and *hospes* – hospes is the origin of 'hospitality', whereas hostis is the origin of 'enemy'. As such strangers/guests can be seen as 'favourable' or 'hostile' especially when they live among the 'local' community. The similar origin can be found in the Greek 'xenos' – meaning stranger – from which the contemporary English word 'xenophobia' is derived. The xenos could easily enter 'xenia', or social contracts. The quirk arises where contemporary English has not evolved an opposing force to xenophobia – such as 'xenophilia' to follow Turner's (2006: 130) example: 'This absence [of an alternative to xenophobia] is telling. It seems that there is no linguistic possibility for the love of strangers; there is simply no social role for a stranger who can become an object of genuine friendship'.

Perhaps partly as a result of this, during times of terror it can be commonplace to see 'hardened attitudes' (Turner, 2006: 133) towards immigration, foreigners and the appearance or image of difference (Pickering, 2005). Pickering (2005: 32) has described this as the 'racialized deviant'. For Pickering (2005: 32) the media employs 'banal opinion' and the doctrine of 'common sense' to frame refugees and asylum seekers as criminal, illegal and deviant. Similarly, I suggest that much of the post-9/11 reporting in

Australia during times of terror has adopted the cultural position of 'us' versus 'them'. This reporting, in Manning's (2006) view, spins and confuses information to the point where there is as much information to be found between the lines as can be found within media discourse itself.

> *It would be easy to argue that Arabs and Muslims are getting bad press because, since September 11, 2001, it is they who have been responsible for some of the worst terrorist excesses in modern history, from the attacks on New York's World Trade Center, to Madrid, then Bali and then London. And how many more have been prevented by vigilant police action? You could argue that but you'd be wrong. Arabs and Muslims were getting bad press long before September 11.*
>
> (Manning, 2006: 13)

More generally, the so-called 'War on Terror' has become a site for anxieties directed towards those who look, speak, dress and act differently. Yet the London bombings were not carried out by foreigners, but members of a city-dwelling and multicultural lifestyle:

> *The aftermath of 7/7 is, at least for Europeans, more significant than 9/11, because the bombings and attempted bombings in London were undertaken by British citizens, the children of migrants and asylum seekers ... the 'friendly stranger' is now the 'hostile stranger'.*
>
> (Turner, 2006: 133)

In this way, terrorists hide in plain sight, and our friends may be enemies. The stories of working people that were explored in Chapters 5 and 6 should be alarming tales for business leaders and managers. 'When I think about terrorists and the terrorist threats I think about *the* certain race'; 'As soon as an Arabian, a Musso, as soon as a Muslim walked in, what I classified as a Mussi, I would genuinely try to stay away from them'; 'I hate them' (Patrick, 21 February 2005) – these are perhaps some of the signposts of the post-9/11 workplace.

How business leaders and managers deal with these dilemmas will have significant consequences for organizational profitability and cohesion. Through the data and information that I have presented in this book, I argue that these dilemmas do not represent an insurmountable challenge. Yet an inability to confront these challenges – even if these confrontations are unsuccessful – may result in legal and moral blowback as a result of a corporate image defined by perceived discrimination and intolerance, a conflictual and demotivated workforce, and poor inter- and extra-organizational relationships.

Designing Out Terrorism Through Social Architecture

So, what can be done? How does one 'respond' to terrorism when it is both an act of violence and an emotion? Perhaps if one can understand what terrorists are seeking to achieve then perhaps steps can be taken to 'design out' the terrorism problem. Wilkinson (1974: 18) argued that terrorists design their violence for 'symbolic' value particularly when they seek to 'implant a sense of insecurity and fear in a specific group'. While I do not suggest that contemporary terrorists are anti-capitalist or that they have a particular vendetta against working people and businesses, I argue that workplaces represent locations where one can reliably expect people to act in a relatively predictable manner. Terrorists in this view should be considered astute social observers – social scientists perhaps. Their unique understanding of what makes people fearful belies the flailing response of some groups to terrorist violence. Terrorists understand that people attend work in cities at somewhere between 8am and 9am each weekday morning. They know that for some time before this people will be travelling to work. They know that lunches will be taken at some point between midday and 2pm. They most likely know that coffee, sugar and nicotine cravings may hit at mid-morning and again in the mid-afternoon. They know that people will finish work at some time around 5pm and will be travelling home some time after. These are sweeping generalizations, and the increasingly casualization of work and the adaptation to new technologies for communication and work continue to deteriorate these mainstays of city-working. Yet, the adherence to these glib generalizations served the 9/11, 3/11 and 7/7 terrorists well! Insecurity and fear has been successfully implanted.

It should therefore be the goal of all business leaders and managers to rigorously 'design out' terrorism and the threat it poses. This could involve building and architectural considerations and physical security improvements. Considerable theorizing and study has been devoted towards designing out security threats and terrorism, and even to designing out fear. Security is deeply ingrained in the Western, city-dwelling psyche and according to de Muynck (2004: 8) 'There can be no doubt that within the contemporary Western condition, fear is the driving force behind the (re-)organization of the public and private space'. The attempt to expel fear and dread from city and organizational spaces can take many forms – security technologies, risk management plans and policies, and a fortress-oriented culture. These 'Prosthetic elements' work to keep 'chance at bay' (de Muynck, 2004: 10). It is an attempt to predict the unpredictable and secure against the 'unsecurable'. After all, terrorism is also an emotion and a state of mind – not merely a political tactic. Organizational security measures are often prosthetic, inherently fictitious, empty and fake. Or, as I have suggested in these pages, *simulated*. As we heard from Louis, a business leader and manager in a Melbourne public transport company, and Sean, a security manager at a major events venue, there is little potential for people in businesses to provide complete, no-gaps security. But the appearance or image of security can be achieved. These appearances combined with some practical security measures such as awareness training can go some way towards mitigating the contranymity of terrorism.

People in organizations can become paralyzed by fear and an obsession with eliminating all risks, dangers and threats (Hauben and Vermeulen, 2004: 6). These obsessions are leaving visible and social traces. Suspicion, hostility and angst have become commonplace in the world's cities and organizations in times of terror. The Twin Towers were once a symbol of power, prosperity and corporate affluence. Their destruction has forged a new view of the proud and tall city-building – they represent 'impotence and fear' (Küng, 2004: 88).

Attempting to design out the dangers, risks and threats of terrorism has long been at the forefront of architectural thinking. The buildings and architecture of mediaeval Europe are locations for historical curiosity (Harbison, 1991: 67), but they also represent an important insight into the lives of people living in Europe at that time. The security oriented and designed fortresses of Europe point to an underlying anxiety associated with the built environment. Viewed in this way the built environment represent 'bits of conscious display' (Harbison, 1991: 67). I suggest that this same anxiety can be seen in the world's cities. Grosz (1995) has similarly emphasized the importance of understanding the relationship between people and the built environment. For Grosz (1995: 105) 'The city is a product not simply of the muscles and energy of the body, but of the conceptual and reflective possibilities of consciousness itself'. For example:

> *In certain parts of Scotland one comes across fortified churches as one does in southwestern France. To us it is an impossible contradiction and sends us looking for signs of religious conflict, not just an unsettled political climate. We assume that this form would never have been hit on until the building's predecessor or another nearby had been flattened in a raid; it only makes sense as the fruit of bitter experience.*
>
> (Harbison, 1991: 74)

It is this 'bitter experience' that partly constitutes the contemporary organizational experience with terrorism and security in cities. In a complex 21st century where time and space have been shrunk – in some respects, shrunk to a singular point of time and space as in the cases of virtual and televisual spaces – by rapid advances in communication and travel technologies, the concept of 'nearby' is not as clear as it first appears. Indeed, I have argued at length in this book that images of contemporary terrorism – best exemplified in simulations and images of 9/11, 3/11 and 7/7 – make cities throughout the world in many respects 'nearby'. Melbourne may not be 'nearby' to London, Madrid and New York in a geographical sense, but they are certainly nearby in spirit. As I argued in Chapter 2, the problematic nature of distance in understanding terrorism brings images of terrorism to the forefront of understanding the consequences of terror for working people and businesses.

It is within the confines of organizational spaces in cities that the human body interacts with other bodies forming the social architecture of precarious and vulnerable city-living (see Grosz, 1995: 104–110). In this way we can view the body and the city as intersecting architectures – the body, the social, and the city – and each are as vulnerable and precarious as the next. Organizations, corporations, managers and employees are at home in the city. The city is a place to which people flock to benefit from the social, cultural and employment opportunities that organizations in cities provide.

Risk, Dread and the Human Brain

Throughout this book, I have steered away from the language of risk for understanding the meanings and consequences of terrorism for working people and businesses. I did this because just as the imperfect human-mind cannot be relied upon for rational judgements and decision-making based on cost-benefit analyses, nor can the 'organization' – made up as it is of fleshy and precarious humans – be relied upon to make decisions about risk, safety and security when these decisions do not improve efficiency, effectiveness and profitability. Human risk evaluation has been theorized by Slovic (in Gardner, 2008: 17) to be a product of two decision-making logics – 'System One and System Two'. System One represents 'Feeling' – a type of instinctual response that works often outside of conscious awareness (Gardner, 2008: 18). It is a reflex reaction that tells the observer when to fear, when to run and hide, and when to flee to safety. System two represents 'Reason'. It calculates the risks, makes a judgement, and plans the most efficient and effective course of action. Gardner's (2008) explanation of biological responses to fear shares many commonalities with my conceptions of *the order of risk* and *the order of dread*. Generally speaking, system one represents a dread response and system two represents a risk response. One embodies calculation, one embodies reaction.

Following for a moment the metaphor of the organization as a brain as argued by Morgan (1997: 73), is not the organization subject to the same kinds of system one and two logics? Does the organization not – in a whole host of ways – sometimes offer a calculated response, sometimes a knee-jerk reaction? The board of directors, the managers and company stewards will routinely respond to fear and dread in the system two manner – through rational, calculated, well organized and well-conceived responses. Yet, what of the throngs of precarious and vulnerable employees? Most can be expected to respond on instinct, not burdened by many of the crucial and everyday decisions that keep organizational wheels in motion. When employees see the snake in the grass, their instinct may be to flee to safety. For managers, business leaders and stewards – people who are paid to make calculated decisions – the response can be expected to be calculated, organized and considered. But what are the consequences of these responses?

In the aftermath of 9/11, America's Vice President Dick Cheney explained that there may never be an 'end date' in the struggle against terrorism (in Mueller, 2008: 7). This certainly seems to be true. As I write there seems to be little scope for forgetting the most spectacular acts of terrorism on 9/11, 3/11 and 7/7. It is perhaps likely that at some point new date coordinates will join the big three. I do not suggest that terrorism should be considered a likely occurrence – as Mueller (2008) points out, while around 300 people die every year at the hands of international terrorists, more will drown in their baths – but as I have argued, I don't believe that people are well equipped to consider probability, likelihood and consequences in responding to terrorism, especially when terror is delivered as high-impact and spectacular media images. As Mueller (2008: 7) argues: 'Terrorism and the attendant "war" thereon have become fully embedded in the public consciousness, with the effect that politicians and bureaucrats have become as wary of appearing soft on terrorism as they are about appearing soft on drugs, or as they once were about appearing soft on Communism'.

Keeping up appearances is vitally important for responding to terrorism. The power of images and simulations of terrorism depicted in the global media can perhaps be cured by the power of images and simulations of safety and security. There is perhaps an amusing irony in this. Žižek (2004: 508) argues that 'action and reaction should coincide' and that in an idealized world the danger – 'the very thing that causes damage' – should also be the medicine. For Žižek (2004) the ultimate example is chocolate laxatives – the relief from constipation finds itself captured within the cause of constipation. Another example is Cherry Beer. Cherry syrup and juice has been used to treat gout – alcohol contributes to gout. Žižek (2004: 508) believes that throughout society and culture people strive to find solutions that 'reproduce the paradox of the chocolate laxative' and 'the structure of a product containing the agent of its own containment can be discerned throughout today's ideological landscape'. I suggest that images of terrorism and the business response epitomizes this paradox. Images of safety and security are crucial in combating the terrorism contranym – both terrorism as political violence, and the emotional terrorism, are vulnerable to the appearance of effective security.

I do not intend to suggest that security should be lax, ill-thought out, or shallow. What I am suggesting is that security will never be complete. This incompleteness, however, can be filled with simulated security. Would-be terrorists will likely not risk an unsuccessful attack by attempting to target a secure-looking business and the emotional consequences of terrorism can be mitigated by creating the right images of a safe and secure workplace. There is an inherent danger in this though as these measures may do little more than displace terrorism from one workplace, mass gathering or public transport network to another.

> *We can ... expect continued efforts to reduce the country's 'vulnerability' despite at least three confounding realities: There is an essentially infinite number of potential terrorist targets; the probability that any one of those targets will be hit by a terrorist attack is essentially zero; and inventive terrorists, should they ever actually show up, are free to redirect their attention from a target that might enjoy a degree of protection to one of the many that don't.*
> (Mueller, 2008: 10)

But simulated security does answer one important question for business leaders and managers – 'What would I say to the Coroner's Court or the Royal Commission to defend the company's and my actions?' (Louis, 20 November 2005).

Certainly, despite the unlikelihood of terrorism, no business leader or manager – or employee for that matter – could simply suggest that terrorism will not happen and declare that no safety and security measures will be undertaken. In many of the world's cities there is some shared consensus that terrorism poses some sort of threat. This notion is perpetuated in political and 'expert' commentary and by spectacular journalism to the point where it becomes 'unwise, even disastrous' to suggest that the terrorist threat is overblown, exaggerated, or unlikely to eventuate (Mueller, 2008: 8). Moreover, terrorism has generated a 'political atmosphere' that creates a space for 'government and assorted pork-barrelers' to fill with excessive expenditures devoted towards countering terrorism and the threat it poses.

The Everydayness of Terror-work

Wessely (2005: 548) tells a story of his experiences in the aftermath of the 7/7 bombings:

> *Three days after the bombings, I joined the crowds celebrating the 60th anniversary of the end of the Second World War. The sun shone, and the Mall was full of old, proud men, wearing polished medals and fading berets ... The following day, England played Australia at cricket, and all seemed normal – including the resounding English defeat. True, there were more police than usual and we now had to enter the grounds by way of metal detectors, but the rituals of a London summer had returned.*

For many other Londoners, there was no quick recovery. Some people's lives in London – and indeed Madrid, New York and Washington DC – have changed dramatically and irreversibly. Some have experienced 'intense mental anguish, an anguish that is painful for the rest of us even to witness' (Wessely, 2005: 548). Quick recovery or slow recovery – either way life has to return to normal. Terrorism has to be incorporated into the routines, mundaneness and banality of living and working in the city. Then, as London was reeling from the 7/7 attacks, the attempted attacks of 21 July showed Londoners that their city was a prime target for international terrorism. Again, the target was public transport. London was perhaps becoming, as some journalists suggested, 'a city in trauma' (see Wessely, 2005: 550). Traumascapes like the contemporary city during times of terror are a place where the seemingly constant threat of terrorism is accommodated into everydayness and routines of living and working in the city.

Consider ABC news-anchor Charles Gibson's (in Mueller, 2008: 8) assessment on the fifth anniversary of 9/11: 'Putting your child on a school bus or driving across a bridge or just going to the mall – each of these things is a small act of courage – and peril is part of everyday life'. These 'small acts of courage' perhaps characterize the routine, everyday and most banal aspects of life and work in the city – terrorism may arrive in spectacular imagery, but it is quickly incorporated into the existential happenings of mundane working and living.

Witnessing is the key to understanding the everydayness of terrorism. Witnessing should be viewed in this context as 'seeing; attesting; standing publicly accountable for, and psychically vulnerable to, one's visions and representations' (Haraway, 1997: 267). Witnesses and victims of terrorism become core components in the corporate and 'sociotechnical' order of society bound to time and space, sites and locations, institutions and routines where 'Witnessing is a collective, limited practice that depends on the constructed and never finished credibility of those who do it, all of whom are mortal, fallible, and fraught with the consequences of unconscious and disowned desires and fears' (Haraway, 1997: 267).

This would seem to be a crucial point for working people as witnesses and victims of terrorism. These 'desires and fears' – the desire for security and safety both physically and emotionally, embodied in the quest to hold perceptions of vulnerability and precariousness at bay, and the quite natural and routine fear and dread of being caught up in a time of terror – structure our lives, our homes, our cities and our workplaces as evidenced in physical and social architectures and security. The situated knowledges of witnesses and victims involve all of these dimensions and are expressed through the many stories that have emerged following moments when terrorists targeted workers.

Bartel (2002: 240) shares a series of 'personal observations' of the emotional, psychological and behavioural consequences of the 9/11 terrorist attacks for New Yorkers. Bartel (2002) is the stereotypical New Yorker that audiences of popular culture have become accustomed to in situated comedies such as *Seinfeld* and *Friends*. Caroline Bartel (2002: 240) is a native of New York – 'born in Queens and raised in Long Island' – the same locations where many of the characters in *Friends* were raised. She describes the 9/11 attacks as terror against the city itself and against the identity of New Yorkers. Bartel (2002: 241) argues that New Yorkers turned to public congregation and social networks to deal with the grief, the anxiety and the renewed sense of precariousness and vulnerability that 9/11 caused. Social organization and cooperation offers a potential 'antidote' for anxiety and fear. The business, the corporation, and the organization would seem to have a crucial role to play in managing terrorist threats. The corporation becomes a critical site for not just social cohesion, networking and socialization. The corporation is transformed in the post-9/11 world to a critical site for counter-terrorism policy and practice – a social laboratory for counter-terrorism.

It is in this spirit that Wrzesniewski (2002) proclaims her post-9/11 workplace to represent more than just a job. In a time of terror people reassess life priorities. Family and friendships enjoy renewed significance, social and cultural communities confront new challenges, and the mundane and routine pursuit of work and a career can suddenly seem insignificant. Alexander and Alexander (2002) theorize that during terror scares managers can expect working people to be absent more frequently, to take leave as soon as it accrues, and be less motivated, efficient and productive. Wrzesniewski (2002) argues that the very meaning of work needs to be critically re-examined in times of terror.

Richard Sennett (1998: 135) once wrote, 'In the flexible, fragmented present it may seem possible only to create coherent narratives about what has been, and no longer possible to create predictive narratives about what will be'. The workplace in a time of terror shares the dilemmas that Sennett's research identifies. Terrorism as a whole has been reanimated in the latest particular terror scare many times in the contemporary city in routine, mundane and everyday ways and in multiple configurations of time and space. Whether on television, in newspapers, on the internet or in the minds of a distant audience of witnesses and victims, images of terrorism at critical moments in time and space appear and reappear in routine and banal ways – terrorism quickly becomes formative of a new narrative of life and work. I suggest that this is a reasonable response to the dreaded consequences of a threat that is difficult to define. Perhaps this is why terrorism and the images that it generates and sustains, like football teams, has spectators – cheering, screaming spectators. As such, spectators can encounter television news and journalistic spaces daily to see terrorism reported and reanimated. Spectators can view terrifying and powerful images and choose sides in debates about terrorism. Am I for or against strict terror laws? Are terrorists evil-doers or freedom fighters? These spectators can contribute to the spectacle that they are subjected to. They can write journalistic articles, opinion editorials and letters to the editor. They are fans of terrorism as spectacle. They are the spectators of terror-work.

But what is the driving force behind this spectatorship? I suggest that what people desired more than anything was the 'spectacle of banality' (Baudrillard, 2001).

It is the obscene spectacle of nullity, insignificance, and platitude. This stands as the complete opposite of the theatre of cruelty. But perhaps there is still a form of cruelty, at least a virtual one, attached to such a banality. At a time when television and the media in general are less and less capable of accounting for the world's (unbearable) events, they rediscover daily life.

Perhaps this rediscovery of daily life is the reason that counter-terrorism and security is the theme of Australia's highest rating television programme *Border Patrol*. Or why the drama series *24* rates highly all over the world, and why people flock to blockbuster disaster movies based on the 9/11 terrorist attacks that contain *real* flight crews. They all represent the ushering of terrorism into the everyday as a way of making routine these otherwise unbearable world events. In the post-9/11 world,[1] the event is reanimated, reconstituted, and re-depicted in images that simulate violence and offer it for consumption – this, I argue, is a crucial coordinate of terror-work.

Terror-work represents the mundane and everyday image that belies deep anxieties and fears held by consuming audiences – audiences in which city-dwelling workers are contemporarily well represented. As Elliott (2007: 145) argues 'the flickering media surfaces of postmodern culture are … mirrored internally, so that a narcissistic preoccupation with

---

1 And indeed the pre-9/11 world. See Laqueur (1987), Chapter 5, pp. 174–202.

appearance, image and style dominates the regulation of the self'. A popular image from New York City on 9/11 illustrates my argument. The image represents the most mundane and routine of scenarios. Five young men and women sit chatting on a sunny morning next to a body of water. They appear relaxed, comfortable and jovial. In the background, smoke billows from the island of Manhattan as the Twin Towers burn. The young people are relaxed, enjoying a sunny New York morning. I suggest that this photograph can be viewed as a reminder that spectacular events such as terrorism can be depicted as everyday parts of life in the city, and that their occurrence is banal, everyday and routine.

Terrorism, counter-terrorism, security, and images of safety have all equally become part of the everyday. We all accept extra security at airports and at major events. Banal stories appear in newspapers, on television and radio news, and images of terrorism are always available on the Internet. Terrorism features in television dramas, major movies, and advertising. But banal events and banal images can have considerable consequences. I suggest that 'images' of terrorism are not merely images. They are special, and represent something more. They represent critical points where images become spectacles. The word 'image', much like the word 'witness', suggests something passive. The spectacle suggests something engaging and interactive. People passively observe images, but actively engage – and sometimes help create – spectacles. Terror-work relies on this spectacular quality of images. Images are dull, banal and often boring. I argue that spectacles may be as well, but they appear as though they are not. Baudrillard (2005) argued that images matter most in their impact: 'whether they are true or false is beside the point'.

> *We are henceforth – and forever – in a state of uncertainty where images are concerned. Only their impact counts ... They no longer represent; they no longer imply either distance or perception or judgement. They are no longer of the order of representation, or of information in the strict sense and, as a result, the question of whether they should be produced, reproduced, broadcast or banned, and even the 'essential' question of whether they are true or false, is 'irrelevant'.*
>
> (Baudrillard, 2005: 24)

I argue, like Baudrillard, that the impact of the spectacle is one of excess: an excess of seeing, an excess of destruction, and an excess of attraction. Predictably, the response was also excessive. It should be of little surprise that whilst the 9/11 terrorist attacks cost around $500,000 to carry out, recent estimates have put the self-inflicted economic and political consequences of 9/11 at a cost of $500 billion (Mueller, 2008: 13). Invasion and war in the name of 9/11 has claimed far more lives than the terror itself. Yet it could be argued that the response to 9/11 was no more or less proportionate than the reaction to other spectacles. Marilyn Manson's tours still attract protests from various segments of the community, as do those of Eminem and Snoop Doggy Dogg. The release of the film *American Psycho,* based on the novel about the serial killer Patrick Bateman written by Bret Easton Ellis, also attracted protesters at publishing houses that distributed the book. For some, spectacles spark horror and disgust. For others they are consumable commodities that fulfill fantasies. The spectacle can sometimes be sickly sweet through its paradoxical abhorrence and the excitement it exerts. Its appeal is as predictable as the outcries of opposition.

A Witness, a Worker, a Theatre

As a witness walking the streets of Melbourne one may see many sites where the theatre of terrorism might be performed and who the players might be. An opportune image strikes witnesses peering across the street to Southern Cross station from the corner of Spencer and Collins streets. This vantage point captures the prominent signage over the walkway into Southern Cross in the foreground – the bold lettering at the entrance to the stylishly renovated station completed just prior to the 2006 Commonwealth Games – and the glistening neon highlighting one of Melbourne's major sporting stadiums, the *Telstra Dome*, in the background. Turning around on that spot has the witness facing one of the Southern Hemisphere's tallest buildings, the Rialto, that has an entirely glass façade. It is a shared space for terror scares, witnessing, victimizing, working and business and the potential reanimation of terrorism as a spectacle. Any terrorist attack in this corridor of notable locations would create witnesses and victims both near and far and would strike at the heart of Melbourne as a place for business, a travel destination and a centre for leisure. Cameras would closely follow, deployed from the major television networks with head offices in Melbourne's inner suburbs a few kilometres away. The offices of the major Australian newspapers *The Age*, the *Herald Sun* and *The Australian* are within a few hundred metres.

I will most likely always get a little jolt from standing on the corner of Collins and Spencer. The site for the spectacle of terrorism may be at major sporting events and other major events, at rail and bus stations, at tall buildings, and at prominent mall strips and street corners in the world's cities. Simply stated, terrorism occurs not where there are flames and explosions, this is violence, but where the image potential is optimal. This is where the fear and dread reside – this is terrorism.

Melbourne – like most of the world's cities – possesses many stages from which terror can be theatrically displayed. I was a spectator at the Melbourne Cricket Ground (MCG) on days two and three of the Boxing Day Test in 2006 where two leading cricketing nations faced off in the 'Battle for the Ashes'. Adversaries on the cricket field, off it Australia and the United Kingdom are powerful strategic and political allies that share ideologies, spirituality and bloodline. The nations are militarily and economically aligned and are actively engaged and linked in many ways, in many parts of the world. The venue for this sports mega-spectacle, the MCG, was nearly full as play commenced on the second day (first-day tickets remain elusive) and I sat among fellow witnesses and victims of terrorism and its reanimation in terror scares in this distant city. As always, security was highly visible yet relaxed and friendly. With the world's cameras fixed on the centre pitch, the match proceeded and concluded without incident. I wondered at how different the game had seemed on television, as attending spectator sports is always a different experience to watching from home with its real-time statistics, the hyper-knowability of the athletes and their lives, and the slow motion and freeze frames of the human form at moments of stunning athletic prowess, embodied beauty, and sickening collision. I wondered, if a terrorist attack had occurred that day, how it would have seemed to witnesses watching at home and in distant cities.

We're Proceeding, at Least on the Surface, as if Things are Normal

I would like to conclude here by suggesting that managers and business leaders must assume that terrorists will target their businesses, even though they almost certainly will not. According to Penn State's Dean of the Smeal College of Business, Judy Olian (n.d), the message from managers to workers should be clear – 'We are here, everyone's at work, and though we are going to be hyper-vigilant, we're proceeding, at least on the surface, as if things are normal'. Yet things will never be normal. Consider again ABC news-anchor Charles Gibson's (in Mueller, 2008: 8) assessment on the fifth anniversary of 9/11: everyday life in a time of terror requires 'small act[s] of courage ... peril is part of everyday life'.

Bret Easton Ellis (1991: 384) ends his novel *American Psycho* with the phrase: 'THIS IS NOT AN EXIT'. The suggestion is that not every story needs to end with a happy ending, or even with closure. Sometimes the space at the end of a story does not contain redemption or catharsis. I would like to suggest that this is one such story. I have tried to show in this book that contemporary terrorism in New York, Washington DC, Madrid and London has had significant consequences for working people and businesses in cities throughout the world. I suggested that these consequences can at least partly be understood by exploring the relationship between witnesses and victims, simulations and images of violence, distance and cities.

In examining these relationships, other relationships begin to emerge between spectacles, spectatorship, locations and people. Where these forces merge, terror-work can be found. Commercial media providers willingly traded on these forces when offering commodified 'jingoistic and spiritual message[s]' (Miller, 2002) that focused on how terrorism makes people *feel*. On the streets of New York it was eyewitness accounts from Ground Zero. In London and Madrid these stories emerged from the staggering survivors who climbed from the wreckage of the public transport networks. On the streets of Melbourne they were eyewitness accounts from Flinders Street Station, Docklands, and below the Rialto Towers. As Latour (1999: 17) has argued, a strange outcome of research for people commanding scientific discourse is to suggest that 'only scientists should speak about science'. In this research the perceptions of the unruly mob, of which I undoubtedly form a part, are central – it is we who walk the streets of the city, occupy its buildings, attend its major sporting, cultural and social events, and linger in its crowds. We are the witnesses of images and violence in distant cities and we are spectators and consumers of terrorism. It is we who toil in the desert of the real.

But what can we do? Is there anything that can be altered, changed or expressed differently in order to not be the victims of international terrorism? Witnesses will continue to *be*, to think, act, develop ideas, explore happenings, be overwhelmed by events, make sense of images, and carry on in the midst of terrorism and its reanimation in media spaces that we all help create. Many will act/think/be in ways that unsettle, trouble, and disrupt meanings relating to the continuing reanimation of terrorism at work and in daily life.

After 9/11, Miller (2002) writes of giving himself 'over to television, like so many others around the world, even though these events were happening only a mile away'. For most witnesses of contemporary terrorism the distance was merely the few feet between themselves and their televisions and newspapers. In much the same way that 9/11 gave

New Yorkers a referent for 'The sounds of lower Manhattan that used to serve as white noise for residents – sirens, screeches, screams', it gave city dwellers the world over a referent for terrorism, violence, images, risk, commodity, entertainment, witnessing and spectatorship (Miller, 2002).

Working people, business leaders and managers will continue to struggle over the meanings and consequences of contemporary terrorism even as they reanimate it. Wars are still fought in Iraq and Afghanistan. George W. Bush's 'Mission Accomplished' banner can seem shocking, humiliating or amusing. Individuals continue to be detained without trial. Torture at Abu Ghraib, and in other anti-terror prisons, has been repackaged as rendition or coercive interrogation. Terrorism is still reported incessantly as Muslim extremists target apostates and infidels. Non-Muslims still attack Muslims for being potential terrorists – both on the streets and in media spaces. In many respects there is no redemption, no catharsis, no way out, and no exit. But the struggles over the meanings and consequences of contemporary terrorism for working people and businesses in the world's cities will go on and should be conjoined in multiple ways. So while this book locates itself in this struggle for meaning that terrorism provokes, it does not pretend to offer solutions. Solutions will be unique to different workplaces, different people and different cities. Solutions will emerge though they can rarely be universally applied from a distance.

In this book I have explored the consequences and meanings of terrorism for working people and businesses. The city of Melbourne, Australia was my case study, but it could have been any major, multicultural city throughout the world. If people living and working in Melbourne – a city whose people are mostly untouched by the menace of terrorism – can be so significantly affected by terrorism then surely all cities are positioned as vulnerable and precarious. The analogy of Melbourne is a telling one – the consequences of reacting to the emotion terror – to date – have far outweighed the consequences of terrorism as a violent political act. It is a needlessly self-inflicted problem – an 'own goal' in the so-called 'Global War on Terror'. Businesses leaders, managers, and workers have a role to play in this war. Workers must attempt 'small acts of courage' in going about their daily lives knowing that they are for the time being the preferred target of choice for international terrorism.

Bibliography

Ackerman, M. (2008) 'The 10 Ackerman Principles for Counterterrorism', *Chief Security Officer Online* [website], September 25, http://www.csoonline.com/article/451067/The_Ackerman_Principles_of_Counterterrorism, accessed 10 December 2008.

Adler, K. (2004), 'Passengers Weigh the Risks in Spain', *BBC News* [website], http://mews.bbc.co.uk/go/pr/fr/-/2/hi/europe/3597015.stm, accessed 1 May 2007.

Agamben, G. (2001), 'On Security and Terror', *European Graduate School Homepage* [website], http://egs.edu/faculty/agamben/agamben-on-securtiy-and-terror.html, accessed April 30, 2007.

Aglionby, J. and Ressa, M. (2005), 'Security Tightened After Bali Suicide Bombings', *CNN.com* [website], http://www.cnn.com/2005/WORLD/asiapcf/10/02/bali.blasts, accessed 21 June 2007.

Alexander, D. and Alexander, Y. (2002), *Terrorism and Business: The Impact of September 11, 2001* (Ardsley: Transnational Publishers).

Alexander, D. (2004), *Business Confronts Terrorism: Risks and Responses* (Madison: University of Wisconsin Press).

Alexander, Y. and Kilmarx, R. (1979), 'Introduction', in Y. Alexander and R. Kilmarx (eds), *Political Terrorism and Business: The Threat and Response* (New York: Praeger), x–xiii.

Alexander, Y. and Latter, R. (eds) (1990), *Terrorism and the Media: Dilemmas for Government, Journalists and the Public* (Washington: Brassey's).

Appelbaum, S., Adeland, E. and Harris, J. (2005), 'Management of Sports Facilities: Stress and Terrorism Since 9/11', *Management Research News*, 28(7): 69–83.

Argenti, P. (2002), 'Crisis Communication: Lessons From 9/11', *Harvard Business Review,* December, 103–109.

Associated Free Press (AFP) (2006), 'Two-year-old Emirati Boy Held as Airport Threat', *Middle East Times* [website], http://www.metimes.com/storyview.php?StoryID=20061107-094010-5779r, accessed 15 May 2007.

Associated Press, Knight Ridder Tribune, and Australian Associated Press (2005), 'Subway Alert Fizzles', *Herald Sun*, October 8, 19.

Atwater, T. (1990), 'Network Evening News Coverage of the TWA Hostage Crisis', in Y. Alexander and R. Latter (eds), *Terrorism and the Media: Dilemmas for Government, Journalists and the Public* (Washington: Brassey's), 85–92.

Australian Associated Press [AAP] (2005), 'Neo-Nazi's in Race Riots: Police', *The Sydney Morning Herald* [website], http://www.smh.com.au/news/national/neonazis-in-race-riots-police/2005/12/12/1134235970427.html, accessed 2 February 2007.

Australian Broadcasting Corporation [ABC] (2005), 'Suspects in Custody After Anti-Terror Raids', *ABC Online* [website], http://www.abc.net.au/news/newsitems/200511/s1500718.htm, accessed 8 January 2007.

Australian Bureau of Statistics (2005), 'Population Projections', *Australian Bureau of Statistics* [website], http://www.ausstats.abs.gov.au/Ausstats/subscriber.nsf/0/B1E6E31CD9A3EA61CA2570C7007296DD/$File/32220_2004%20to%202101.pdf, accessed 4 October 2006.

Australian Federal Police (n.d.), 'Bali Bombings 2002', http://www.afp.gov.au/international/operations/previous_operations/bali_bombings_2002.html, accessed 2 June 2008.

Australian Financial Review (n.d.), 'About the Newspaper', *Financial Review* [website], http://afr.com/home/newspaper.aspx#history, accessed 22 July 2007.
Bagaric, M. (2005a), 'Your Rights or Your Life? It's No Contest', *Herald Sun*, October 4, 21.
Bagaric, M. (2005b), 'A Case for Torture', *The Age*, May 17, 13.
Barnes, R. and Ker, P. (2005), 'Games Faces Up to Bio-Terror Threat', *The Age* [website], http://www.theage.com.au/articles/2005/09/20/112698203484.html?from=rss, accessed 20 August 2006.
Barnett, M. (2002), 'From Me to We ... and Back Again: Returning to Business as Usual', *Journal of Management Inquiry*, 11(3): 249–52.
Bartel, C. (2002), 'I Love New York, More Than Ever: Changes in People's Identities as New Yorkers Following the World Trade Center Terrorist Attacks', *Journal of Management Inquiry*, 11(3): 240–48.
Baudrillard, J. (1983), 'The Implosion of Meaning in the Media', in *In the Shadows of the Silent Majority or, The End of the Social: and Other Essays* (New York: Semiotext(e)), 95–112.
Baudrillard, J. (1987a), *The Evil Demon of Images* (New South Wales: The Power Institute of Fine Arts).
Baudrillard, J. (1988), *The Ecstasy of Communication* (New York: Semiotext(e)).
Baudrillard, J. (1994), *Simulacra and Simulation* (Ann Arbor: The University of Michigan Press).
Baudrillard, J. (2001), 'Dust Breeding', in A. Kroker and M. Kroker (eds), *CTheory* [website] http://www.ctheory.net/articles.aspx?id=293, accessed 7 August 2006.
Baudrillard, J. (2002), *The Spirit of Terrorism and Requiem for the Twin Towers* (London: Verso).
Baudrillard, J. (2005), *The Intelligence of Evil or the Lucidity Pact* (Oxford: Berg).
Bauman, Z. (2005), *Liquid Life* (Cambridge: Polity).
Bauman, Z. (2006), *Liquid Fear* (Cambridge: Polity).
Beck, U. (1999), *World Risk Society* (Malden: Polity).
Berg, R. (1986), 'Losing Vietnam: Covering the War in an Age of Technology', *Cultural Critique*, 3: 92–125.
Bergin, A. (2005), 'Australia Faces Counter-Terrorism Challenges', transcript of interview with Tony Jones on *Lateline*, Australian Broadcasting Corporation [ABC], [website] http://www.abc.net.au/lateline/content/2005/s1411905.htm, accessed 3 May 2006.
Bergin, A. and Yates, A. (2006), 'Challenges Ahead for Australian Homeland Security', *Asian Security Review*, July/August, 8.
Birmingham, J. (2005), 'A Time For War: Australia as a Military Power', *Quarterly Essay*, Issue 20.
Blanchot, M. (1995), *The Writing of the Disaster: L'ecriture du Desastre* (Lincoln: University of Nebraska Press).
Bolt, A. (2005a), 'Terror by Degrees', *Herald Sun*, October 7, 23.
Bolt, A. (2005b), 'The Threat is Real', *Herald Sun*, November 9, 23.
Braithwaite, D. and Petrie, A. (2007), 'Chaser Comic Convoy Beats Summit Security', *The Age* [website], http://www.theage.com.au/news/national/chaser-comic-convoy-beats-summit-security/2007/09/06/1188773415730.html, accessed 12 January 2008.
Buzan, B. (2006), 'Will the 'Global War on Terrorism' be the New Cold War?', *International Affairs*, 82(6): 1101–118.
Chulov, M. (2006), *Australian Jihad: The Battle Against Terrorism From Within and Without* (Sydney: Macmillan).
Churchill, W. (2003), '"Some People Push Back": On the Justice of Roosting Chickens', http://www.kersplebedeb.com/mystuff/s11/churchill.html, accessed 1 May 2007.
City of Melbourne (2006), 'Events and Festivals – Introduction', http://www.melbourne.vic.gov.au/info.cfm?top=12&pg=945, accessed 4 October 2006.

Cline, R. (1979), 'Foreword', in Y. Alexander and R. Kilmarx (eds), *Political Terrorism and Business: The Threat and Response* (Praeger: New York).

Coaffee, J. (2003), *Terrorism, Risk and the City: The Making of a Contemporary Urban Landscape* (Aldershot: Ashgate).

Committee on Government Reform (2006), 'Telecommuting: A 21st Century Solution to Traffic Jams and Terrorism: Hearing Before the Subcommittee on the Federal Workforce and Agency Organization of the Committee on Government Reform, House of Representatives, One Hundred Ninth Congress, Second Session, July 18, 2006', http://purl.access.gpo.gov/GPO/LPS85694, accessed 15 February 2009.

Conlin, M., Thornton, E., Foust, D. and Welch, D. (2001), 'When the Office is the War Zone', *Business Week*, 37(58): 38.

Coogan, T. (2000), *The I.R.A.* (London: Harper Collins).

Cook, I. (2005), *Australians Speak 2005: Public Opinion and Foreign Policy* (Sydney: Lowy Institute for International Policy).

Cornish, A., Stout, R., Swan, K and Glendinning, C. (1996), 'Memories of the Bureau of Meteorology', *Metarch Papers*, No. 8 February 1996, Bureau of Meteorology [website], http://www.austehc.unimelb.edu.au/fam/0490.html, accessed 20 June 2007.

Czinkota, M., Knight, G., Liesch, P. and Steen, J. (2005), 'Positioning Terrorism in Management and Marketing: Research Propositions', *Journal of International Management*, 11(4): 581–604.

Debord, G. (1983), *Society of the Spectacle* (Detroit: Black & Red).

Deleuze, G. (2004), *The Logic of Sense* (London: Continuum).

de Muynck, B. (2004), 'The Prosthetic Paradox', in T. Hauben, M. Vermeulen and V. Patteeuw (eds), *Fear & Space: The View of Young Designers in the Netherlands* (Netherlands: NAi Uitgevers/Publishers), 8–15.

Dickinson, L. (2006), 'Public Law Values in a Privatized World', *Yale Journal of International Law*, 31: 383–426.

Dunn, C. (1998), 'The Attempted Assassination of Prince Alfred at Clontarf 1868', http://www.shoalhaven.net.au/~cathyd/history/prince.html, accessed 11 April 2006.

Dunn, M. (2005), 'Brereton Undeterred', *Herald Sun*, October 4, 8.

Dunn, M. and Anderson, P. (2005), 'A Day That Forever Changed Our Lives', *Herald Sun*, November 9, 2.

Eastley, T. (2006), 'Games Terror Attack Feasible: ASIO', *AM* [website], http://www.abc.net.au/am/content/2006/s1587340.html, accessed 3 May 2006.

Editor – *Financial Review* (2005), 'Nation Right to Trust PM', *Financial Review*, November 9, 62.

Editor – *Herald Sun* (2005), 'Bali and the Games', *Herald Sun*, October 4, 20.

Editor – *The Age* (2005), 'Finding a Balance Between Security and Freedom', *The Age*, September 24, 10.

Editor – *The Australian* (2005), 'Domestic Dangers', *The Australian*, November 9, 17.

Editor – *The Sydney Morning Herald* (2005), 'The Crossing of Terrorism's Threshold', *The Sydney Morning Herald*, November 9, 16.

Edkins, J. (2002), 'Forget Trauma? Response to September 11', *International Relations*, 16(2): 243–256.

Edmund, S. (2005), 'Train Lover Denied Photos', *Herald Sun*, October 4, 12.

Eisinger, P. (2004), 'The American City in the Age of Terror', *Urban Affairs Review*, 40(1): 115–130.

Elliott, A. (2007), *Concepts of the Self*, 2nd edition (Cambridge: Polity).

Elliott, M. (2003), 'So, What Went Wrong', *Time* [website], http://www.time.com/time/magazine/article/0,9171,1101031006-490595,00.html, accessed 20 October 2007.

Ellis, B. (1991), *American Psycho: A Novel* (London: Picador).
Fine, M. (2002), '2001 Carolyn Sherif Award Address: The Presence of an Absence', *Psychology of Women Quarterly*, 26(1): 9–24.
Fischer III, H. (1998a), *Behavioral Response to Chemical and Biological Terrorism*, Research Planning, Inc., Church Falls, White Paper.
Fischer III, H. (1998b), *Response to Disaster: Fact Versus Fiction and Its Perpetuation*, 2nd ed. (Landam: University Press of America).
Fischer III, H. (2002), 'Terrorism and 11 September 2001: Does the "Behavioral Response to Disaster" Model Fit?', *Disaster Prevention and Management: An International Journal*, 11(2): 123–127.
Fleckner, A. and Stevens, A. (2005), *Meeting the Obligations of Critical Infrastructure Under the Victorian Terrorism (Community Protection) Act 2003*, Emergency Management Experts and Australian Homeland Security Research Centre, Mount Waverley and Canberra.
Forbes, M., Nicholson, B. and Hudson, P. (2005), 'Bombs Rock Bali', *Sunday Age*, October 2, 1.
Frenkel, J. (2005), 'Leaders Plea for Calm', *Herald Sun*, November 10, 5.
Freyd, J. (2002), 'In the Wake of Terrorist Attack, Hatred May Mask Fear', *Analyses of Social Issues and Public Policy*, 2(1): 5–8.
Friedland, N. and Merari, A. (1985), 'The Psychological Impact of Terrorism: A Double-Edged Sword', *Political Psychology*, 6(4): 591–604.
Fromkin, D. (1975), 'The Strategy of Terrorism', *Foreign Affairs*, 53(4): 684–5.
Gardner, D. (2008), *Risk: The Science and Politics of Fear* (Melbourne: Scribe).
George, A. (ed.) (1991), *Western State Terrorism* (New York: Routledge).
Giddens, A. (1991), *Modernity and Self-identity: Self and Society in the Late Modern Age* (Stanford: Stanford University Press).
Gilroy, L. (2001), 'Our Relationship with the Built Environment in the Aftermath of Terrorist Attacks', *Reason Public Policy Institute* [website], http://www.rppi.org/opeds/092801.html, accessed 24 December 2006.
Gordon, M. (2005), 'PM Not Gloating, But Makes His Point', *The Age*, November 9, 4.
Gosch, E. and Makin, L. (2005), 'Raids Leave Neighbours "Traumatised, Sleepless"', *The Australian*, November 10, 5.
Graham, S. (2004), 'Introduction: Cities, Warfare, and States of Emergency', in S. Graham (ed.), *Cities, War, and Terrorism: Towards an Urban Geopolitics* (Malden: Blackwell Publishing), 1–25.
Gray, P. (2005), 'Bill of Rights Debate Unclear', *Herald Sun*, October 3, 21.
Grosz, E. (1995), *Space, Time and Perversion: The Politics of Bodies* (St Leonards: Allen & Unwin).
Gupta, S. (2002), *The Replication of Violence: Thoughts on International Terrorism after September 11th 2001* (London: Pluto Press).
Haraway, D. (1997), *Modest_Witness@Second_Millenium.FemaleMale©_Meets_OncoMouse: Feminism and Technoscience* (New York: Routledge).
Haraway, D. (2000), 'Birth of the Kennel: A Lecture by Donna Haraway', *European Graduate School* [website], http://www.egs.edu/faculty/haraway/haraway-birth-of-the-kennel-2000.html, accessed 13 March 2008.
Harbison, R. (1991), *The Built, The Unbuilt and the Unbuildable: In Pursuit of Architectural Meaning* (London: Thames and Hudson).
Hargest, J. (2005), 'Waiting Game', *Herald Sun*, November 10, 5.
Hauben, T. and Vermeulen, M. (2004), 'Preface', in T. Hauben, M. Vermeulen and V. Patteeuw (eds), *Fear & Space: The View of Young Designers in the Netherlands* (Netherlands: NAi Uitgevers/Publishers), 6–7.
Haywood, B. (2005), 'On the Attack', *The Age*, October 3, 8.

Healey, J. (ed.) (2004), *Religions and Beliefs in Australia* (Thirroul: The Spinney Press).
Heidegger, M. (1929), 'What is Metaphysics?', lecture delivered at the University of Freiburg, http://www.msu.org/e&r/content_e&r/text/heidegger/heidegger_wm2.html, accessed 1 August 2005.
Heidegger, M. (1962), *Being and Time* (San Francisco: Harper Collins).
Herald Sun (2005a), 'Trail of Destruction', *Herald Sun*, October 3, 8–9.
Herald Sun (2005b), 'Your Say', *Herald Sun*, October 3, 18–19.
Herald Sun (2005c), 'World Police Team Up To Hunt Bali Bombers', *Herald Sun*, October 6, 1.
Herald Sun (2005d), 'It's Not For Everyone', *Herald Sun*, October 7, 3.
Herald Sun (2005e), 'Stones Throw', *Herald Sun*, October 8, 19.
Herald Sun (2005f), 'Your Say', *Herald Sun*, October 5, 18–19.
Herald Sun (2005g), 'Your Say', *Herald Sun*, October 7, 20–21.
Herald Sun (2005h), 'Your Say', *Herald Sun*, November 9, 18.
Herald Sun (2005i), 'Your Say', *Herald Sun*, November 10, 20.
Herman, E. (1982), *The Real Terror Network: Terrorism in Fact and Propaganda* (Boston: South End Press).
Herman, E. (1986), 'Power and Semantics of Terrorism', in E. Ray and W. Schaap (eds) (2003), *Covert Action: The Roots of Terrorism* (Melbourne: Ocean Press), 40–46.
Herman, E. and Chomsky, N. (1994), *Manufacturing Consent: The Political Economy of the Mass Media* (London: Vintage).
Hirst, R. (2003), *Willie's Bar and Grill: A Rock 'n' Roll Tour of North America in the Age of Terror* (Sydney: Picador).
Hocking, J. (1993), *Beyond Terrorism: The Development of the Australian Security State* (St Leonards: Allen & Unwin).
Hocking, J. (2004), *Terror Laws: ASIO, Counter-Terrorism, and the Threat to Democracy* (Sydney: University of New South Wales Press).
Holt, A. (2006), 'Al-Qaeda and the Threat to Mass Surface Transportation', *Terrorism Monitor* [website], 4(9): http://jamestown.org/terrorism/news/article.php?articleid=2369984, accessed 3 November 2006.
Horgan, J. (2005), *The Psychology of Terrorism* (London: Routledge).
Houlihan, L. (2005), 'Prayer Call', *Herald Sun*, October 8, 13.
Hunt, E., Dunn, M. and Whinnett, E. (2005), 'Terror Alarm on Map', *Herald Sun*, November 10, 1.
Hunt, G. Wood, J. (2005), 'Gather Facts, Foil the Plots', *Herald Sun*, November 10, 22.
Isaacs, V. and Kirkpatrick, R. (n.d.), 'Two Hundred Years of Sydney Newspapers: A Short History', http://eprint.uq.edu.au/archive/00000391/01/sydnews.pdf, accessed 19 June 2007.
Jackson, A. (2005), 'Back to Bali: Australians' Devotion to the Island Resilient', *The Age*, October 5, 4.
Jackson, G. (2007), 'Defending economic growth against leftwing fanatics, part I', *BrookesNews.com* [website], http://www.brookesnews.com/071604trainer1.html, accessed 19 June 2007.
Jenkins, B. (1987), 'The Future Course of International Terrorism', in P. Wilkinson and A. Stewart (eds), *Contemporary Research on Terrorism* (Aberdeen: Aberdeen University Press), 581–89.
Kantor, P. (2002), 'Terrorism and Governability in New York City: Old Problem, New Dilemma', *Urban Affairs Review*, 38(1): 120–27.
Kellner, D. (2004), 'Baudrillard, Globalization and Terrorism: Some Comments on Recent Adventures of the Image and Spectacle on the Occasion of Baudrillard's 75th Birthday', http://www.gseis.ucla.edu/faculty/kellner/, accessed 1 December 2006.
Kellner, D. (2005), 'Media Culture and the Triumph of the Spectacle', *Fast Capitalism* [website], 1(1): http://www.uta.edu/huma/agger/fastcapitalism/1_1/fastcap_left2.htm, accessed 13 March 2007.
Kelly, J. (2005), 'High Flyers Can Go Jump', *Herald Sun*, Friday, October 7, 3.

Kennedy, S. (2001), 'Community, Leadership and the Emerging Social Importance of the Workplace: Lessons Learned as a Result of the September 11 Tragedies', *Customer Interface*, November, 18–19.

Kerin, J. (2005), 'Attacks on Big Events Possible: Police Chief – Terror Revisits Bali', *The Australian*, October 5, 8.

Kierkegaard, S. (1957), *The Concept of Dread* (Princeton: Princeton University Press).

Kissane, K. (2005), 'Conspiracy Theories Air a New Wave of Views About Bali Bombings', *The Australian*, October 6, 10.

Koltnow, B. (2006), '9/11 Families United Over Must-See Tale', *Sunday Mail*, August 6, 92.

Küng, M. (2004), 'Fear as an Associative Space', in T. Hauben, M. Vermeulen and V. Patteeuw (eds), *Fear & Space: The View of Young Designers in the Netherlands* (Netherlands: NAi Uitgevers/Publishers), 88–91.

Kunstler, J. and Salingaros, N. (2001), 'The End of Tall Buildings', *Planetizen.com* [website], http://www.planetizen.com/node/27, accessed 28 September 2005.

Kupperman, R. (1979), 'Countermeasures: Some Technological Considerations', in Y. Alexander and R. Kilmarx (eds), *Political Terrorism and Business: The Threat and Response* (New York: Praeger), 97–105.

Lake, G. (2005), 'Building Partnerships for a Safer Australia', *Security in Government Conference* [website], http://www.alga.asn.au/newsroom/speeches/2005/20050512.php, accessed 3 May 2006.

Laqueur, W. (1977), *Terrorism: A Study of National and International Political Violence* (Boston: Little, Brown and Company).

Laqueur, W. (1987), *The Age of Terrorism*, (Boston: Little, Brown and Company).

Laqueur, W. (1999), *The New Terrorism: Fanaticism and the Arms of Mass Destruction* (London: Phoenix Press).

Laqueur, W. (2003), *No End to War: Terrorism in the Twenty-First Century* (New York: Continuum).

Latour, B. (1999), *Pandora's Hope: Essays on the Reality of Science Studies* (Cambridge: Harvard University Press).

Liverant, G., Hofmann, S. and Litz, B. (2004), 'Coping and Anxiety in College Students After the September 11th Terrorist Attacks', *Anxiety, Stress, & Coping*, 17(2): 127–39.

Loukaitou-Sideris, A., Taylor, B. and Fink, C. (2006), 'Rail Transit Security in an International Context: Lessons From Four Cities', *Urban Affairs Review*, 41(6): 727–48.

Lule, J. (1991), 'Sacrifice and the Body on the Tarmac: Symbolic Significance of U.S News About a Terrorist Victim', in Y. Alexander and R. Picard (eds), *In the Camera's Eye: News Coverage of Terrorist Events* (Washington: Brassey's), 30–45.

MacDonald, F. (2004), 'Powers of Surveillance' *HR Monthly*, March, 34.

Macnamara, L. (2005), 'Terrorists 'Will be Tourists' – Terror Revisits Bali', *The Australian*, October 5, 7.

McCartney, J. (2003), *Jason McCartney: After Bali* (Docklands and South Melbourne: Geoff Slattery Publishing and Lothian).

McCulloch, J. and Tham, J. (2005), 'Secret State, Transparent Subject: The Australian Security Intelligence Organisation in the Age of Terror', *Australian and New Zealand Journal of Criminology*, 38(3): 400–415.

McHoul, A. and Miller, T. (1998), *Popular Culture and Everyday Life* (London: Sage).

McNair, B. (2006), 'The Information Flood', *The Age*, July 3, 7.

Mainiero, L. and Gibson, D. (2003), 'Managing Employee Trauma: Dealing With the Emotional Fallout From 9-11', *Academy of Management Executive*, 17(3): 130–44.

Mahmud, V. (2003), 'Virtual Workplace: Take It or Leave It', *Jakarta Post*, March 31.

Mankin, L. and Perry, R. (2004), 'Terrorism Challenges for Human Resource Management', *Review of Public Personnel Administration*, 24(1): 3–17.

Manning, P. (2006), *Us and Them: A Journalist's Investigation of Media, Muslims and the Middle East* (Milsons Point: Random House).

Marren, P. (2002), 'Business in the Age of Terrorism', *Journal of Business Strategy*, 23(4): 19–23.

Mayo, E. (1923), 'The Irrational Factor in Human Behavior. The "Night-Mind" in Industry', *Annals of the American Academy of Political and Social Science*, 110, 'Psychology in Business', November, 117–130.

Meade, A. (2005), 'Networks Finetune Their Responses to Terror', *The Australian*, October 7, 17.

Media Transparency (n.d.), 'Reason Foundation', *Media Transparency* [website], http://www.mediatransparency.org/recipientgrants.php?recipient10=286, accessed 29 October 2007.

Melvin, D. (2005), 'Terror Probe's Scope Widens London Bombing Suspects Traced to Four Countries', *The Atlanta Journal – Constitution*, July 27, A3.

Michaelsen, C. (2005), 'Anti-Terrorism Legislation in Australia: A Proportionate Response to the Terrorist Threat?', *Studies in Conflict and Terrorism*, 28(4): 321–39.

Mickelburough, P. (2005), 'Attack Inevitable – Police Chief', *Herald Sun*, October 4, 9.

Mickolus, E. (1979), 'Chronology of Transnational Terrorist Attacks Upon American Business People, 1968–1978', in Y. Alexander and R. Kilmarx (eds), *Political Terrorism and Business: The Threat and Response* (New York: Praeger), 297–318.

Miller, B. and Russell, C. (1979), 'Terrorism and the Corporate Target', in Y. Alexander and R. Kilmarx (eds), *Political Terrorism and Business: The Threat and Response* (Praeger: New York), 56–65.

Miller, T. (2002), 'Being Ignorant, Living in Manhattan', www.portalcomunicacion.com/bcn2002/n_eng/contents/11/miller.pdf, accessed 1 February 2007.

Miller, T. (2007), *Cultural Citizenship: Cosmopolitanism, Consumerism, and Television in a Neoliberal Age* (Philadelphia: Temple University Press).

Mitchell, N. (2005a), 'It's Coming: Ready or Not', *Herald Sun*, October 6, 23.

Mitchell, N. (2005b), 'Fairness Must Survive', *Herald Sun*, November 10, 23.

Moran, S. and Drummond, M. (2005), 'Police: We Had to Act Quickly', *Financial Review*, November 9, 5.

Moreno, L. (2005), 'The Madrid Bombings in the Domestic and Regional Politics of Spain', *Irish Studies in International Affairs*, 16: 65–72.

Morgan, G. (1997), *Images of Organization* (Thousand Oaks: Sage).

Mourtada, R. (2004), 'A Climate of Fear', *Canadian Business*, 77(7): 24–5.

Mueller, J. (2006), *Overblown: How Politicians and the Terrorism Industry Inflate National Security Threats, and Why We Believe Them* (New York: Free Press).

Mueller, J. (2008), 'Terrorphobia: Our False Sense of Insecurity', *The American Interest*, 3(5): 6–13.

Mydans, S. (2005), 'A Government on the Move to a Half-Built Capital', *International Herald Tribune: Asia Pacific* [website], http://www.iht.com/articles/2005/11/10/news/burma.php, accessed 22 July 2007.

Myriad Mint (2005), 'Loosened Cross-media Ownership Means More Media Bias – A Tale From the 2004 Election', *Your Democracy* [website], http://www.yourdemocracy.net.au/drupal/node/1041, accessed 19 June 2007.

Nacos, B. (1994), *Terrorism and the Media: From the Iran Hostage Crisis to the Oklahoma City Bombing* (New York: Columbia University Press).

Nacos, B. (2002), *Mass-Mediated Terrorism: The Central Role of the Media in Terrorism and Counter-terrorism* (Lanham: Rowman and Littlefield Publishers).

Nacos, B. (2006), *Terrorism and Counterterrorism: Understanding Threats and Responses in the Post-9/11 World* (New York: Pearson Longman).

Nancy, J. (2000), *Being Singular Plural* (Stanford: Stanford University Press).

Neighbour, S. (2005), 'Aussies Schooled by Al-Qa'ida', *The Australian*, November 9, 3.

Nicholson, B. and Grattan, M. (2005), 'Top Muslims Seek PM's Help to Stop Backlash', *The Age*, November 10, 4.

Nighswonger, T. (2002), 'Threat of Terror Impacts Workplace Safety', *Occupational Hazards*, 64(7): 24–27.

Nohria, N. (2006), 'Corporate Security 21st Century … The Business of Resilience', *Security 360*, 1(3): 19.

Nolan, K. (2005), 'Too Much At Risk, Says McCartney', *Herald Sun*, October 3, 15.

Nunn, S. (2006), 'Tell Us What's Going to Happen: Information Feeds to the War on Terror', in A. Kroker and M. Kroker (eds), *CTheory: 1000 Days of Theory* [website], http://www.ctheory.net/articles.aspx?id=518, accessed 8 January 2007.

Ochberg, F. (1979), 'Preparing for Terrorist Victimization', in Y. Alexander and R. Kilmarx (eds), *Political Terrorism and Business: The Threat and Response* (New York: Praeger), 113–22.

O'Connor, C. (2006), 'Cut Together', *Film Philosophy*, 10(2): http://www.film-philosophy.com/2006v10n2/o'connor.pdf, accessed 5 February 2007.

Olian, J. (n. d.), 'When Terrorism Targets Business', Penn State's Smeal College of Business [website], http://www.smeal.psu.edu/news/latest-news/aug04/terror.html, accessed 25 August 2008.

Paletz, D. and Schmid, A. (eds) (1992), *Terrorism and the Media* (Sage: Newbury Park).

Parker, M. (1995), 'Organisational Gothic', *Culture and Organization*, 11(3): 153–66.

Parker, M. (2002), *Against Management: Organization in the Age of Managerialism* (Cambridge: Polity).

Paust, J. (1977), 'A Definitional Focus', in Y. Alexander and S. Finger (eds), *Terrorism: Interdisciplinary Perspectives* (New York: John Jay Press), 18–29.

Pearson, C. (2005), 'Torture is not the Answer', *The Australian*, 28 May: 20.

Perry, R. and Lindell, M. (2003), 'Understanding Citizen Response to Disasters With Implications for Terrorism', *Journal of Contingencies and Crisis Management*, 11(2): 49–60.

Petersen, A. (1997), 'Risk, Governance and the New Public Health', in A. Peterson and R. Bunton (eds), *Foucault, Health and Medicine* (London: Routledge), 189–206.

Pfefferbaum, B., Seale, T., McDonald, N., Brandt, N., Rainwater, S., Maynard, B., Meierhoefer, B. and Miller, P. (2000), 'Posttraumatic Stress Two Years After the Oklahoma City Bombing in Youths Geographically Distant From the Explosion', *Psychiatry*, 64(4): 358–70.

Pickering, S. (2005), *Refugees and State Crime* (Annandale: The Federation Press).

Plotnik, R. (2005), *Introduction to Psychology*, 7th edn (Southbank: Thomson Wadsworth).

Poe, A. (2001), 'Aftershocks of the 11th', *HR Magazine*, 46(12): 46–52.

Poynting, S. and Noble, G. (2004), 'Living With Racism: The Experience and Reporting by Arab and Muslim Australians of Discrimination, Abuse and Violence Since 11 September 2001', report to The Human Rights and Equal Opportunity Commission, http://www.hreoc.gov.au/racial_discrimination/isma/research/UWSReport.pdf, accessed 8 August 2006.

Rapoport, D. (1984), 'Fear and Trembling: Terrorism in Three Religious Traditions', *American Political Science Review*, 78(3): 658–77.

Rapoport, D. (2006), 'The Four Waves of Modern Terrorism', in D. Gupta (ed.), *Terrorism and Homeland Security* (Belmont: Thomson Wadsworth), 9–37.

Rauchway, E. (2003), 'The President and the Assassin', *The Boston Globe* [website], http://www.boston.com/news/globe/ideas/articles/2003/09/07/the_president_and_the_assassin/, accessed 15 April 2005.

Reich, W. (ed.) (1998), *Origins of Terrorism: Psychologies, Ideologies, Theologies, States of Mind* (Washington DC: Woodrow Wilson Center Press).

Richardson, L. (2006), *What Terrorists Want: Understanding the Terrorist Threat* (London: John Murray).

Robbins, S., Bergman, R., Stagg, I. and Coulter, M. (2003), *Management,* 3rd edn (Frenchs Forest: Prentice Hall).

Robinson, M. and Whinnett, E. (2005), 'Tourists Torn on Making a Stand', *Herald Sun*, October 4, 11.

Rosen, B. (1990), 'The Media Dilemma and Terrorism', in Y. Alexander and R. Latter (eds), *Terrorism and the Media: Dilemmas for Government, Journalists and the Public* (Washington: Brassey's), 57–60.

Rubin, B. and Rubin, J. (2004), *Hating America: A History* (Oxford: Oxford University Press).

Saleh, L., Cummings, L. and Yamine, E. (2005), 'Soap Actor on Murder Bid Charges', *Herald Sun*, November 10, 7.

Savitch, H. (2003), 'Does 9-11 Portend a New Paradigm for Cities?', *Urban Affairs Review*, 39(1): 103–27.

Schimmel, K. (2006), 'Deep Play: Sports Mega-Events and Urban Social Conditions in the USA', *The Sociological Review*, 54(s2): 160–74.

Schmid, A. and Jongman, A. (1988), *Political Terrorism: A New Guide to Actors, Authors, Concepts, Data Bases, Theories and Literature* (Oxford: North Holland).

Schmid, A. (1993), 'Defining Terrorism: The Response Problem as a Definition Problem', in A. Schmid and R. Crelinsten (eds), *Western Responses to Terrorism* (London: Frank Cass), 7–13.

Schuster, M., Stein, B., Jaycox, L., Collins, R., Marshall, G., Elliot, M., Zhou, A., Kanouse, D., Morrison, J. and Berry, S. (2001), 'A National Survey of Stress: Reactions After the September 11, 2001, Terrorist Attacks', *The New England Journal of Medicine*, 345(20): 1507–12.

Sennett, R. (1998), *The Corrosion of Character* (New York: Norton).

Shaw, I. (2005), 'Soft Target Strategy', *Herald Sun*, October 3, 21.

Shaw, M. (1996), *Civil Society and Media in Global Crises: Representing Distant Violence* (London: Pinter).

Simmel, G. (1903), 'The Metropolis and Mental Life', in G. Simmel (ed.) (1971), *On Individuality and Social Forms: Selected Writings* (Chicago: The University of Chicago Press), 324–39.

Simpson, C. (1996), 'The Uses of "Counterterrorism"', in E. Ray and W. Schaap (eds) (2003), *Covert Action: The Roots of Terrorism* (Melbourne: Ocean Press), 75–83.

Singh, B. (1977), 'An Overview', in Y. Alexander and S. Finger (eds), *Terrorism: Interdisciplinary Perspectives* (New York: John Jay Press), 18–29.

Sixel, L. (2003), 'EEOC Suit Claims Firing Prompted by Terrorism Fear', *Houston Chronicle* [website], http://www.chron.com/cs/CDA/printstory.mpl/business/sixel/206095, accessed 22 March 2004.

Sleeman, J. (1933), *Thugs; Or a Million Murders* (London: S. Low and Marston).

Stanley, T. (2005), 'Australian Anti-Terror Raids: A Serious Plot Thwarted', *Terrorism Monitor*, 3(23): http://www.jamestown.org (home page), accessed 12 February 2007.

Stewart, C. (2002), 'Soul Time', *Potentials,* 35(9): 92.

Stewart, C. (2005), 'Terror Link to Radical Sheiks', *The Australian*, November 10, 1.

Stewart, C. and Leys, N. (2005), 'Osama's Aussie Offspring – Terror Plot Foiled After 17 Arrested', *The Australian*, November 9, 1.

Stiglitz, J. and Bilmes, L. (2008), *The Three Trillion Dollar War: The True Cost of the Iraq Conflict* (New York: W. W. Norton).

St. John, P. (1991), *Air Piracy, Airport Security, and International Terrorism: Winning the War Against Hijackers* (New York: Quorum Books).

Sullivan, J. and Anderson, L. (2004), 'How Should HR React in the Aftermath of Terrorism Events?', http://www.drjohnsullivan.com/newsletter/091201.htm, accessed 22 March 2004.

Summers, T. (2001), 'Responding to Terror: What Employers are Doing', *Clemson University, Department of Management*, http://people.clemson.edu/~summers/RespondingtoTerror.htm, accessed 22 March 2004.

Taureck, R. (2006), 'Securitisation Theory – The Story So Far: Theoretical Inheritance and What it Means to be a Post-Structural Realist', *4th Annual CEEISA Convention* [website], www.ceeisaconf.ut.ee/orb.aw/class=file/action=preview/id=164452/TAURECK.doc, accessed 10 March 2007.

Tham, J. (2002), 'ASIO and the Rule of Law', *Alternative Law Journal*, 27(5): 216–19.

The Age (2005a), 'Letters', *The Age*, October 4, 12.

The Age (2005b), 'Letters', *The Age*, October 5, 16.

The Age (2005c), 'Letters', *The Age*, October 7, 12.

The Age (2005d), 'Talking Point', *The Age*, November 9, 18.

The Age (2005e), 'Letters', *The Age*, November 10, 14.

The Age (2005f), 'And Another Thing...', *The Age*, November 10, 14.

The Age – Corporate Information (2007), 'Circulation and Readership', *The Age* [website], http://www.about.theage.com.au/view_circulation.asp, accessed 19 June 2007.

The Australian (2005a), 'Letters to the Editor', *The Australian*, October 5, 15.

The Australian (2005b), 'Letters to the Editor', *The Australian*, October 6, 13.

The Australian (2005c), 'Letters to the Editor', *The Australian*, November 9, 17.

The Australian (2005d), 'Letters to the Editor', *The Australian*, November 10, 13.

The Daily Telegraph (2007), '"Sex Bomb" Sparks Security Alert', *The Daily Telegraph* [website], http://www.news.com.au/dailytelegraph/story/0,22049,21584339-5001028,00.html?from=public_rrs#, accessed 15 May 2007.

The Herald Weekly Time Pty Ltd (no date), 'About Us', *Herald Sun* [website], http://www.news.com.au/heraldsun/aboutus, accessed 19 June 2007.

Then, S. and Loosemore, M. (2006), 'Terrorism Prevention, Preparedness, and Response in Built Facilities', *Facilities*, 24(5/6): 157–76.

The Sydney Morning Herald (2005), 'The Reality of Mass Murder Chills to the Bone', *The Sydney Morning Herald*, October 5, 14.

Thomas, M. (2005), 'No Need For Oppressive Powers', *Herald Sun*, November 10, 23.

Tippet, G. (2005), 'Angry Young Men Come and Go With Intent', *The Age*, November 9, 3.

Toohey, K. and Taylor, T. (2004), 'No Rain Stops Play – How the Drought is Hurting Rural Sport', *The Sports Factor*, Australian Broadcasting Corporation [ABC] Radio National transcript of interview with Warwick Hadfield, http://www.ausport.gov.au/fulltext/2004/sportsf/s1068638.asp, accessed 3 May 2006.

Trist, E. and Bamforth, K. (1951), 'Some Social and Psychological Consequences of the Longwall Method of Coal Getting', *Human Relations*, 4(1): 3–38.

Trusted Information Sharing Network [TISN] (2005), 'Property CEOs Discuss Security', *CIP Newsletter*, 2(2): 1.

Tulloch, J. (2006), *One Day in July: Experiencing 7/7* (London: Little, Brown).

Tumarkin, M. (2005), *Traumascapes: The Power and Fate of Places Transformed by Tragedy* (Carlton: Melbourne University Press).

Turner, B. (2006), *Vulnerability and Human Rights*, (Pennsylvania: The Pennsylvania State University Press).

Virilio, P. (2002), *Ground Zero* (London: Verso).

Volkan, V. (2002), 'September 11 and Societal Regression', *Group Analysis*, 35(4): 456–83.

von Zielbauer, P. (2006), 'G.I. Tells Why He Testified in Rape-Murder Inquiry', *The New York Times* [website], http://www.nytimes.com/2006/08/07/world/middleeast/07cnd-iraq.html?ei=5094, accessed 3 November 2007.

Walters, P. (2005), 'Raids Show How Far We've Come Since 9/11', *The Australian*, November 9, 5.

Watson, R. (2007), 'Top Cop Livid Over Chaser APEC Stunt', *The Daily Telegraph* [website], http://www.news.com.au/dailytelegraph/story/0,22049,22378184-5001021,00.html, accessed 12 January 2008.

Waugh, Jr., W. (1982), *International Terrorism: How Nations Respond to Terrorists* (Salisbury: Documentary Publications).

Waugh, Jr., W. (1990), *Terrorism and Emergency Management* (New York: Marcel Dekker Inc.).

Weimann, G. and Winn, C. (1994), *The Theatre of Terrorism: Mass Media and International Terrorism* (New York: Longman).

Weinberg, L., Pedahzur, A. and Hirsch-Hoefler, S. (2004), 'The Challenges of Conceptualizing Terrorism', *Terrorism and Political Violence*, 16(4): 777–94.

Wessely, S. (2005), 'Victimhood and Resilience', *New England Journal of Medicine*, 353(6): 548–50.

West, A. and Stein, B. (2005), 'Vindicated for Proving a Scientific Consensus Untrue', *The Australian*, October 5, 15.

West, D. and Orr, M. (2005), 'Managing Citizen Fears: Public Attitudes Toward Urban Terrorism', *Urban Affairs Review*, 41(1): 93–105.

Whitaker, D. (2007), *Terrorism: Understanding the Global Threat* (Harlow: Pearson Longman).

White, E. (1999), *Here is New York* (New York: The Little Book Room).

White, H. (2005a), 'Learning to Live with Terror in Our Own Land', *The Age*, November 10, 15.

White, H. (2005b), 'With a Terrorist Threat Out in the Open, it is Time to Confront the Causes', *The Sydney Morning Herald*, November 10, 11.

Whinnett, E. (2005), 'Small Victory Worth Winning', *Herald Sun*, October 8, 13.

Wilkinson, P. (1974), *Political Terrorism* (London: Macmillan).

Williams, C. (2004), *Terrorism Explained: The Facts About Terrorism and Terrorist Groups* (Sydney: New Holland).

Wilson, H. (2008), 'Editorial: Walking with Apathy into Disaster', *Disaster Prevention and Management: An International Journal*, 17(2): 2.

Wilson, K. (2007), 'Guns, Guards and Gates', *Overland* [website], No. 188, http://www.overlandexpress.org/188%20wilson.html, accessed 21 May 2008.

Wonkette (2007), 'Terror Porn Fantasy Puts WALNUTS! McCain In the White House', *Wonkette: The D.C. Gossip* [website], http://wonkette.com/politics/john-mccain/terror-porn-fantasy-puts-walnuts-mccain-in-the-white-house-238906.php, accessed 8 May 2007.

Wood, J. and Dupont, B. (eds) (2006), *Democracy, Society and the Governance of Security* (Cambridge: Cambridge University Press).

Wrzesniewski, A. (2002), '"It's Not Just a Job": Shifting Meanings of Work in the Wake of 9/11', *Journal of Management Inquiry*, 11(3): 230–234.

Yates, A. (2005), 'Australia Faces Counter-Terrorism Challenges', transcript of interview with Tony Jones on *Lateline*, Australian Broadcasting Corporation [ABC], http://www.abc.net.au/lateline/content/2005/s1411905.htm, accessed 3 May 2006.

Zedner, L. (2003), 'The Concept of Security: An Agenda for Comparative Analysis', *Legal Studies*, 23(1): 153–76.
Ziffer, D. (2006), 'Threat of Terror Keeps Us Tuned In', *The Age*, Friday, July 21, 8.
Zinn, H. (2002), *Terrorism and War* (Crows Nest: Allen and Unwin).
Žižek, S. (2002a), *Welcome to the Desert of the Real* (London: Verso).
Žižek, S. (2002b), 'The Matrix: Or, The Two Sides of Perversion', in W. Irwin (ed.), *The Matrix and Philosophy: Welcome to the Desert of the Real* (Chicago: Open Court), 240–66.
Žižek, S. (2004), 'From Politics to Biopolitics ... and Back', *South Atlantic Quarterly*, 103(2/3): 501–21.
Žižek, S. (2006), *The Pervert's Guide to Cinema: Parts 1, 2, 3*, A Lone Star, Mischief Films, Amoeba Film Production.

Index

Abu Ghraib 1, 177
Afghanistan War
    post-9/11 1, 23, 44, 80, 113, 128, 177
    pre-9/11 26
Agamben, Georgio 71, 73, 137
Age, The 78, 85–7, 90, 93–102, 175
Alexander, Dean 44–51, 57, 64–5, 68–72, 79, 129, 173,
Alexander, Yonah 44–51, 57, 64–5, 68–72, 129, 173
al-Qaeda 47, 75, 80, 84, 101, 154
ASIO (Australian Security Intelligence Organisation) 74, 96, 100, 102, 149
Aum Shinrikyo 21, 48
Australian, The 85, 90, 93–4, 96–8, 100, 102, 175

Bali bombings 2–3, 5, 26, 28, 30, 80–97, 120–21, 123, 131–32, 144–47, 153
Baudrillard, Jean 4–11, 27, 39, 46, 88, 104–6, 126, 141–42, 144, 163, 174
Bauman, Zygmunt 2–3, 31, 36
Beck, Ulrich 57–8
black museum of journalism 12, 80, 103–7
Black September *see* Munich Olympics
Blair, Tony 47, 83, 155
built environment
    as a terrorist target 34–5, 64
    anxiety 168–169
Bush, George W. 1, 19, 23, 42, 47, 72, 164, 177
business leaders
    and corporate counter-terrorism 12, 42, 57, 61–71, 135
    and managing terrorism 3, 5, 8, 12–15, 29, 41, 56–61, 134–5, 165, 167–8, 170–1, 176–7
    and the media 78, 80
    and simulated security 33, 57, 137–162

Chaser's, The 72–73
Chomsky, Noam
    media and culture 112, 125
    and the 'propaganda model' 19
cities
    and businesses 41–42, 45, 56, 62, 65–66, 69, 73–4, 78
    and the desert of the real 10–1, 116
    and the human body 13
    and media 77–107
    and terrorism 3–4, 11–15, 18, 24, 31–36, 41, 46–7, 58, 60, 81–3, 91, 95, 126–131, 164–177
    as a theatre of terrorism 17, 172
    as a traumascape 36–39, 171–2
    and work 43, 49, 56, 84, 90, 92, 109–10, 112, 115–6, 119, 122, 133–158, 164–177
Coaffee, John 36, 58, 73
contranym
    of security 71–3
    of terrorism 45, 56, 71, 163, 168, 170
corporate counter-terrorism 13, 42, 49–50, 52, 55–7, 61–71, 74–5, 78, 135, 150, 157–162, 172
counter-terrorism
    and business (*see* corporate counter-terrorism)
    counterterrorism 38, 56
    and critical infrastructure 147
    and everyday life 129, 174
    and Islam 132
    and managers 12, 56, 61–2, 114, 135, 157–162
    and the media 100, 102
    and the Melbourne Commonwealth Games 149
    organizations 8

policing 48, 72–3, 96, 100, 102
spending 33
television 78–9, 173
and the Trusted Information Sharing Network (TISN) 149
counterterrorism 22, 38, 56, 59–60, 64, 69, 79, 166
CSI (Crime Scene Investigation) 94

da-sein 14
Debord, Guy 15, 78–9, 84, 105
Deep Impact (1999) 7
desert of the real 10–11, 81, 116, 153, 176
Die Hard (1988) 7, 142
Disneyland 80, 138, 143
distance
   and indirectly affected populations 29–31, 146
   and the media 105, 124
   from terrorism 5, 11, 14, 17, 19, 24, 28–9, 39–41, 74–5, 80, 82–3, 103, 109, 128, 162, 164, 169, 176
   and traveling to work 3, 134, 143
dread 14, 35, 38, 45–6, 58–60, 104, 109, 120–21, 125–27, 132, 135, 142, 153, 161–62, 165–66, 168, 169–73, 175

Edgware Road 47, 79, 82
Elliott, Anthony 173
ETA 35, 47, 132

fear
   and the city 39, 45, 60, 62, 77, 81, 92, 116, 149, 156, 168
   and distance 28
   and dread (*see* dread)
   and the Hashashin 20
   and the human brain 169–170
   and human precariousness and vulnerability 3, 39, 66, 81
   of Muslims 94, 99, 101, 123–126
   and risk 58
   and stress 8, 38, 62–64, 121–23, 127, 134
   in the terrorism definition 22–4, 27, 155
   and the theatre of terrorism 2
   and witnessing 9, 15, 17, 42, 44, 47, 57, 82, 102, 129–30
   and working people 2, 15, 18, 30, 52–6, 64, 66, 120, 122, 129–33, 135, 140, 150, 161, 163, 168
Fear TV 78, 129
Financial Review, The 86, 96, 98
Fine, Michele 35
football
   all codes 173
   American 39
   Australian 81, 87–9, 131, 151
Friends 143, 172

George, Alexander 22
Giddens, Anthony 57
Ground Zero 1–2, 9, 18, 34, 45, 49, 79, 107, 176
Grosz, Elizabeth 13, 169
Guantánamo Bay, Cuba 1
Haraway, Donna 58, 65–6, 172
Hashashsin 20–21
Heidegger, Martin 1 4, 120
Herald Sun 85–96, 98–101, 125, 131, 147, 153, 175
Herman, Edward 19, 22
hijab 119
Hilton bombing 83, 120–21, 145
Hollywood 6–7, 10, 46, 104, 115, 142
Howard, John 94, 97, 99–102
hyperreality 7–8, 101–02, 106–07

images
   of business 3, 50
   of the city 143–44, 169, 176
   of Islam 116–119
   of the Russell Street bombing 145–146
   of security 147–62, 170–71, 174
   of the Self and Others 110, 128–32, 137
   and simulations 4, 7–10, 12–14, 41, 74, 109, 124, 137, 160, 170, 173
   of society 81, 128–32
   of terrorism 4–7, 10–12, 17, 19, 21, 24–32, 37–40, 45, 47, 78–84, 88, 93–4, 97, 102, 104–07, 126–128, 137, 140–42, 146, 153, 155, 160, 169–70, 173–174
   of terrorists 101
   of war 23, 25–6

and witnesses 19–24, 27, 29, 78, 96, 110, 112, 125, 153, 164, 176
Independence Day (1996) 7, 142
indirectly affected populations 29–31, 40, 52, 146
Islamic Jihad 26
Israeli/Palestinian conflict 25–6, 35, 74, 154
Iraq War 1, 23, 47, 80, 92, 113, 117, 128, 145, 149, 156, 177

jihad 85, 97

Kierkegaard, Sören 60, 120

Laqueur, Walter 7, 11, 13, 19–21, 24, 43, 173
London
    and Australians 82
    bombings 2–6, 10–1, 15, 18–9, 26, 28–31, 38, 42, 47–50, 60, 69–70, 80, 83, 87–88, 93, 96–98, 102–03, 126, 128, 134, 137, 140, 142–150, 154–56, 167, 171–172, 176
    the desert of the real 10
    and Jean Charles de Menezes 47, 155–56
    organizations in 66
    as a symbol 24, 166
    and working people 40, 77–8, 146–50, 176

Los Angeles 77

Madrid
    ETA 35, 47
    3/11 bombings 2–6, 10–1, 14–5, 18–9, 24, 26, 28–31, 38, 40, 42, 46–50, 60, 77–8, 82, 87–88, 93, 97–98, 102–03, 112, 121, 127, 134, 145, 149, 154, 156, 158, 166–67, 169, 171, 176
    organizations in 66
    major events 33, 35–36, 39, 50, 88, 137, 139, 144, 147, 149, 151–53, 168, 174–75
Matrix, The (1999) 10, 104
MCG (Melbourne Cricket Ground) 91, 93, 131, 175
media
    Islam in the 118–19, 157, 177
    newspaper 77–107

security and the 152
terrorism and the 1, 3–7, 18–20, 22–32, 38, 43, 45, 48, 63, 74, 123–31, 153, 155, 166–67, 170, 176
working people and the 112, 115, 139, 141, 146–48, 153, 155
Melbourne
    Commonwealth Games 35
    interviews in 14
    managers in 137–62
    newspapers 1, 77–107
    University 61–62
    workers in 3, 29, 109–36
Miller, Toby 13, 19, 27, 79–80, 176–77
Mumbai 26, 128
Munich (2005) 112
Munich Olympics 35, 112

Nacos, Brigitte 5–6, 27
New York City
    as a desert of the real 10–11
    Fire Department 46
    and New Yorkers 2, 37–8, 60, 86, 124, 142, 172, 174, 176–77
    skyline 28, 35, 143
    subway 92, 159
    Twin Towers (World Trade Center) 1–4, 27, 45–46, 97, 103, 107, 116, 127, 142, 144, 148, 154–55, 167, 174;
    working people 18–9, 29–30, 39–40, 42, 49, 52, 66, 78, 92, 103, 122
Night at the Museum (2006) 8, 71, 80, 104, 107, 128

Osama bin Laden 72, 91, 98
Overland, Simon 88, 131

Parker, Martin 8, 12, 50
Permanent Vacation (1980) 143
propaganda model *see* Chomsky, Noam
PTSD (Post-traumatic Stress Disorder) 51, 122
public transport
    and Aum Shinrikyo 48
    in London 2–3, 6, 10, 18, 28, 38, 47–8, 50, 60, 77, 82, 142, 147–48, 166, 172, 176
    in Madrid 2, 6, 10, 18, 28, 38, 46–7, 50, 77, 82, 166, 176

in Melbourne 114, 122, 133–34,
  138–40, 154–61, 168
as a potential terrorist target 10, 33–4,
  36, 50, 59, 171
and security 12, 63–9, 154–61

Rapoport, David 11, 19–22, 24–6, 28
Richardson, Louise 7, 23–4, 27–30, 48
Russell Street bombing 145–46

Simmel, Georg 36
Scrubs 163
Seinfeld 1 72
Sennett, Richard 173
Shanksville, Pennsylvania 18, 45, 116
Sicarii 20
Simpsons, The 143
simulations
  and images 4, 7–12, 14, 17, 45, 109,
    124, 169–70, 176
  and the media 78, 84, 103, 106, 124
  and popular culture 8–11
  of security 13, 32–3, 71–4, 151–53,
    160–62, 170
  in social theory 4, 7–11, 162, 164
South Park 103
sport 10–11, 33, 35–6, 81, 85, 87, 92–3, 95,
  97, 113–14, 122, 124, 131–32, 144,
  148, 175–76
stress
  and the city 157
  and simulations 8
  and terrorism 29–30, 64
  and trauma 38
  and witnesses and victims 60
  work 29, 51–3, 56, 62–3, 120–23, 125,
    127, 133–34, 139, 150, 161
Sydney Morning Herald, The 60, 85–6, 94,
  98–100, 131

Team America: World Police (2004) 121
television
  audiences; and simulations; and terrorism
terrorism as spectacle 5–8, 14–5, 28, 32, 36,
  40, 78–79, 86, 101, 103–104, 153,
  173
terror-work 12–4, 163–64, 171, 173–74, 176

theatre of terror 1–7, 11, 14, 17, 20, 24,
  27–8, 30–7, 40, 63, 77, 81, 88, 93,
  105–06, 109, 128, 131–32, 175
Thuggee 20–1
traumascape 28, 36–9, 95, 172
Tulloch, John 2, 47–9, 66, 79–80, 82–3
Turner, Bryan 3, 23, 31, 36, 49, 166–67
Twin Towers 1–2, 6, 10–1, 24, 27–8, 34–5,
  38–9, 45–6, 50, 55, 77, 97, 107,
  115–17, 126, 142, 144, 164, 168, 174

Underground Zero 2, 4, 18–9, 49, 79

victims
  in Bali 86, 92, 94
  of discrimination 115
  and interpersonal distance 146
  and the media 29, 36, 105, 124, 132
  victimized distinction 3, 27, 29–30, 36,
    38
  witnesses and 4, 8–12, 14–5, 17–24,
    26–9, 32–3, 39–42, 44, 46–8, 57, 60,
    63, 66, 72, 74–5, 78–84, 88, 103–06,
    109–10, 124–25, 127–29, 135–38,
    149, 155, 164, 166, 172–73, 175–76
  working people as 2, 18, 30–1, 46, 49,
    52–53, 80, 91, 100, 103, 109–10,
    122, 138
Vietnam War 24–6, 81, 111

Washington D.C. 1, 3–4, 10, 15, 18–9, 31,
  40, 42, 45, 49, 52, 60, 66, 77, 103,
  142, 149, 154, 171, 176
West Wing, The 81, 115
Wilkinson, Paul 28, 164–65, 167
witnesses
  of 9/11 1, 7, 11, 13, 15, 47, 79, 99–100,
    106, 128, 130, 142, 146, 176
  in the Beaubourg 104–05
  in the definition of terrorism 23–24
  distant 3, 9, 30, 97, 103, 106, 153, 155,
    157
  in the history of terrorism 19–21, 24–8
  and indirectly affected populations 29–31
  and the media 12, 21, 83, 88, 93–4,
    96–7, 100–05, 109–110, 131
  and simulations 7, 9, 11

the stories of 109–62
to terrorism on television 9–10, 17, 23, 38, 40, 78, 81, 94, 106–07, 110, 124, 129, 175
and victims (*see* victims)
World Trade Center (2006) 6

X-Files 163

Žižek, Slavoj
commodities 11, 162
desert of the real 10, 81, 153
images 24, 28, 39, 162, 170
the media 19
multiculturalism 166
popular culture 7, 10
risk society 58–9

If you have found this book useful you may be interested in other titles from Gower

Spaces of Security and Insecurity:
Geographies of the War on Terror
Edited by Alan Ingram and Klaus Dodds
Hardback: 978-0-7546-7349-1
E-book: 978-0-7546-9041-2

Responding to Terrorism:
Political, Philosophical and Legal Perspectives
Robert Imre, T. Brian Mooney and Benjamin Clarke
Hardback: 978-0-7546-7277-7
E-book: 978-0-7546-8527-2

Countering Terrorist Finance
Tim Parkman and Gill Peeling
Hardback: 978-0-566-08725-7

Terrorism, Risk and the Global City:
Towards Urban Resilience
Jon Coaffee
Hardback: 978-0-7546-7428-3
E-book: 978-0-7546-9046-7

Visit **www.gowerpublishing.com** and

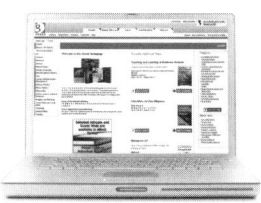

- search the entire catalogue of Gower books in print
- order titles online at 10% discount
- take advantage of special offers
- sign up for our monthly e-mail update service
- download free sample chapters from all recent titles
- download or order our catalogue